T0305833

East Asian Entrepreneurs

A Study of State Role, Education and Mindsets

East Asian Entrepreneurs

A Study of State Role, Education and Mindsets

Tai Wei LIM

National University of Singapore, Singapore
Soka University, Japan

World Scientific

EW JERSEY · LONDON · SINGAPORE · BEIJING · SHANGHAI · HONG KONG · TAIPEI · CHENNAI · TOKYO

Published by

World Scientific Publishing Co. Pte. Ltd.

5 Toh Tuck Link, Singapore 596224

USA office: 27 Warren Street, Suite 401-402, Hackensack, NJ 07601

UK office: 57 Shelton Street, Covent Garden, London WC2H 9HE

Library of Congress Cataloging-in-Publication Data

Names: Lim, Tai-Wei, author.

Title: East Asian entrepreneurs : a study of state role, education and mindsets /
 Tai Wei Lim, National University of Singapore, Singapore, Soka University, Japan.

Description: Hackensack, NJ : World Scientific, 2022. |
 Includes bibliographical references and index.

Identifiers: LCCN 2021021072 | ISBN 9789811240263 (hardcover) |
 ISBN 9789811240270 (ebook) | ISBN 9789811240287 (ebook other)

Subjects: LCSH: Entrepreneurship--Government policy--Asia, East. |
 Entrepreneurship--Study and teaching--Asia, East. | Success in business--Asia, East.

Classification: LCC HB615 .L49446 2022 | DDC 338/.04095--dc23

LC record available at https://lccn.loc.gov/2021021072

British Library Cataloguing-in-Publication Data

A catalogue record for this book is available from the British Library.

For any available supplementary material, please visit
https://www.worldscientific.com/worldscibooks/10.1142/12371#t=suppl

Desk Editors: Aanand Jayaraman/Lixi Dong

Typeset by Stallion Press
Email: enquiries@stallionpress.com

Printed in Singapore

About the Author

Prof Tai Wei LIM is an Associate Professor with Soka University of Japan Faculty of Business. He teaches international business, sustainable management, multicultural management, Japanese management courses at the undergraduate level and business ethics courses in the graduate masters level. He is also a East Asian area studies specialist.

About the Chapter 8 Contributor

Wong, Kenneth, PBM. Wong started to be involved in community service as young as 13 years old. Inspired and motivated in serving the community in a greater capacity, Kenneth pursued his undergraduate with the National University of Singapore, majoring in Social Work. In 2016, Kenneth attained his Master Degree in Community Leadership and Social Development with the Singapore University of Social Sciences.

In 2006, Kenneth began to serve as a Grassroots Leader with Joo Chiat Constituency. Since then, he has engaged the youth meaningfully in various environmental, community and social programmes for the needy.

At the National level, Kenneth served as the Council member for People's Association Youth Movement (PAYM) Central Youth Council and led in the organizing of PAYM Chingay Contingent since its participation in 2008. He was the Organizing Chairperson for PAYM Chingay Contingent in 2011, 2015 and 2018.

Having assembled a strong team to take over, Kenneth relinquished his Chairmanship for the YEC and concurrently was appointed as Chairman for Joo Chiat Community Sports Club.

Currently, a lecturer with the Institute of Technical Education (ITE), Kenneth continues to engage youths meaningfully, both academically and non-academically, to contribute to the community through Service-Learning programme.

In recognition for Kenneth's contributions to the community, he was conferred the National Day Award 2017 — Pingat Bakti Masyarakat (PBM) and in May 2018, he was awarded the PAYM Excellent Youth Award in recognition for his service and contributions.

Contents

Chapter 1

Introduction

Working Definitions of Entrepreneurship

Klaus Schwab, the founder of World Economic Forum (WEF) provided the following definition for entrepreneurship: "Entrepreneurship is the engine fuelling innovation employment generation and economic growth ... the power that education has in developing the skills that generate an entrepreneurial mindset and in preparing future leaders for solving more complex, interlinked and fast-changing problems".[1] Others defined entrepreneurship in terms of mode of doing business (including those trading online). For example, Yokoyama and Birchley included online entrepreneurs, consumers as well as online communities who profit from cross-boundary economic activities to produce and distribute products (including through e-commerce platforms) and defined them as "consumers-as-international entrepreneurs who do business overseas through their own firms without being employed known as 'self-initiated expatriate entrepreneurs'".[2]

---

[1] Penaluna, Andrew and Kathryn Penaluna, "Entrepreneurial education in practice part 2 — building motivations and competencies" dated 2015 in Entrepreneurship 360 Thematic Paper (EU: European Commission LEED), 2015 [downloaded on 1 December 2020], available at http://www.oecd.org/cfe/leed/Entrepreneurial-Education-Practice-pt2.pdf, p. 6.

[2] Yokoyama, Kazuko and Sarah Louisa Birchley, Transnational Entrepreneurship in South East Asia (US: Springer Link), 2019, p. 8.

Individuals who are located overseas without being employed and establish their own firms and still make a significant impact on their home country are known as "high-impact self-initiated expatriate social entrepreneur" while migrants (and their descendants) who set up create entrepreneurial activities that reaches across national business environments and their country of residence are known as "diaspora entrepreneurs".[3] A case study of diaspora entrepreneurs is covered in the chapter on overseas ethnic Chinese entrepreneurs while civic tech entrepreneurs are featured in the chapter on Japan's civic technopreneurship.

Yokoyama and Birchley define "immigrant/migrant entrepreneurs" as individuals who settled in a country besides their own and start their own companies for economic survival while the entrepreneurial spouse of an individual who was posted overseas by his/her company who start businesses in the countries that their other half is located in is known as a "trailing spouse entrepreneur".[4] Finally, entrepreneurs with regular connections and interactions with other national backgrounds are known as "ethnic entrepreneurs", while business owners that are not the majority in their population are defined as "minority entrepreneur" and "expatpreneurs" are those who relocated overseas on their own and started a new venture in the host country.[5] The broad implications of all these definitions is that entrepreneurship has reached a high level of trans-nationality and are now effectively globalized in nature.

Other literatures prefer to conceptualize entrepreneurship in terms of stages of development rather than their trans-nationality statuses. In other definitions found in Singapore-oriented studies, there are different stages of entrepreneurship. For example, Gomulya and team has defined entrepreneurial in several stages. They include: the stage of "intent to start a business in three years" (i.e. starting from zero), "total early-stage entrepreneurial activity (TEA)" (new entrepreneurs), "nascent entrepreneurs" (those active in a start-up and no wages have been paid for 3 months) and "new firm entrepreneurs" (business owners who have been paid salaries between 3 and 42 months).[6] Yet others adopt a reductionist view by asso-

---

[3] *Ibid.*

[4] *Ibid.*

[5] *Ibid.*

[6] Gomulya, David, Olexander Chernyshenko, Marilyn Ang Uy, Wong Lun Kai Francis, Ho Moon-Ho Ringo, Chan Kim Yin and Calvin Ong He Lu, "Entrepreneurship in Singapore: Growth and challenges chapter" dated January 2015 in Nanyang Business School website [downloaded on 1 December 2020], (Singapore: Nanyang Business School Nanyang

ciating certain concepts with entrepreneurship, for example, the idea of "thinking big". The mindset concept of "thinking big" refers to high risk and high reward proceeding in tandem and this means the need for a risk-taking investor community and a large receptive market for encouraging disruptive innovation and breakthrough technologies in entrepreneurship instead of only on incremental innovations or imitations of already-successful innovative models.[7]

The Global University Entrepreneurial Spirit Students' Survey (GUESSS) included more categories of entrepreneurs. Additional terms include: short-term entrepreneurs (defined as founder or successor after studies), long-term entrepreneurial aspiration (i.e. becoming a founder or successor after five year of studies), nascent entrepreneurs (attempting to start their own business or self-employment), active entrepreneurs (currently in her/his own founded firm), successors (individuals with family businesses).[8]

There is also a cultivation component to entrepreneurship as well. The nexus between entrepreneurship education and an entrepreneurial mindset is well-established in the existing literature on this subject matter. The entrepreneurial mindset is intimately connected with how an individual formulates thoughts or conscious/sub-conscious states of mind or forms a worldview that can influence the outcome for success in entrepreneurial activities and entrepreneurship education has the role of enhancing this mindset of entrepreneurship.[9] Entrepreneurship education trains minds/

Technological University), available at https://www.researchgate.net/publication/304864757_Entrepreneurship_in_Singapore_Growth_and_Challenges/link/5b3c3be30f7e9b0df5ec7b38/download, p. 3.

[7] Narasimhalu, Arcot Desai, "Thinking bigger: Pushing Singaporean entrepreneurship to the next level" dated March 2015 at Singapore Management University (SMU) Research Collection School of Information Systems School of Information Systems (Singapore: SMU), 2015, available at https://ink.library.smu.edu.sg/cgi/viewcontent.cgi?article=4446&context=sis_research, p. 44.

[8] Wong, Poh-Kam, Yuen-Ping Ho and Su-Juan-Crystal Ng, "Global University Entrepreneurial Spirit Students' Survey 2013/2014 Singapore Report" dated March 2015 in NUS Entrepreneurship Center and Guess Survey.org [downloaded on 1 December 2020], (Singapore: NUS), available at https://www.guesssurvey.org/resources/nat_2013/GUESSS-2013_14_Singapore_-FinalReport.pdf, p. 3.

[9] Saptono, Ari, Agus Wibowo, Bagus Shandy Narmaditya, Rr Ponco Dewi Karyaningsih and Heri Yanto, "Does entrepreneurial education matter for Indonesian students' entrepreneurial preparation: The mediating role of entrepreneurial mindset and knowledge" dated 2020 in Education 7:1 (Taylor and Francis/Cogent), 2020 [downloaded on 1 January

mindsets for business start-ups and self-employment.[10] Embedded within the entrepreneurship narrative is the idea of whether entrepreneurship can be "learned" (and to what extent) and some believe that that mindset attributes, characteristics and skills can be imparted but others argue that entrepreneurship is both an "art" (inherent creative features) and a "science" (practical management skills and strategizing that can be acquired through entrepreneurial education).[11] This is a perennial debate.

Yet, others argue that it does not matter. The mindset is just one of the individual attributes amongst others that are equally important in making or breaking a new entrepreneurial venture. Stakeholders in entrepreneurial venture form ecosystems to cultivate and maintain interest and practice in entrepreneurship through public policies/political leadership, cultural cultivation, funding provision, human resources capital availability, market system and other forms of support.[12] There are some intellectuals like Arcot Desai Narasimhalu from Singapore Management University (SMU) who argued that, in Silicon Valley, a start-up firm can locate lawyers, accountants and service providers offering their services at a discounted rate in exchange for equity in the company.[13] He argued for the transplan-

---

2021], available at https://www.tandfonline.com/doi/full/10.1080/2331186X.2020. 1836728, p. 4.

[10] Yu, Min-Chun, Mark Goh, Hao-Yun Kao and Wen-Hsiung Wu, "A comparative study of entrepreneurship education between Singapore and Taiwan" dated 2017 in *Management Decision*, 55(7) (Emerald Insight), 2017 [downloaded on 1 December 2020], available at https://doi.org/10.1108/MD-06–2016–0415 and https://www.researchgate.net/publication/ 318288513_A_Comparative_Study_of_Entrepreneurship_Education_between_ Singapore_and_Taiwan/link/5992652ea6fdcc53b79b6e30/download, p. 1427.

[11] Yokoyama, Kazuko and Sarah Louisa Birchley, Transnational Entrepreneurship in South East Asia (US: Springer Link), 2019, p. 30.

[12] Yu, Min-Chun, Mark Goh, Hao-Yun Kao and Wen-Hsiung Wu, "A comparative study of entrepreneurship education between Singapore and Taiwan" dated 2017 in *Management Decision*, 55(7) (Emerald Insight), 2017 [downloaded on 1 December 2020], available at https://doi.org/10.1108/MD-06–2016–0415 and https://www.researchgate.net/publication/ 318288513_A_Comparative_Study_of_Entrepreneurship_Education_between_ Singapore_and_Taiwan/link/5992652ea6fdcc53b79b6e30/download, p. 1428.

[13] Narasimhalu, Arcot Desai, "Thinking bigger: Pushing Singaporean entrepreneurship to the next level" dated March 2015 at Singapore Management University (SMU) Research Collection School Of Information Systems School of Information Systems (Singapore: SMU), 2015, available at https://ink.library.smu.edu.sg/cgi/viewcontent.cgi?article=4446 &context=sis_research, p. 42.

tation of these practices to Singapore so as to avoid expensive legal service bills that start-ups cannot afford so a change of mindsets of the service providers is needed to service local start-ups with good potential instead of asking for money upfront to strengthen Singapore's entrepreneurship ecosystem.[14]

Without such incentives, especially in East Asia, even if an individual is imbued naturally with the art of entrepreneurship, his ventures may not succeed without the right amount of resource support from the state and government. Unlike universities in Western countries, the Singapore government and the governments of many other East Asian countries play a significant role in formulating policies for entrepreneurship education, often collaborating with economic departments/agencies to cultivate entrepreneurship through specialized entrepreneurship education.[15] In working with the entrepreneurial mindset, entrepreneur education creates a culture that penetrates all businesses and non-business projects and motivates students to learn more about entrepreneurship through presenting new ventures.[16] The close relationship between state policies and entrepreneurial education is another feature of East Asian entrepreneurship. Some East Asian states also have their own policy definitions of entrepreneurship education; for example, the Japanese Ministry of Trade and Industry policy paper mentions: "Entrepreneurship education refers to education provided to train people to develop "entrepreneurship" and "entrepreneurial skills" and to be able to find their own mission, discover themselves what to do with it, and carry it out themselves".[17]

[14] *Ibid.*

[15] Yu, Min-Chun, Mark Goh, Hao-Yun Kao and Wen-Hsiung Wu, "A comparative study of entrepreneurship education between Singapore and Taiwan" dated 2017 in *Management Decision*, 55(7) (Emerald Insight), 2017 [downloaded on 1 December 2020], available at https://doi.org/10.1108/MD-06–2016–0415 and https://www.researchgate.net/publication/318288513_A_Comparative_Study_of_Entrepreneurship_Education_between_Singapore_and_Taiwan/link/5992652ea6fdcc53b79b6e30/download, p. 1437.

[16] Saptono, Ari, Agus Wibowo, Bagus Shandy Narmaditya, Rr Ponco Dewi Karyaningsih and Heri Yanto, "Does entrepreneurial education matter for Indonesian students' entrepreneurial preparation: The mediating role of entrepreneurial mindset and knowledge" dated 2020 in Education 7:1 (Taylor and Francis/Cogent), 2020 [downloaded on 1 January 2021], available at https://www.tandfonline.com/doi/full/10.1080/2331186X.2020.1836728, p. 30.

[17] Yokoyama, Kazuko and Sarah Louisa Birchley, Transnational Entrepreneurship in South East Asia (US: Springer Link), 2019, p.

Education cultivation also involves shaping or changing mindsets. An entrepreneurial mindset is defined as "a feeling and belief with a unique way of seeking the opportunities and challenges" as well as an integrated realization of the importance of novel ideas, seeking opportunities, overcoming hindrances, managing a business and the process of internal assessment of his/her perspectives from holistic ideas rather than practical attributes.[18] The entrepreneurial mindset proactively locates economic opportunities instead of only obstacles, evaluates opportunities rather than consider failures, searches for solutions and not grumble about problems; in general, it is a state of mind that orientates individual behavior towards activities/outcomes concerned with entrepreneurship.[19]

Literature Review: Mindsets, Education and Environmental Factors

In the literature on mindsets, some characteristics/behaviors are associated with entrepreneurs like risk-tolerance and problem-solving aptitude, and entrepreneurs in private companies show characteristics of being risk-taking, innovative and proactive.[20] Some specific case studies are analysed below.

Singapore Case Study

Some existing studies have focused on the case study of Singapore. In the Global University Entrepreneurial Spirit Students' Survey (GUESSS) biennial research project to understand entrepreneurial attitudes,

---

[18] Saptono, Ari, Agus Wibowo, Bagus Shandy Narmaditya, Rr Ponco Dewi Karyaningsih and Heri Yanto, "Does entrepreneurial education matter for Indonesian students' entrepreneurial preparation: The mediating role of entrepreneurial mindset and knowledge" dated 2020 in Education 7:1 (Taylor and Francis/Cogent), 2020 [downloaded on 1 January 2021], available at https://www.tandfonline.com/doi/full/10.1080/2331186X.2020.1836728, p. 3.

[19] *Ibid*, pp. 3–4.

[20] Ahlstrom, David and Zhujun Ding, "Entrepreneurship in China: An overview" in International Small Business Journal, 32(6) (UK: Sage), [downloaded on 1 December 2020], 2014, available at http://sites.utexas.edu/chinaecon/files/2015/06/Scholarly_Entrepreneurship-in-China_2014–1.pdf, p. 613.

intentions and activities of students at institutes of higher learning (IHLs), the NUS Entrepreneurship Center (NEC)'s 2013/2014 component study was useful for gauging and evaluating the entrepreneurship intentions and aspirations amongst Singaporean university students.[21] In the GUESSS study, entrepreneurial intentions were profiled and the role of IHLs were highlighted. In terms of Singaporean profiles, students in business schools, polytechnics, male students, those who considered themselves better academic performers and those with family businesses (parental occupational background) appears to show greater intentions in entrepreneurship while 56% of Singaporean students stated their IHLs motivated students to participate in entrepreneurial activities.[22]

Fifty percent of the surveyed Singaporeans have the opinion that IHLs had a positive environment for them to become entrepreneurs and develop ideas for new ventures although approximately two-thirds of Singaporean students have not taken any entrepreneurship classes in the IHLs (which are comparable with global average).[23] Singaporean students who participated in IHL entrepreneurship classes were generally satisfied with their experience because, compared to the global average, Singapore IHLs are perceived to have programs that are helpful in providing students with entrepreneurial skills while nascent and active student entrepreneurs in Singapore opined that IHL entrepreneurship programs augmented their ability to locate opportunities.[24]

Gomulya and his team's study concluded that the reasons why more Singaporeans were not entrepreneurs was the perceived absence of skills and opportunities to establish a new business venture.[25] Some mindset

---

[21] It started in 2003 by the Swiss Research Institute of Small Business and Entrepreneurship at the University of St. Gallen in Switzerland [Source: Wong, Poh-Kam, Yuen-Ping Ho and Su-Juan-Crystal Ng, "Global University Entrepreneurial Spirit Students' Survey 2013/2014 Singapore Report" dated March 2015 in NUS Entrepreneurship Center and Guess Survey.org [downloaded on 1 December 2020], (Singapore: NUS), available at https://www.guesssurvey.org/resources/nat_2013/GUESSS-2013_14_Singapore_-FinalReport.pdf, p. 1].

[22] *Ibid*, p. 3.

[23] *Ibid*.

[24] *Ibid*.

[25] Gomulya, David, Olexander Chernyshenko, Marilyn Ang Uy, Wong Lun Kai Francis, Ho Moon-Ho Ringo, Chan Kim Yin and Calvin Ong He Lu, "Entrepreneurship in Singapore: Growth and challenges chapter" dated January 2015 in Nanyang Business School website [downloaded on 1 December 2020], (Singapore: Nanyang Business

attitudinal factors identified as obstacles to the respondents' plans to initiate a business venture and open up opportunities for new firms include the perception of fear of failure.[26] Arcot Desai Narasimhalu argues that, in term of societal mindset, a pre-emptive constraints faced by Singaporean young start-ups is the societal perception of entrepreneurship as a risky occupation in comparison with a paid employee and the initial hindrance for an enthusiastic entrepreneur is: "How do I convince my parents?".[27] As parental and familial influences highlight the difficulties/challenges/odds of business start-up successes, they urge their children to assume "secure" jobs.[28]

Narasimhalu argued that, for Singapore to have a vibrant entrepreneurial culture, the business can learn from generations of business leaders before them and derive mileage from the "entrepreneurial intelligence" of successful entrepreneurs and he opined that newly entrepreneurial Singapore still has room to develop a critical mass of successful "serial entrepreneurs".[29] He urged local entrepreneurs not to think small and give up easily as, statistically, there are very few start-ups that can become a US$1 billion business but successful Singaporean entrepreneurs can gradually invest their knowledge, expertise and experience to grooming new business ideas into billion dollar firms to build momentum.[30]

Tackling the confidence factor and skills component, Wong Poh-Kam and his team's data may be useful. It indicated that Singaporean students with stronger entrepreneurial interest tended to show stronger confidence in controlling their decisions/directions, especially for company founders, but interestingly, in terms of entrepreneurial self-efficacy, entrepreneurial students saw themselves as most competent in leadership and communicator and least competent in innovation (creating new products

---

School Nanyang Technological University), available at https://www.researchgate.net/publication/304864757_Entrepreneurship_in_Singapore_Growth_and_Challenges/link/5b3c3be30f7e9b0df5ec7b38/download, p. 5.

[26] *Ibid*, p. 9.

[27] Narasimhalu, Arcot Desai, "Thinking bigger: Pushing Singaporean entrepreneurship to the next level" dated March 2015 at Singapore Management University (SMU) Research Collection School Of Information Systems School of Information Systems (Singapore: SMU), 2015, available at https://ink.library.smu.edu.sg/cgi/viewcontent.cgi?article=4446&context=sis_research, p. 41.

[28] *Ibid*.

[29] *Ibid*, p. 42.

[30] *Ibid*.

and services).[31] Singaporean IHL students viewed business ownership and initiation as more risky compared to managing their own business and, despite fairly consistent Singaporean perceptions that entrepreneurship is risky, willingness to take risks is higher among polytechnic students, business school students, those with entrepreneurial aspirations and strong entrepreneurial intentions.[32]

The mass media in Singapore has tracked some of the trends in entrepreneurship in Singapore. In terms of mindsets, there have been global surveys covering Singaporeans too. The 2019 WEF-Sea World survey released on 16 August 2019 uncovered that Singapore respondents were less keen than their foreign peers to work overseas in the next three years with only 17% surveyed wanting to be self-employed whereas the global average for the survey was 33%.[33] About two-thirds of Singaporean youths (66% of them) do not want to work overseas, according to the WEF report "Asean Youth: Skills, Technology and the Future of Work" published on 16 August 2019.[34] Singaporeans surveyed were less keen to work overseas in 2019–2022 with just 34% indicating a desire to work overseas compared with overall share of 47%.[35]

The survey covered 56 000 individuals aged between 15 and 35 years from Indonesia, Malaysia, the Philippines, Singapore, Thailand and Vietnam in July 2019 with 9% of the respondents being employees of

---

[31] Wong, Poh-Kam, Yuen-Ping Ho and Su-Juan-Crystal Ng, "Global University Entrepreneurial Spirit Students' Survey 2013/2014 Singapore Report" dated March 2015 in NUS Entrepreneurship Center and Guess Survey.org [downloaded on 1 December 2020], (Singapore: NUS), available at https://www.guesssurvey.org/resources/nat_2013/GUESSS-2013_14_Singapore_-FinalReport.pdf, p. 4.

[32] *Ibid.*

[33] Seow, Joanna, "Poll: Singapore youth less keen on being entrepreneurs than Asean peers" dated 17 August 2019 in The Straits Times [downloaded on 17 August 2019], available at https://www.straitstimes.com/business/poll-spore-youth-less-keen-on-being-entrepreneurs-than-asean-peers.

[34] Lim, Kimberly, "Few Singaporean youths aim to be entrepreneurs, most have no plans to work overseas: WEF survey" dated 16 August 2019 in TodayOnline [downloaded on 16 August 2019], available at https://www.todayonline.com/singapore/singapore-youths-come-last-survey-six-nations-entrepreneurial-ambition.

[35] Seow, Joanna, "Poll: Singapore youth less keen on being entrepreneurs than Asean peers" dated 17 August 2019 in The Straits Times [downloaded on 17 August 2019], available at https://www.straitstimes.com/business/poll-spore-youth-less-keen-on-being-entrepreneurs-than-asean-peers.

multinational corporations (MNCs) and 19% with the same plans of working for others in the future (though non-start-up traditional small and
medium enterprises [SMEs] were viewed less positively as employers).[36]
Although 18% of the young people surveyed indicated they are employed
by SMEs now, just 8% want to find employment with these firms in the
future due to perceived lower levels of training at smaller companies, thus
suggesting SME recruitment may run into difficulties in the near future.[37]

Other studies cited in WEF indicate bright sparks though. Asia's 18-
to 34-year-olds have one of the highest start-up rates globally (approximately 40% creating jobs for others) and 1.3% of entrepreneurs (all ages)
run a nascent firm that was hi-tech or medium-tech, and young people in
the region are more likely to start in small firms (plumbing or street-
vending than the likes of next WeChat or Grab).[38] More than 50% of
ASEAN youths surveyed are interested in skills upgrading particularly in
creativity and innovation, linguistic skills and technology capabilities.[39]
Singaporean youths also considered analytical and critical thinking skills
to be important for entrepreneurship.[40]

There are gender-specific studies on entrepreneurship in Singapore
too. Existing literatures appear to indicate that women entrepreneurs are
more alike with their male counterparts than dissimilar in terms of mindsets and psychological dimensions, but Seet and team's study of Singapore
women appears to show there are differences in terms of motivation.[41]

[36] *Ibid.*

[37] *Ibid.*

[38] Xu, Haoliang, "Asia's young entrepreneurs need help with the hustle" dated 10 August
2018 in World Economic Forum (WEF) [downloaded on 10 August 2018], available at
https://www.weforum.org/agenda/2018/08/asias-young-entrepreneurs-need-help-
with-the-hustle/.

[39] Seow, Joanna, "Poll: Singapore youth less keen on being entrepreneurs than Asean
peers" dated 17 August 2019 in *The Straits Times* [downloaded on 17 August 2019],
available at https://www.straitstimes.com/business/poll-spore-youth-less-keen-on-being-
entrepreneurs-than-asean-peers.

[40] Lim, Kimberly, "Few Singaporean youths aim to be entrepreneurs, most have no plans
to work overseas: WEF survey" dated 16 August 2019 in TodayOnline [downloaded on
16 August 2019], available at https://www.todayonline.com/singapore/singapore-youths-
come-last-survey-six-nations-entrepreneurial-ambition.

[41] Seet, Pi-Shen, Noor Hazlina Ahmad and Lip-Chai Seet, "Singapore's female entrepreneurs — are they different?" dated 2008 in International Journal Entrepreneurship and
Small Business, 5(3/4), 257 (UK: Inderscience Enterprises Ltd.) 2008 [downloaded on

While Seet and her team's study focused on studying the important topic of gender differences between female and male entrepreneurs in Singapore, gender issues in entrepreneurship falls outside the purview of this writing. Readers can pick up more gender perspectives from reading Seet's study and the questions that Seet and team asked in their writing are useful for understanding entrepreneurial mindset and motivations for entrepreneurship in Singapore in terms of gender perspectives.

Briefly stated here, Seet and her team's study showed that there were no significant differences in terms of motivational needs for female/male entrepreneurs in Singapore, and both genders considered their "need for achievement" as the most important motivation for being an entrepreneur and the "need for autonomy" the lowest impetus in their study.[42] The reason was attributed by Seet and her team to Singapore's meritocratic worldview based on the idea of success evaluated through monetary rewards, reinforced by the presence of successful entrepreneurs located in the country's top income earners, therefore they argued that this was likely why Singaporean entrepreneurs have a strong need for achievement.[43]

The moderate rating for "need for autonomy" in Seet and team's study indicates that entrepreneurs feel they have some latitude of autonomy in running their businesses (offset by burdensome responsibilities) and the reason for its lower rating was attributed to Singapore's collectivist society where social bonding is essential in many aspects of daily lives.[44] Therefore, real (complete and unmitigated) autonomy was not really feasible in that sense. There are other studies that discuss the element of autonomy amongst certain groups of Asian entrepreneurs like the overseas Chinese. Ethnic Chinese entrepreneurs show an inclination to become business owners and this desire is often stereotyped by a traditional Chinese proverb: "better be the beak of a cock than the rump of an ox", resulting in a powerful mindset that drives entrepreneurial spirit.[45]

---

1 December 2020], available at https://www.researchgate.net/publication/228630880_ Singapore's_female_entrepreneurs_are_they_different/link/02e7e53befd938b369000000/ download, pp. 260–261.

[42] *Ibid*, pp. 266–267.

[43] *Ibid*, p. 267.

[44] *Ibid*.

[45] Yeung, Henry Wai-chung and Kris Olds, "Globalizing Chinese business firms: where are they coming from, where are they heading?" dated 2000 in The Globalization of Chinese Business Firms Henry Wai-chung Yeung and Kris Olds (eds.), (London: Macmillan),

According to the study by Po published by DLSU, certain cultural/ethnic groups like the overseas ethnic Chinese like to run their own businesses and became their own bosses with a compulsion for autonomy/independence while creating something of value that they can contribute to society or improve their social statuses by transcending poor work environments or family finances.[46]

In general literature on entrepreneurship thinking/mindset and education, S.S. Tan and Frank Ng argued that skills/knowledge for building and managing new firms are fundamental business concepts found outside traditional business ideas such as the creativity, cross-functional thinking and ambiguity tolerance.[47] With the complexities of starting a contemporary business, all stakeholders in entrepreneurial ventures requires cross-functional management skills: students want skills that can help them start businesses to cope with corporate downsizing and outsourcing; employers want employees who can think like entrepreneurs and practice corporate entrepreneurship to cope with global competition and technological disruptions.[48] The intellectual stakeholders are also inclined to work towards the ideas that entrepreneurship can be learned/taught and not only subscribe to the idea of "born" entrepreneurs while catering to experienced executives desiring to learn skills to expand their businesses.[49]

A local case study was used to demonstrate Tan and Ng's arguments. In the implementation of the entrepreneurship program at the Republic Polytechnic, students were exposed to a problem-solving syllabus with specific learning outcomes through self-motivated learning,

---

[downloaded on 1 January 2020], available at https://courses.nus.edu.sg/course/geoywc/publication/Macmillan.PDF, p.17 [online edition].

[46]Po, Gerley Q., "A comparative analysis of the entrepreneurial styles of second, third, and fourth generation overseas Chinese and filipinos in the philippines" dated 2010 in DLSU (De La Salle University) *Business & Economics Review* 19.2 [downloaded on 1 January 2021], available at https://www.dlsu.edu.ph/wp-content/uploads/2019/10/AComparativeAnalysisoftheEntrepreneurialStylesofSecondThirdandFourthGeneration OverseasChineseandFilipinosinthePhilippines.pdf, p, 17.

[47]Tan, Siok San and Frank Ng CK, "An innovative approach to entrepreneurship education using problem-based learning" undated in Boston Entrepreneur Center Bostonec.com [downloaded on 1 December 2020], available at http://www.bostonec.com/uploads/1/4/0/0/14008812/entrepreneurship_education_using_problem-based_learning_.pdf, un-paginated online edition.

[48]*Ibid.*

[49]*Ibid.*

self-generated enquiry of knowledge and peer teaching with teams working together based on role-playing scenarios and class presentations.[50] This is based on the conceptual idea that a large body of collective knowledge can be distilled from veteran entrepreneurs for classroom teaching and practical problem-solving and it can tease out "some of the anxiety, excitement and action associated with a new venture" on the part of the students.[51]

This however comes with the caveat that the actual world is the optimal teaching environment for entrepreneurship although with the embedded idea that many entrepreneurs would have executed decisions differently if they had awareness that there are potential pitfalls prevalent in business activities.[52] Thus, the classroom environment pre-empts students of upcoming challenges in business activities, assist students to manage critical issues with broad ideas on problem-solving, enable students to work in teams, engage in peer discussion (alongside teaching) for better conceptual learning and engaged with different affective aspects of the business, offering reasonable insights for application in practical situation.[53]

The idea of creative solutions for business problems is discussed in Organization for Economic Co-operation and Development (OECD) literature. Andrew Penaluna and Kathryn Penaluna argued in their OECD report on entrepreneurial education that fostering creativity may involve unlearning knowledge that was formerly valid and conceptualizing matters in new ways and drop ways of doing things that are no longer useful.[54] Penaluna and Penaluna also highlighted how an entrepreneurial mindset is motivated by being an adaptive, inquisitive learner who searches for new opportunities by questioning established norms and spotting multiple rather than unitary resolutions to challenges/problems, thus entrepreneurial education has emphasized managing changing objectives and dynamic

---

[50] *Ibid.*

[51] *Ibid.*

[52] *Ibid.*

[53] *Ibid.*

[54] Penaluna, Andrew and Kathryn Penaluna, "Entrepreneurial education in practice part 2- building motivations and competencies" dated 2015 in Entrepreneurship 360 Thematic Paper (EU: European Commission LEED), 2015 [downloaded on 1 December 2020], available at http://www.oecd.org/cfe/leed/Entrepreneurial-Education-Practice-pt2.pdf, p. 9.

scenarios rather than a fixed pathway.[55] This is in line with Seet and Ng's study which was also cited in the Penaluna and Penaluna's OECD report.

Methodology

The monograph will also take a social-constructivist approach, using interpretive work, perspectives and paradigms to analyze case studies (case method) and take a qualitative approach to analyze narratives in these case studies. The narratives assist the author to understand how individuals think about their environments. The writing includes case studies, life stories and career paths to understand the growth and development of entrepreneurs and some of their worldviews. It will also seek to find out how these entrepreneurs understand the development of their own businesses. In appreciating their views and experiences, it may be possible to link some concepts, definitions and theories with the way entrepreneurs and students of entrepreneurship recognize opportunities to create companies and the way they view host societies/economies.

The Asian Entrepreneur Mindset

The 2015 Global Entrepreneurship Index noted the diversity of entrepreneurship in Asia. Asia's diverse economic landscape includes leading entrepreneurial economies like Australia, Taiwan and Singapore co-existing with economies that have underdeveloped potential like Myanmar, Indonesia, Pakistan and Bangladesh. Asia's economic system also varies. Some countries have the state as a key stakeholder in their economy like Singapore and Malaysia, while Hong Kong and Indonesia are private sector-led, resulting in the fragmentation of Asia as a market accommodating all kinds of businesses.[56]

Despite East Asian success, many challenges remain for the region. Four out of 42 Asia-Pacific countries are low-income economies

---

[55] *Ibid*, p. 10.

[56] Narasimhalu, Arcot Desai, "Thinking bigger: Pushing Singaporean entrepreneurship to the next level" dated March 2015 at Singapore Management University (SMU) Research Collection School Of Information Systems School of Information Systems (Singapore: SMU), 2015, available at https://ink.library.smu.edu.sg/cgi/viewcontent.cgi?article=4446 &context=sis_research, pp. 42–43.

(450 million extreme poor in middle-income economies), Industry 4.0 automation risks loom large, 700 million Asian youngsters reaching working age at a rate faster than industrial jobs creation, 220.5 million youngsters are neither in education or employment (NEETs) and the region is ageing fast (becoming old before it gets wealthy).[57] International organizations (IOs) like the United Nations (UN) are well aware of the acute need for Asian job creation to forestall these abovementioned challenges. On a regional basis, the United Nations Development Program (UNDP)'s Youth Co: Lab initiative is eliminating legal/funding barriers for youngsters and connecting social entrepreneurs with incubators like TechStars to foreground pitching ideas and skills for national skills enhancement, business-making or employment.[58]

The fear of failure appears to be the largest hindrance for Asian entrepreneurs, contrasting with their US counterparts as CEO Mykolas Rambus of Wealth-X, a research firm that monitors the ultra-rich, explained:

> There are huge numbers of graduates in Asia and that's fine. But entrepreneurs — individuals that have a like mindset and are prepared to take a risk to start a business?, I'm not sure about that ... The price of failure in the U.S. is that you learn from your mistakes and try again — banks can be accepting of that, the community can be accepting of that, your family can be accepting of that ... I don't see that being the case in Asia. Failure is branded that way permanently.[59]

Compared with East Asia, the United States has a number of entrepreneurial heroes they can look up to who experienced failure before succeeding. They include Walt Disney (his initial animation firm was bankrupt), Harvard dropout Bill Gates and Microsoft co-founder Paul Allen (and his failed initial venture Traf-O-Data), all of whom thrived

---

[57]Xu, Haoliang, "Asia's young entrepreneurs need help with the hustle" dated 10 August 2018 in World Economic Forum (WEF) [downloaded on 10 August 2018], available at https://www.weforum.org/agenda/2018/08/asias-young-entrepreneurs-need-help-with-the-hustle/.

[58]*Ibid.*

[59]Ranasinghe, Dhara and Katie Holliday, "What are Asian entrepreneurs afraid of?" dated 29 April 2013 in CNBC.com [downloaded on 1 December 2020], available at https://www.cnbc.com/id/100682512.

because failure in the United States is seen as a learning experience.[60] A 2015 KPMG report stated, "Invariably, most start-ups struggle to grow and failure rates are extremely high. Although young entrepreneurs may demonstrate ideas, motivation and expertise, they lack experience and capital assets".[61]

In Asia, failure is stigmatized, restraining entrepreneurship despite the region's expanding consumer markets and ample economic opportunities for risk-takers because obtaining a stable occupation and moving up the hierarchy of reputable firms are more broadly accepted as a benchmark of success than a risky new venture.[62] Experts opined the fear of failure in Asia is more prominent than other world regions due to traditional family expectations with parental encouragement/pressuring their off-springs to take on an established professional pathway like becoming a lawyer or engineer, more so in conservative societies (Japan, Taiwan and Singapore) than Asian countries that have has strong roots in entrepreneurship (India).[63]

Experts like Rambus have also argued that Asian countries with strong familial structures like Japan (compared to Indian social structures, for example) require a mindset change. For example, Damien Duhamel, managing partner at Singapore-based consultancy Solidiance argued:

> Singapore is risk-averse traditionally, a lot of Singaporean entrepreneurs are not necessarily Singaporean born and bred [e.g. TWG established by two expatriates in Singapore] … Fifteen years ago entrepreneurs in Asia were viewed as outcasts from society. This is because peer pressure in Asia is stronger than in Europe — there is greater pressure to get married, stay put, and buy a house and a car. It was not the norm to take a

---

[60] *Ibid.*

[61] Narasimhalu, Arcot Desai, "Thinking bigger: Pushing Singaporean entrepreneurship to the next level" dated March 2015 at Singapore Management University (SMU) Research Collection School Of Information Systems School of Information Systems (Singapore: SMU), 2015, available at https://ink.library.smu.edu.sg/cgi/viewcontent.cgi?article=4446&context=sis_research, p. 44.

[62] Ranasinghe, Dhara and Katie Holliday, "What are Asian entrepreneurs afraid of?" dated 29 April 2013 in CNBC.com [downloaded on 1 December 2020], available at https://www.cnbc.com/id/100682512.

[63] *Ibid.*

year off, go travelling etc … The younger crowd does seem happier to stick its neck out [now].[64]

But, some successful Singaporean entrepreneurs appear to be accommodating risks as part of their worldview and company philosophy. Singapore's home-grown Forrest Li highlighted an important part of his responsibilities as an entrepreneur is to encourage a "day one mentality" of curiosity and experimentation in his company:

> One of my job's very important parts is to constantly remind the entire organization (of) what really matters to us … We always believe that we can do more in the future and that we are still at the very beginning of the journey. We encourage people to try things without certainty and we tolerate some failure … I think this [adaptability and openness] has become a key thing that differentiates ourselves as an organization, compared to our peers who are competitors. In a very unplanned situation, whoever adapts better and embraces change … will do better.[65]

There are also mitigating factors to offset the fear of failure in Singapore's entrepreneurship ecosystem. Singaporean entrepreneurs also enjoy strong ecological support. For example, Singapore's Action Community for Entrepreneurship (ACE) has assisted the creation of thousands of successful start-ups and jobs for more than 15 years.[66] Such support may help to overcome risk-adverse mindsets.

East Asian Entrepreneurship

Southeast Asian economies are expected to grow significantly, especially after the quiet formation of the ASEAN Economic Community (AEC) in 2015. It has vast markets like the huge population of Indonesia, the largest

---

[64] *Ibid.*

[65] Pillai, Sharanya, "Don't miss forrest for the trees" dated 25 November 2020 in *Business Times* [downloaded on 25 November 2020], available at https://www.businesstimes.com.sg/garage/news/singapore-business-awards-2020/dont-miss-forrest-for-the-trees.

[66] Xu, Haoliang, "Asia's young entrepreneurs need help with the hustle" dated 10 August 2018 in World Economic Forum (WEF) [downloaded on 10 August 2018], available at https://www.weforum.org/agenda/2018/08/asias-young-entrepreneurs-need-help-with-the-hustle/.

Muslim country on Earth and a sizable market and underdeveloped markets like Laos. All of which are growing markets with consumer demand. Part of the entrepreneurs' learning process (including those from Singapore) will be learning how to navigate foreign markets, something that can be supported by training. Political stability will be essential for entrepreneurial activities while others need to upgrade their infrastructures, institutional and legal systems to cultivate entrepreneurial skills.

There are local characteristics of entrepreneurial mindsets in East Asia. East Asia is not a homogenous world region when it comes to entrepreneurship. Xu Haoliang from the UN mentioned the profiles of successful entrepreneurs in Asia in his WEF article. His group's research indicated entrepreneurs over 35 years old manage the most successful firms in Asia and typically armed with the most education.[67] In the case of Japan, Yokoyama and Birchley's study quoted Inter Nations, an independent research firm's survey of 14,000 individuals which uncovered that Japanese entrepreneurs who work overseas (expatriate entrepreneurs) are typically male, employed in business services/consulting, satisfied with work/life balance with a relationship (7 out of 10) and bringing up kids (25% of them).[68] The same study indicated that 19% of Japanese business owners/entrepreneurs are keen to establish their own companies in their destination (more the global average of 3%) and 12% of them are interested to have a better quality of life overseas.[69] In the next chapter, this publication will look at the case study of how young, tech-savvy technopreneurs are trying to capitalize on a growing industry while tackling Japan's social challenges at the same time.

---

[67] *Ibid.*

[68] Yokoyama, Kazuko and Sarah Louisa Birchley, Transnational Entrepreneurship in South East Asia (US: Springer Link), 2019, p. 7.

[69] *Ibid.*

Chapter 2

Northeast Asia, A Japanese Case Study: Entrepreneurship and Civic Tech in Japan

Introduction

Some commentators like Stacy Donohue, an investment partner at Omidyar Network dealing with innovations in civic tech, contextualized civic technopreneurship development in contemporary history. She argued that civic tech is not new as humans have been utilizing technology to empower citizenry and enhance government functions even before 2005, but what has different now is the new enthusiasm shown by more entrepreneurs, innovators, private-/public-sector leaders who are excited about its prospects for disruptions.[1] While the promise of disruptions appear to be a major driving force in civic technopreneurship in the United States, Japanese civic technopreneurship appears to be catalyzed by major national crises and disasters. This is not surprising given that Japanese culture tends to favor stability and inertial in times of peace and prosperity and are only prodded into making major changes when there are major external shocks to the system. Historians often cite how the crisis of foreign intervention and *gaiastsu* (foreign pressure) prodded Japan into the bloodless Meiji Restoration (1868), transforming Japan

---

[1] Donohue, Stacy, "Civic tech is ready for investment" dated 30 April 2015 in *TechCrunch* [downloaded on 30 April 2015], available at https://techcrunch.com/2015/04/29/civic-tech-is-ready-for-investment/.

from the backwaters of a late feudal nation with a self-imposed isolation-ist (*sakoku*) policy to a modern nation (*fukoku kyohei* or wealthy nation, strong army) that joined the ranks of leading powers in the world.

Crisis Entrepreneurship in Japan

The hope that civic tech holds for Japan's economic rejuvenation is based on the idea that Japan has undergone economic slowdown and recession-ary conditions since 1989. Between 1945 and 1952, Japan was devastated by World War II and came under the Allied Occupation. Between 1952 and 1960, Japan quickly restored its economic growth and heavy industrial as well as business vitality. The period of 1960s was Japan's income-doubling economic growth period that propelled it the world's third largest economy in the late 1970s. The 1980s nearly saw Japan taking over as the world's largest economy from the United States (a pro-jection popularized by Professor Ezra Vogel's publication *Japan as Number One*). In 1985, Japan was compelled to increase the value of its yen to satisfy its major G-5 trading partners who were concerned with Japan's undervalued yen and the unfair economic competitiveness associ-ated with it.

But, the sudden revaluation of the yen after 1985 saw a period of irrational exuberance as Japanese local and foreign investments bal-looned. This "bubble" was eventually unsustainable and came to an end in 1989. Some argue that Japan has been on a steady mature state of slower economic growth since the bubble economy burst in 1989. They opined that its technological and industrial growth has slowed down or/ and facing challenges and entire sectors have been slow to innovate with a less optimistic future for tech start-ups and it is in this context that some observers argued civic tech start-ups represents a understated but bright spark in this scenario.[2]

The end of the bubble economy in Japan in 1989 was not the only event that jolted the Japanese state and its civic techies into action. The Great East Japan Earthquake 2011 (nicknamed popularly as "311") is another crisis that has triggered civic technopreneurs to come up with

---

[2]Gingold, Naomi, "There's new life in Japan's tech start-up scene" dated 28 July 2015 in *The World* [downloaded on 1 January 2020], available at https://www.pri.org/stories/2015-07-28/theres-new-life-japans-tech-startup-scene.

solutions. Upon the advisory of civic techie and entrepreneur Hal Seki, the Japanese government offered tablets to the former residents of Namie in Fukushima that provided them with the schedules of making safe return to their hometown as well as the area's restoration progress in 2014.[3] Seki put together a team of professional hackers for an annual government contractor employment to create "Code for Namie" to perform these functions (especially for the elderly residents) and also hold classroom sessions for them on how to use the six apps to access daily local updates, photo-share Namie's reconstruction and use digital technologies "meet" their scattered family members.[4] Disasters have been major impetus for changes in technopreneur–government relations. Expert hackers who were sub-contracted to work on government projects in a natural disaster area stimulated changes in government thinking, resulting in the Code for Namie fellowship project for institutionalizing state cooperation with hackers for a tenure of up to three years and training successive generations of hackers to manage such projects.[5]

The latest COVID-19 pandemic is the latest series of crises triggering off civic tech entrepreneurship. To mitigate the pandemic, the IT Strategic Headquarters of the Cabinet Secretariat, Ministry of Internal Affairs and Communications (MIC), Ministry of Economy, Trade and Industry (METI), Japan's industries and a Civic Tech association collaborated closely together. They worked on Project "#Navigation of Information on Private Support Services" to collect data on private sector support services for mitigating the novel coronavirus disease and then publish the data into a standardized format.[6]

---

[3]Liu, Chih-hsin and Aaron Wytze (contributor and translator), "Code for Japan: How a Tsunami Ushered in the age of the hacker" dated 16 May 2017 [downloaded on 16 May 2017], available at https://g0v.news/code-for-japan-how-a-nuclear-disaster-ushered-in-the-age-of-the-hacker-c624d6f5bf66.

[4]*Ibid.*

[5]*Ibid.*

[6]Ministry of Economy, Trade and Industry (METI), "Publish information on free-of-charge and discounted Support Services Provided by Private Companies as Responses to Novel Coronavirus Disease with Standardized Open Data — Project for "#Navigation of information on private support services" dated 9 March 2020 in METI website [downloaded on 9 March 2020], available at https://www.meti.go.jp/english/press/2020/0309_002.html.

The objective of this initiative is for the government to facilitate businesses in accessing free and discounted services offered by private sector tech firms to stimulate business activities in COVID-19 coronavirus pandemic conditions.[7] These services are aggregated by the Cabinet Secretariat, MIC and METI in Project "#Navigation of Information on Private Support Services" in a user-friendly format on an accessible platform while offering industrial associations standard data forms to input information on support services and asking them for help to reach out to other member companies and entrepreneurs to do likewise.[8]

Civic Tech Entrepreneurship and Morale Boost

Some leading civic tech firms like Murashiki's (a website and digital consulting firm) founder Yuu Sumiyoshi insisted they started their specialized e-commerce sites because Japan's economy had been stagnant in the post-bubble economic era. He articulated: "I wanted to do something to throw off that sense of despair … [opining that traditional Japanese companies have been risk-averse, slow to change, and rigidly hierarchical, but Japan still has the skill and know-how to make amazing things, especially by fusing together old craft with new technology]".[9] Concurrent CEO Yuu Sumiyoshi's Murashiki office is typical of civic tech start-ups, located in a hipster surrounding inside a traditional Japanese house in a bamboo grove with tatami mats and sliding shoji paper screens that facilitates his concentration power: "it's easy to think of good ideas when you brainstorm here. It's just a more creative environment than being surrounded by concrete".[10] Tokyo appears to be a major attractor of civic tech start-ups. Sumiyoshi moved his office to metropolitan Tokyo from Kamakura (south of Tokyo with a Zen-like atmosphere well-known for its temples, Buddha idols and sea-sides) in 2008.[11]

A signature Murashiki project is designing the marketplace Iichi for artisanal products that eventually became a company of its own and

---

[7] *Ibid.*

[8] *Ibid.*

[9] Gingold, Naomi, "There's new life in Japan's tech start-up scene" dated 28 July 2015 in *The World* [downloaded on 1 January 2020], available at https://www.pri.org/stories/2015-07-28/theres-new-life-japans-tech-startup-scene.

[10] *Ibid.*

[11] *Ibid.*

another one is Crazy Japan whose selling point is: "For Kings, Lords and Billionaires of the World. Welcome to Crazy Japan Murashiki: A Marketplace for Everything Crazy and Japanese".[12] The e-commerce marketplace sells zany items like pet samurai armor for only US$480,000 (actual price from a local artisan), an example of the idiosyncratic oddity of Kamakura-based start-ups that are innovative in terms of businesses management and physical office setups.[13]

Commercial items are not the only items aggregated in civic tech sites. The government has also worked with private sector companies and entrepreneurs to offer their services in collaborative sites to keep businesses running in a pandemic. In reaction to the COVID-19 disruptions of economic activities, companies offered free and discounted services to support members of the public, including commercial activities like online studies and telework and so the government brought all these disparate services under a single one-stop online information counter for users.[14]

In pulling the state and civic technopreneurs closer together, there are evangelists who form a bridge between the two stakeholders, founder of New Stories and Policy Advisor of Ministry of Internal Affairs. One example is Naoki Ota who is a former Boston Consulting Group (BCG) Asian Technology Group management member, representative of New Stories and is appointed Policy Advisor of Ministry of Internal Affairs.[15] He designs and manages future proto-typing by working with governments, private companies, academics/intellectuals and social businesses in local cities that serve as "living laboratories" for the prototyping process.[16] He is also a civic tech advocate in Code for Japan while he was

---

[12] *Ibid.*

[13] *Ibid.*

[14] Ministry of Economy, Trade and Industry (METI), "Publish information on free-of-charge and discounted Support Services Provided by Private Companies as Responses to Novel Coronavirus Disease with Standardized Open Data — Project for "#Navigation of information on private support services" dated 9 March 2020 in METI website [downloaded on 9 March 2020], available at https://www.meti.go.jp/english/press/2020/0309_002.html.

[15] Swiss Re, "Naoki Ota" dated 2021 in Swiss Re website [downloaded on 1 February 2021], available at https://www.swissre.com/en/japan/profile/Naoki_Ota/ep_4d5e41.

[16] He has a BA at Tokyo University and an MBA at London Business School. (Source: Swiss Re, "Naoki Ota" dated 2021 in Swiss Re website [downloaded on 1 February 2021], available at https://www.swissre.com/en/japan/profile/Naoki_Ota/ep_4d5e41).

executing his responsibility as the Special Advisor of Minister of Internal Affairs from 2015 to 2018 in policy planning and execution in the local revitalization and Proof of Concept (PoC) of IoT, AI, and so on.[17]

Entrepreneurs and Government Relations

Some entrepreneurs nurse idealistic aspirations to contribute to government reforms, especially in the aspect of offering better services to society. Hal Seki is a case study in this aspect. Before 2014, civic techie Hal Seki was an ordinary idealistic entrepreneur with ambitions to bring about Japanese government reforms through civic tech inspired by American public–private collaborations with companies but ran into funding issues: "Everything depended on money. Nobody was willing to pay up".[18] Seki also found it difficult to employ individuals for shorter-term project basis and was told by civil servants that it was difficult to sell the idea palatably to elected politicians and civil service unions.[19]

In this aspect, not only is the United States appointing top officials in the government's tech hierarchy who believed in civic tech entrepreneurship in 2015, increasing government interest in this sector appears to be attracting private sector investors as well. Betting on civic tech, Omidyar Network is investing in both expanding non-profits and for-profits sectors and, for funding sustainability, both grants and venture capital are deployed to back up organizations like civic tech Non Profit Organization (NPOs) like Code for America and Sunlight Foundation and profit-making tech outfits like NationBuilder and SeeClickFix with early-stage funding for catalyzing innovation in the civic tech industry.[20]

---

[17] Swiss Re, "Naoki Ota" dated 2021 in Swiss Re website [downloaded on 1 February 2021], available at https://www.swissre.com/en/japan/profile/Naoki_Ota/ep_4d5e41.

[18] Liu, Chih-hsin and Aaron Wytze (contributor and translator), "Code for Japan: How a Tsunami Ushered in the age of the hacker" dated 16 May 2017 [downloaded on 16 May 2017], available at https://g0v.news/code-for-japan-how-a-nuclear-disaster-ushered-in-the-age-of-the-hacker-c624d6f5bf66.

[19] *Ibid.*

[20] Donohue, Stacy, "Civic tech is ready for investment" dated 30 April 2015 in *TechCrunch* [downloaded on 30 April 2015], available at https://techcrunch.com/2015/04/29/civic-tech-is-ready-for-investment/.

The Kamacon

One of the most important districts when it comes to running civic tech entrepreneurship is probably found in the hipster and trendy Silicon Valley-type neighborhood of Kamakura in the southern periphery of Tokyo. Perhaps the most distinguishing feature of the Kamakura start-ups is their adoption of civic tech methodologies in community development of applications. Historically, it started in 2012 when there were only seven start-ups in Kamakura but they seldom have meetings and then a brain-wave occurred one night when these CEOs met for social drinking and collectively said: "you know, we're here — we might as well do something together" to improve Kamakura for all community stakeholders.[21]

This was the accidental genesis of Kamacon Valley (Silicon Valley + Kamakura) and the idea of a tech hub snowballed with an increase in start-ups and local community participants and, before long, the technopreneurs started asking what the local communities needed and then offered their services for free.[22] There appears to be a genuine love for Kamakura and contribute back to the local host community, a sentiment expressed by the information technologists, designers engineers, entrepreneurs, Kamakura-based CEOs. So Craig Mod (author/designer for American/Japanese start-ups) argued:

> I feel like Kamakura is the greatest hack of Tokyo ... You can live in a great place for not a lot of money, you have incredible access to nature, and yet Tokyo is right there ... creating a real culture, and it is attracting a certain kind of innovator and a certain kind of entrepreneur ... I think that we won't see what the results of those people coming together is until ten years from now.[23]

Some observers noted that such arrangements are not common in San Francisco's Silicon Valley where the tech constituents are somewhat disparately organized and have tensions with the local resident

---

[21] Gingold, Naomi, "There's new life in Japan's tech start-up scene" dated 28 July 2015 in *The World* [downloaded on 1 January 2020], available at https://www.pri.org/stories/2015-07-28/theres-new-life-japans-tech-startup-scene.

[22] *Ibid.*

[23] *Ibid.*

communities.[24] Having said that, US investors are progressive when it comes to investing in the sector. In terms of revenue growth and expansion of civic tech services users, civic tech start-ups are required to show success to secure investor confidence but the regular venture fund has a 10-year period and some cutting-edge innovations require decades to materialize and produce results.[25] Civic tech start-ups are also dependent on government procurement procedures so any would-be investors (a major stakeholder in the future of civic technopreneurship) need to calibrate their profit expectations and returns by taking a long-term approach.[26]

In Japan, Kamacon's techie enthusiasm appears to rub off nationally with some participants articulating: "we can make Japan alive again. And not just Japan, but the world. There are a lot of people here who think that way", inspiring other Japanese to learn and experience Kamacon to replicate it in their own communities (Iwaki, Fukushima and Fukuoka are just some examples).[27] Some Japanese metropolitan cities have implemented their own technopreneur–local government–civic tech cooperation. For example, in 2017, metropolitan Kobe City city's dynamic young mayor who is an advocate of open government employed civic technopreneur Hal Seki as the city's "innovation officer" with the city budget funding Seki's office space and a one-year Kobe city fellowship program to encourage hackers to collaborate with civil servants in enhancing the city bureaucracy's internal work culture.[28] This is especially pertinent to the local bureaucracy's implementation of technology.

Some even opine Kamacon is becoming a civic tech showcase with features that even techie mecca Silicon Valley and other global tech

---

[24] *Ibid.*

[25] Donohue, Stacy, "Civic tech is ready for investment" dated 30 April 2015 in *TechCrunch* [downloaded on 30 April 2015], available at https://techcrunch.com/2015/04/29/civic-tech-is-ready-for-investment/.

[26] *Ibid.*

[27] Gingold, Naomi, "There's new life in Japan's tech start-up scene" dated 28 July 2015 in *The World* [downloaded on 1 January 2020], available at https://www.pri.org/stories/2015-07-28/theres-new-life-japans-tech-startup-scene.

[28] Liu, Chih-hsin and Aaron Wytze (contributor and translator), "Code for Japan: How a Tsunami Ushered in the age of the hacker" dated 16 May 2017 [downloaded on 16 May 2017], available at https://g0v.news/code-for-japan-how-a-nuclear-disaster-ushered-in-the-age-of-the-hacker-c624d6f5bf66.

communities can look at.[29] Kamacon's inclusion of local government officials into their events like hackathons is something that governments in the West are also keen on doing. In the United States, state-funded tech solutions are transforming how governments work, provide public services, carry out data-driven policies, enhance efficiency, create smart governments, interpret charts/graphs, pull out historical data, reduce spending, carry out better planning and store big data in cloud for entrepreneurs to work with the government.[30]

Because of government enthusiasm warming up, investors are also taking notice of the emerging growth industry. Civic technopreneurship excited investors with its investment opportunities. They spot a growing civic tech industry where the US government is spending billions and appointing tech talents into the ranks of the government starting from 2015 with ex-Googler Megan Smith assuming the country's chief technology officer (2014) while former Twitter and Medium exec DJ Patil rose to be the United States' first digital scientist in that year.[31] With civic tech promising to generate both revenues while effecting social impacts, savvy investors have been surfacing in this industry since 2015. Andreessen Horowitz (investor in profitable start-ups like Airbnb, Facebook, Lyft, Twitter) led OpenGov's US$15 million funding exercise while Change.org (biggest global petition platform with 100 million users) came up with US$25 million Series C funding from investors like Arianna Huffington, Bill Gates, Richard Branson and Omidyar Network.[32]

Government resources may be hard to secure in bad times but once tech entrepreneurs secure work with them, they may enjoy security in partnership given that state budgets tend to work in blocks of several years in places like the United States, thus providing secure revenues in those

---

[29]Gingold, Naomi, "There's new life in Japan's tech start-up scene" dated 28 July 2015 in *The World* [downloaded on 1 January 2020], available at https://www.pri.org/stories/2015-07-28/theres-new-life-japans-tech-startup-scene.

[30]Montgomery, Mike, "Why civic tech is the next big thing" dated 24 June 2015 in Forbes [downloaded on 24 June 2015], available at https://www.forbes.com/sites/mikemontgomery/2015/06/24/why-civic-tech-is-the-next-big-thing/?sh=c84b77f369a9.

[31]Donohue, Stacy, "Civic tech is ready for investment" dated 30 April 2015 in *TechCrunch* [downloaded on 30 April 2015], available at https://techcrunch.com/2015/04/29/civic-tech-is-ready-for-investment/.

[32]*Ibid.*

years.[33] Kamacon is not the only example of state–society–civic techno-preneur cooperation. Hal Seki's post-311 app accessible by state-subsidized tablets were all part of the 770 ideas generated by 400 Namie residents and Seki translated his experiences from Yahoo! Japan's user-centered methodology to the project as well as the tablet apps (released after 12 prototypes and ten trial runs).[34]

For most part, civic tech entrepreneurship is entirely driven by non-profits and private sector techies. They are not dependent on state-led initiatives, going against the grain in a country whose economic development has been closely associated with a state-led model. In the United States, up till 1995, state involvement in the tech sector was shunned by tech entrepreneurs due to their tendencies for red tape, perceived circum-scribed resources (especially at the municipal levels) while private sector funding have less strings attached and diverse in nature.[35] At the same time, however, the state and local authorities are equal community stake-holders and should not be left out. Therefore, while civic tech initiatives in Japan may not be catalyzed by the government, civic techies welcome all stakeholders, including the government and their feedback/inputs on their initiatives.

This is certainly true in the case of civic technopreneur Hal Seki. By persuading the Kobe City government to offer him an innovation officer seat in the bureaucracy, Hal Seki located the "sweet spot" for actualizing corporation-technopreneur–government collaboration with services funded by the private sector and coders offering free services that were "sweet enough carrots" to get this triangular relationship going.[36]

---

[33] Montgomery, Mike, "Why civic tech is the next big thing" dated 24 June 2015 in Forbes [downloaded on 24 June 2015], available at https://www.forbes.com/sites/mikemontgomery/2015/06/24/why-civic-tech-is-the-next-big-thing/?sh=c84b77f369a9.

[34] Liu, Chih-hsin and Aaron Wytze (contributor and translator), "Code for Japan: How a Tsunami Ushered in the age of the hacker" dated 16 May 2017 [downloaded on 16 May 2017], available at https://g0v.news/code-for-japan-how-a-nuclear-disaster-ushered-in-the-age-of-the-hacker-c624d6f5bf66.

[35] Montgomery, Mike, "Why civic tech is the next big thing" dated 24 June 2015 in Forbes [downloaded on 24 June 2015], available at https://www.forbes.com/sites/mikemontgomery/2015/06/24/why-civic-tech-is-the-next-big-thing/?sh=c84b77f369a9.

[36] Liu, Chih-hsin and Aaron Wytze (contributor and translator), "Code for Japan: How a Tsunami Ushered in the age of the hacker" dated 16 May 2017 [downloaded on 16 May 2017], available at https://g0v.news/code-for-japan-how-a-nuclear-disaster-ushered-in-the-age-of-the-hacker-c624d6f5bf66.

It has introduced socially conscious entrepreneurs into the halls of the government while shaping the government to be technologically savvy and embrace elements of civil society.

In the Kamacon town hall gathering, some of the attendees are students, women in their sixties, local assembly members, nursery school teachers, tech CEOs, people of all genders, the mayor, all coming to brainstorm the local community issues, collectively coming up with "cool" solutions and democratically speak their minds.[37] These cool projects have taken on the formats of movie fest, open data initiatives, app-based guide to local elections, tsunami alert apps, nostalgic curation of old photos in Kamakura for a heritage tour app, a musical with the Fukushima meltdown theme, entrepreneurship programs for local kids, a bi-annual hackathon in a temple and crowdfunding start-up for local projects.[38]

Local regulatory authorities would be a great ally to have for civic tech entrepreneurship as they are the traditional guardians of community data and information. The state realizes the potential of technology to effect social and socio-economic change in the 21st century. In turn, civic techies can unlock the potential of data for public initiatives and economic activities instead of sealing them up in cabinets and reports, especially at a time of citizen demand for government transparency, calls for accountability to the public and a desire to see how tax payer revenues are utilized.[39]

Many define "civic tech" in a broad manner to mean any technology to empower citizens or help make government more accessible, efficient and effective, inclusively embracing diverse stakeholders with many working on local government projects that are perceived as better living labs for civic tech innovations, despite the fact that national governments tend to have bigger budgets and nationwide applicability.[40] Civic technopreneur innovations also helped to save governments tax dollars while

---

[37] Gingold, Naomi, "There's new life in Japan's tech start-up scene" dated 28 July 2015 in *The World* [downloaded on 1 January 2020], available at https://www.pri.org/stories/2015-07-28/theres-new-life-japans-tech-startup-scene.

[38] *Ibid.*

[39] Montgomery, Mike, "Why civic tech is the next big thing" dated 24 June 2015 in Forbes [downloaded on 24 June 2015], available at https://www.forbes.com/sites/mikemontgomery/2015/06/24/why-civic-tech-is-the-next-big-thing/?sh=c84b77f369a9.

[40] Donohue, Stacy, "Civic tech is ready for investment" dated 30 April 2015 in *TechCrunch* [downloaded on 30 April 2015], available at https://techcrunch.com/2015/04/29/civic-tech-is-ready-for-investment/.

being compensated from public revenues by coming up with cost-saving and effective solutions for the local communities. For example, the Code for Namie civic technopreneurs' digital solutions for the affected families of 311 (Great East Japan Earthquake) managed to optimize the local authority's three-year budget and was still below a million US dollars cheaper than other local authorities' projects in the tech arena.[41] Code for Namie representatives explained: "I think because we understood the procurement process, we knew the rules for tendering a bid. Plus there's a lot of things you can do with open source software, which saved us a lot of money".[42]

Case Study of Code for Japan

Hal Seki from Code4Japan is a Civic-Tech advocate who previously worked for smartphone outfits as a Geo developer since 2002, former CEO of Sinsai (cloud sourcing crisis information platform using Ushah) and then became the CEO of Georepublic Japan, founder and CEO of HackCamp Inc. (Hackathons and Ideathons organizer).[43] He founded a new civic tech organization in 2013 known as Code for Japan (expanded to 80 branches) with the slogan "Think together, Create together" that mainly earn profit from governments through consultancy and fund community-building activities.[44] The civic tech outfit works in small teams. The small-team units are autonomous and self-driven and snowballs personnel on a project basis, such as running workshops for the government, sourcing human resources to be government contractors, connecting governments with private sector firms, organizing bi-monthly hackathons, collaborating with the global Code for All (CFA) network to get network exchange funding to organize workshops on collaborative

---

[41] Liu, Chih-hsin and Aaron Wytze (contributor and translator), "Code for Japan: How a Tsunami Ushered in the age of the hacker" dated 16 May 2017 [downloaded on 16 May 2017], available at https://g0v.news/code-for-japan-how-a-nuclear-disaster-ushered-in-the-age-of-the-hacker-c624d6f5bf66.

[42] *Ibid.*

[43] Maurel, Roxane, "Une entrevue au Japon – Code 4 Japan" dated 17 April 2020 in Open by Design website [downloaded on 17 April 2020], available at https://openbydesign.io/2020/04/17/une-entrevue-au-japon-code-4-japan/.

[44] *Ibid.*

policy-making.[45] The outfit is creating a comprehensive network of NPOs and social entrepreneurs to brainstorm for solutions to social challenges faced by all stakeholders in society, link up social entrepreneurs, work with the private sectors in areas like FIWARE interoperability between smart cities.[46]

In his technopreneurship consultancy, Hal Seki is also forging closer ties between the government and companies, facilitating the state's borrowing of top private sector hackers with little costs and even getting private companies to pay for getting their engineers to work on state projects.[47] "Corporate fellowships" proved to be ideal for filling in the government's difficulties in locating suitable human resource, thus if a private sector IT engineer or coder applies for "Code for Japan" fellowship, she/he can opt to be sub-contracted for a three month period to a state unit requiring their expertise.[48] The participating private sector company offers their expert personnel for three months subcontracting periods while Code for Japan intermediates as a results-oriented quality assurance entity to ensure government assignments/requirements are met by each contracted engineer and deploying them as consultants for two days per week in the relevant government departments.[49] This is a win–win situation for all. Junior engineers in the private corporations may encounter an uphill effort in securing promotions and/or are tired of routinized work, which can all be resolved with short stints of high-innovation work with the government, resulting in a good avenue for companies to retain technicians who are otherwise bored and also build commercial relations with companies through small-scale paid projects.

---

[45] *Ibid.*

[46] *Ibid.*

[47] Liu, Chih-hsin and Aaron Wytze (contributor and translator), "Code for Japan: How a Tsunami Ushered in the age of the hacker" dated 16 May 2017 [downloaded on 16 May 2017], available at https://g0v.news/code-for-japan-how-a-nuclear-disaster-ushered-in-the-age-of-the-hacker-c624d6f5bf66.

[48] *Ibid.*

[49] *Ibid.*

Chapter 3

The Chinese Case Study in Entrepreneurship and the State

China's Domestic Politics and Policies for Entrepreneurship in the Age of Innovation

Laying the Foundations

Pre-modern and early modern China did not have a long history when it came to instituting entrepreneurship policies, lending political support or creating conducive political economic environments for entrepreneurs. In imperial China, the old feudal examination system, strict licensing regime restricting profits/rewards to inventors and China's political instability/warfare obstructed optimal entrepreneurship development in imperial China.[1]

In the early days of the People's Republic of China (PRC) in the 1950s, collectivized agriculture and nationalized industry were instituted. They wiped out the small and medium-sized enterprise (SME) sector carried over from the Kuomintang-era Republican China (1911–1949) because managers in Chinese enterprises during this era had to get permission from superiors to spend more than 50 yuan (US$10) and

---

[1]Ahlstrom, David and Zhujun Ding, "Entrepreneurship in China: An overview" in *International Small Business Journal*, 32(6) (UK: Sage), [downloaded on 1 December 2020], 2014, available at http://sites.utexas.edu/chinaecon/files/2015/06/Scholarly_Entrepreneurship-in-China_2014-1.pdf, p. 610.

entrepreneurship was legally banned.[2] This was followed by the establishment of heavy industrial state-owned enterprises (SOEs), central planning, Sovietization of the economy which all placed a constraint on private sector entrepreneurship.

This situation changed with the rise of paramount leader Deng Xiaoping who instituted the economic reforms in China that transformed China into an economic power. Between 1968 and 1976, just before the onset of economic reforms, the Chinese authorities realized that companies with less than 20 workers generated four times as many new jobs as firms with more than 500 employees.[3] It was an early indication of the power of entrepreneurship. He advocated the "Four Modernizations" in 1978 that were popularly supported by the people and these reforms reached into Chinese households and small businesses that could now have access to vital local goods and stimulated the accelerated growth of township/village enterprises that functioned much like entrepreneurial companies in the capitalist economies.[4] These were the earliest days of entrepreneurial policy-making in China.

According to the *World Bank Doing Business Report 2013*, China was ranked 91 out of 181 countries in terms of regulatory environments that is conducive to establishing/running new firms, with an average of 13 procedures involved and approximately 33 days needed to establish a business (compared with five procedures and 12 days in the Organization for Economic Co-operation and Development [OECD] countries).[5] At that time, only the local Chinese entrepreneurs are adept enough to work within China's institutional, regulatory and legal environment that were still in flux while the international entrepreneurs balked at less ideal property rights and state interference in the economy at that point of time.[6]

21st Century Renaissance

China's economic reforms encouraged more young Chinese to study abroad, pursue degrees and other qualifications locally, and most importantly, imbue them with dreams of becoming rich. This released

---

[2] *Ibid*, pp. 610 and 612.
[3] *Ibid*, pp. 611–612.
[4] *Ibid*, p. 612.
[5] *Ibid*, p. 614.
[6] *Ibid*, p. 614.

tremendous entrepreneurial energies amongst the young Chinese people. By the 2010s, a new class of young (average age: 31 years old) and educated (32% with undergraduate degrees, 27% with community college qualifications and postgraduates make up 4.4%) Chinese entrepreneurs emerged, as well as scientist/engineer overseas returnees and migrant entrepreneurs with strong ties to their families amongst their numbers.[7]

Approximately 80% of entrepreneurs have prior work experience with large groups who are migrant entrepreneurs with strong social ties link to home villages/communities exchange businesses, technologies, information and remittances as well as highly-skilled overseas returnees interested to start business ventures.[8] Existing literatures also show that Chinese managers of state-owned enterprises (SOEs), women, seniors, cadres in hierarchical structures appear to show less capabilities in reacting to changing institutional environments that significantly reduce the probability of becoming an entrepreneur.[9]

Emergence of State Support

Early 2000s

When Xi assumed power in Zhejiang in 2002, Xi led the "New Zhijiang Army" who utilized private investments to assume some of the risks in financing key infrastructure projects and this was recorded in confidential US government cable wires by US ambassador to Beijing Clark Randt Jr in 2007 that was subsequently hacked and revealed publicly by WikiLeaks.[10] In the cable, President Xi acknowledged Zhejiang's wealth was made possible by local entrepreneurs, and he streamlined private sector firms' registration, improved entrepreneur's ability to get funding and supported private property in the interest of generating wealth.[11]

---

[7] *Ibid*, p. 613.
[8] *Ibid*, p. 613.
[9] *Ibid*, p. 613.
[10] McGregor, Richard, "How the state runs business in China" dated 25 July 2019 in *The Guardian* [downloaded on 25 July 2019], available at https://www.theguardian.com/world/2019/jul/25/china-business-xi-jinping-communist-party-state-private-enterprise-huawei.
[11] *Ibid*.

Working with International Organizations (IOs)

China also worked hard with IOs to augment their entrepreneurship capabilities. China's Know About Business (KAB) is an entrepreneurship development curriculum developed by the International Labour Organization (ILO) in over 50 states and it was successful in assisting the creation of new businesses and enhancing public officials' knowledge of entrepreneurship while disseminating entrepreneurship education to more than 100 Chinese universities (and its 15,000 students).[12]

Entrepreneur Education

Education played a big role in cultivating Chinese entrepreneurs in China. Alongside the practices in developed economies, emphasizing entrepreneurship has become the catalyst for highlighting entrepreneurship education in the Asia-Pacific with institutes of higher learning (IHLs) promoting entrepreneurship-related programs and courses to meet the growing demands for such courses.[13] Even mainland Chinese overseas have started entrepreneurial courses abroad, attended by Chinese students overseas along with other students in the general population. Professor of Computer Science, Zhou Yuanyuan, from the University of California San Diego (UCSD) and an entrepreneur herself is offering seminars in entrepreneurship at UCSD from 2019:

> Many people in my generation knew nothing about entrepreneurship, and we preferred a stable career to taking adventures …The new generation is familiar with the stories of Jack Ma, Michael Yu [founder of New Oriental Education and Technology Group], and Robin Li

---

[12]Xu, Haoliang, "Asia's young entrepreneurs need help with the hustle" dated 10 Aug 2018 in World Economic Forum (WEF) [downloaded on 10 August 2018], available at https://www.weforum.org/agenda/2018/08/asias-young-entrepreneurs-need-help-with-the-hustle/.

[13]Wu, Yenchun Jim and Tienhua Wu, "A decade of entrepreneurship education in the Asia Pacific for future directions in theory and practice" dated August 2017 in *Management Decision* 55 (7) [downloaded on 1 January 2020], available at https://www.researchgate.net/publication/318292842_A_decade_of_entrepreneurship_education_in_the_Asia_Pacific_for_future_directions_in_theory_and_practice, pp. 1333–1350. [Online version page 2).

[Baidu's Founder]. Their passion for creating their own companies is much greater.[14]

In 2015, Beijing promulgated directives to drum up entrepreneurship by constructing more incubators, giving rent for start-ups, starting entrepreneurship courses in colleges and permitting university students to temporarily stop their degree studies to establish their own firms and, since 2015, China has come up with 200 model colleges for innovation and entrepreneurship education, offering 2,800 courses for 630,000 students.[15] The average number of new businesses registered in China increased from 7,000 (2013) to 12,000 (end-2015) to 19,700 (October 2019) and 3% of university students graduating in 2017 formed their own businesses within 6 months, twice the speed in 2011 and surveys showed that, by 2018, almost 90% of Chinese university students thought about forming their own companies.[16]

2010s

In the 2010s, the accent of Chinese policies on entrepreneurship has been job creation with people starting their own businesses to increase employment rate. When Chinese President Xi Jinping assumed presidency in 2012, China's fast-growth economy was driven by private entrepreneurs with private sector firms accounting for approximately half of all investments in China and approximately 75% of economic output.[17] Some noted that even at the start of the gold rush for private sector entrepreneur-driven economic growth, the Chinese Communist Party (CCP) remained a stakeholder in the system. This was a highly optimistic period when the incoming Chinese President Xi was hailed as a reformer in the field of business, economy and entrepreneurship.

---

[14]Rong, Xiaoqing, "China is winning the race for young entrepreneurs" dated 14 January 2020 in Foreign Policy [downloaded on 14 Jan 2020], available at https://foreignpolicy.com/2020/01/14/china-is-winning-the-race-for-young-entrepreneurs/.

[15]*Ibid.*

[16]*Ibid.*

[17]McGregor, Richard, "How the state runs business in China" dated 25 July 2019 in *The Guardian* [downloaded on 25 July 2019], available at https://www.theguardian.com/world/2019/jul/25/china-business-xi-jinping-communist-party-state-private-enterprise-huawei.

From 1985 to 2007, President Xi worked diligently in Fujian and Zhejiang that were symbolic of private enterprise successes in China, with Fujian attracting Taiwanese investments from the 1980s and Zhejiang a hotbed of entrepreneurial activities represented by the Jack Ma types and many stakeholders in the Chinese economic success story noted Xi's father was a well-known reformer.[18] Entrepreneurship had strong support from the highest ranks of the CCP.

2015

From 2010, after the large bailouts associated with the 2008 global financial crisis triggered by the "Lehman Shocks", Chinese planners worked hard to reduce debt, augment consumption, go softer on investment/exports and ram up reliance on private business to augment economic growth.[19] By September 2015, Alibaba's Jack Ma confidently argued: "Chinese consumption is not driven by the government but by entrepreneurship, and the market … In the past 20 years, the government was so strong. Now, they are getting weak. It's our opportunity; it's our show time, to see how the market economy, entrepreneurship, can develop real consumption".[20]

Professor Zhu Lijia of the China National School of Administration, which is a state-owned policy and research institution, highlighted: "Public innovation and massive entrepreneurship is one of the major engines powering the slowing economy and more measures should be taken to let the market play the leading role in allocating resources".[21] To put the money where the mouth is, the Chinese state established a 40-billion-yuan fund to boost emerging sectors in early January 2015.[22]

With state encouragement/incentives and driven by bureaucratic reforms to make business founding easier, the number of new Chinese firms increased dramatically. Approximately 844,000 new firms registered in the first quarter of 2015 (increasing 38.4% from the equivalent

---

[18] *Ibid.*

[19] *Ibid.*

[20] *Ibid.*

[21] Xinhua, "New policies encourage entrepreneurship, boost employment" dated 22 April 2015 in *China Daily* [downloaded on 22 April 2015], available at http://www.chinadaily.com.cn/china/2015-05/06/content_20634114_4.htm.

[22] *Ibid.*

period in 2014, based on statistics from the State Administration for Industry and Commerce) and between January and March 2015, new registered companies in tertiary industry increased 41% to 677,000 (80.2% of new companies).[23]

2017

The State Council executive meeting headed by Premier Li Keqiang promulgated the 12 July 2017 guideline to increase support for innovation and entrepreneurship. China will establish an integrated digital business license registry by coming up with an all-in-one registration platform for foreign and local companies that has easier approval procedures for hiring foreign talents and highly qualified student returnees (including HKers/ Macanese) keen to become entrepreneurs in China.[24]

The State Administration for Industry and Commerce data indicated China experienced the registration of 13 million new enterprises between March 2014 and February 2017 with 94.6% of them situated in the private sector, generating an average of 15,600 new firms daily in the first five months 2017 alone.[25] The China Association for Science and Technology report stated, on 7 June 2017, the State Council executive meeting established more high-level demonstration bases for mass entrepreneurship and innovation in the provinces (28 zones were set up in 2016).[26]

Research and Development (R&D) was hailed as a major objective in the state's entrepreneurship drive. Chinese Premier Li Keqiang declared: "We should keep promoting entrepreneurship and innovation, and give full play to the initiative and creativity of the public. The R & D outcomes should be put to full use so that we can better draw on the wisdom of the public ... The internal strength of the new growth drivers should be fully converted into new growth engines of the Chinese economy".[27]

---

[23] *Ibid.*

[24] Xu, Wei, "China to further promote innovation and entrepreneurship" dated 12 July 2017 in The State Council The People Republic of China website [downloaded on 12 July 2017], available at http://english.www.gov.cn/premier/news/2017/07/12/content_281475723086902.htm.

[25] *Ibid.*

[26] *Ibid.*

[27] *Ibid.*

2018

In 2018, the State Council of China supported by Premier Li Keqiang launched a large-scale entrepreneurship and innovation public campaign to increase job opportunities, promote tech innovation and entrepreneurship as a primary motivator and catalyze industrial growth.[28] In the earlier half of 2018, daily averages of 18,100 new businesses were registered, seemingly responding to the government's call and taking advantage of simplified administrative procedures, incentives for research and military personnel who are keen on becoming entrepreneurs.[29]

2020

In 2020, at the height of the COVID-19 pandemic, Chinese Premier Li Keqiang of the Standing Committee of the Political Bureau of the Communist Party of China Central Committee gave a public speech at the opening ceremony of the 2020 National Mass Innovation and Entrepreneurship Week in Beijing on 15 October 2020. He continued to advocate mass entrepreneurship (including amongst China's large numbers of micro, small, and medium-sized enterprises MSMEs as well as individual business owners) and innovation as the panacea to augment the strength and catalysts of economic growth, particularly in the area of job creation.[30]

Potential Challenges

The Detractors, a Western Point of View

American economist and expert on Chinese economy Nicholas Lardy argued in 2019 that 2012 was probably the peak of what the West would consider a private sector-driven economy: "Since 2012, private,

---

[28]Xinhua, "China to upgrade mass entrepreneurship and innovation" dated 6 September 2018 edited by Liangyu [downloaded on 6 September 2018], available at http://www. xinhuanet.com/english/2018-09/06/c_137450275.htm.

[29]*Ibid.*

[30]Xinhua, "Chinese premier stresses innovation, entrepreneurship to drive growth" dated 15 October 2020 in *Xinhuanet* [downloaded on 1 February 2020], available at http://www. xinhuanet.com/english/2020-10/15/c_139443194.htm.

market-driven growth has given way to a resurgence of the role of the state".[31] President Xi's strongman centralized rule and the confidence in which he wielded power is seen as the emergence of a new model in which the state inserts itself into the entrepreneurship system in China. The party is embedding itself into private sector companies and citizenry (including entrepreneurs) are now empowered by a 2017 national intelligence law to have "any organization and citizen … support and cooperate in national intelligence work".[32] This creates a new business economic model that is distinct from the West and the divergence has resulted in some resistance of this model from the West.

The 2019 Director of the US National Counterintelligence and Security Center highlighted the following point about China's entrepreneurs in the context of greater embeddedness of the party in the private sector firms: "Chinese company relationships with the Chinese government aren't like private sector company relationships with governments in the west".[33] A 2019 Central Organization Department survey (CCP's human resource department) revealed that 68% of China's private firms had embedded party bodies in 2016 and 70% in terms of foreign enterprises while provinces like Zhejiang targeted having party cells in 95% of private sector firms in August 2018 to maintain the "revolutionary spirit" in the private sector over generations.[34]

State presence and control in Chinese companies is trending upwards, so even the top billionaire entrepreneurs running large private sector companies need to heed the Party's message and the state views on businesses in China. Even Jack Ma, who retired from active responsibility in Alibaba in September 2018, a Party cadre member since 1980s and praised by state media *People's Daily* newspaper for his contributions, did not escape the fate of "disappearing" (and/or lying low) after he incurred the wrath of the state regulators for comments made in late 2020. Others like Anbang Insurance Group Chairperson Wu Xiaohui disappeared after

---

[31] McGregor, Richard, "How the state runs business in China" dated 25 July 2019 in *The Guardian* [downloaded on 25 July 2019], available at https://www.theguardian.com/world/2019/jul/25/china-business-xi-jinping-communist-party-state-private-enterprise-huawei.

[32] *Ibid.*

[33] *Ibid.*

[34] *Ibid.*

dealing on a US$14 billion deal on American hotels before reappearing to be sentenced to 18 years in prison for fraud in May 2018.[35]

The Defenders: Narratives Highlighting the Attractiveness of This State-oriented System

Those who in support of a great state role or are unsurprised by such developments (unlike Western observers) indicated that the party wants to be part of those companies' successes by being partners with them (both local and foreign entrepreneurs) to share their wealth and not ruin those companies.[36] In this narrative, the Party is merely interested in checking any potential entrepreneurs that can become a political rival to the leadership (and/or an alternative source of power) to guard against countervailing forces analogous to those that broke up the Soviet Union when it collapsed in the Cold War in 1992.[37]

The integration of successful entrepreneurs and/or their companies into the Party's fold meant that they could get richer or maintain their wealth when their personal dreams, aspirations and ambitions coincide with those of the Party. This gives added incentives for rich and successful entrepreneurs to be complementary to the party line. Examples include e-commerce JD.com founder's Richard Liu who predicted the realization of communism and nationalization of private enterprises in his lifetime, property developer Evergrande Group's Xu Jiayin attributed his company's existence to the Party, Sany Heavy Industry's Liang Wengen declared that his life belonged to the Party.[38] Moreover, President Xi's anti-corruption campaign appeared to be popular with the Chinese people. He warned successful entrepreneurs/private sector management to "strengthen self-study, self-education and self-improvement and not feel uncomfortable with this requirement [since] Communist party has similar and stricter requirements on its leaders".[39]

Some also argued that state orientation is not restricted to China only within East Asia. Studies by Wu and Wu have shown a strong nexus

---

[35] *Ibid.*
[36] *Ibid.*
[37] *Ibid.*
[38] *Ibid.*
[39] *Ibid.*

between East Asian governments and the promotion of entrepreneurship. For example, they noted that Malaysia's response to globalization is tapping into entrepreneurship to increase economic growth and maintain competitiveness while Chinese Premier Li Keqiang and the State Council highlighted the significance of mass entrepreneurship and innovation for economic development in the mid-2010s.[40]

Moreover, the Party is flexible and pragmatic. As long as duty calls, the state is willing to back up politically/ideologically complementary entrepreneurs. In 2018, when Sino-US trade war heated up, Xi pragmatically solicited specially selected entrepreneurs (such as Tencent's Pony Ma Huateng) to gather in the Great Hall of the People and reiterated "all [of them are] part of our family" with state-owned media following up in persuading banks to release liquidity to private firms[41] to cope with the trade war. This call was backed up by his Premier after the Sino-US trade war was followed by a global pandemic. During the COVID-19 pandemic, Chinese Premier Li Keqiang also highlighted the market forces aspects and the idea that mass entrepreneurship/innovation led to the proliferation of a large number (hundreds of millions) of market entities in various sectors, stabilized the national economy and created many jobs.[42]

Mindsets of the Chinese Returnee Entrepreneurs and State Policies in the 2020s

A bonanza in entrepreneurship in China came unexpectedly and politically in the last few years of the 2010s. The Trump era's tighter immigration

---

[40]Wu, Yenchun Jim and Tienhua Wu, "A decade of entrepreneurship education in the Asia Pacific for future directions in theory and practice" dated August 2017 in *Management Decision*, 55(7) [downloaded on 1 January 2020], available at https://www.researchgate.net/publication/318292842_A_decade_of_entrepreneurship_education_in_the_Asia_Pacific_for_future_directions_in_theory_and_practice, pp. 1333–1350. [Online version page 2).

[41]McGregor, Richard, "How the state runs business in China" dated 25 July 2019 in *The Guardian* [downloaded on 25 July 2019], available at https://www.theguardian.com/world/2019/jul/25/china-business-xi-jinping-communist-party-state-private-enterprise-huawei.

[42]Xinhua, "Chinese premier stresses innovation, entrepreneurship to drive growth" dated 15 October 2020 in *Xinhuanet* [downloaded on 1 Feb 2020], available at http://www.xinhuanet.com/english/2020-10/15/c_139443194.htm.

restrictions came almost simultaneously with attractive incentives from China to encourage Chinese students in the United States to return to China and many did return, with some becoming entrepreneurs. The mindset of necessity had previously compelled many of these returnees to develop innovative products while they were in the United States. For example, Leo Wen came up with his business plan in 2017 for his map-based social media app Pokke to facilitate subscribers (especially isolated Chinese students studying in the United States) in uploading their activities and circulating updates of activities in their locations for optimal linkages.[43]

Chinese government and corporations are keen to dip into the pool of returnee students and highly skilled labor from China who studied/lived/worked in the United States since 1979 (e.g. 370,000 Chinese studying in the 2018–2019 school year alone).[44] Wen joined China's Ministry of Education and Ministry of Science and Technology's initiatives for attracting overseas Chinese students globally with a sponsored trip to China to tour state-operated start-up incubators, including those interested to host his project.[45] The current generation of Chinese students is significantly wealthier than their predecessors with many coming from comparatively rich families and observed their parents establishing family businesses from its foundations while being influenced by entrepreneurs-at-large like Jack Ma of Alibaba.[46]

The Trump administration's policy on student visas and Chinese reverse migrants accounted for the statistics from Chinese Ministry of Education indicating that 519,400 Chinese students returnees arrived in China from all over the globe in 2018 (8% more than 2017), encouraged by Premier Li Keqiang called for mass entrepreneurship.[47] Chinese venture capital firms invested in American start-ups [from US$2.8 billion (2014) to US$14.8 billion (2018)], organized competitions like Chunhui Cup that assisted 634 start-ups to obtain funding and set up in China since 2006 and, by the end of 2018, China built 350 enterprise parks

---

[43] Rong, Xiaoqing, "China is winning the race for young entrepreneurs" dated 14 January 2020 in *Foreign Policy* [downloaded on 14 January 2020], available at https://foreignpolicy.com/2020/01/14/china-is-winning-the-race-for-young-entrepreneurs/.
[44] *Ibid.*
[45] *Ibid.*
[46] *Ibid.*
[47] *Ibid.*

hosting 25,000 firms with discounted office spaces for returnee entrepreneurs.[48] Some start-ups received more than RMB 100 million (US$14 million) from local authorities while statistics from Hurun Research Institute shows China had 206 unicorns by October 2019 (the largest unicorn hub globally) and Chinese start-ups raised US$35.6 billion in 2047 rounds.[49]

While China is blazing a path in the world of venture start-ups and Japan is on the cusp of a civic technopreneurship renaissance, their Southeast Asian counterparts are preparing for the future of entrepreneurship education in the context of (and in preparation for) the formation of the ASEAN Economic Community (AEC). This topic is discussed in the next chapter.

---

[48] *Ibid.*
[49] *Ibid.*

Chapter 4

Entrepreneurship Education in Southeast Asia

The Association of Southeast Asian Nations (ASEAN) has developed a common curriculum for a bachelor degree in 2012 customized for the ASEAN business contexts with the intention to have a positive impact on micro and small and medium-sized enterprises (MSMEs) development as well as catalyzing new business developments amongst stakeholders like the students, universities and local enterprises.[1] The ASEAN common curriculum is also primed to ensure students can have educational foundations in entrepreneurship in preparation for lifelong learning, manage their own businesses, arm them with the appropriate attitudes to bring about change, recognize continuous improvement, instil a belief in seizing opportunities, embrace innovation, learn from failures and develop an entrepreneurial mindset.[2]

The common curriculum also infuses the element of morality into the mindset, making ethical concerns (such as community development, good law-abiding citizenry, patriotism, awareness of local cultures, global solidarity, lifelong learning values) as important as profits.[3] The course also defines culture as shared ideas/meanings (explicit and implicit) to

---

[1]ASEAN, "Common curriculum for entrepreneurship in ASEAN" dated May 2012 in the ASEAN website [downloaded on 1 January 2021], Jakarta: Asia Seed), 2012, available at https://asean.org/wp-content/uploads/2012/05/8.-Common-Curriculum-for-Entrepreneurship-in-ASEAN.pdf, p. 1.

[2]*Ibid*, pp. 1–2.

[3]*Ibid*, p. 3.

interpret the world and guide their behavior and this extends to cultural mindsets and understanding of arts, literature, and history of a society as well as studying attitudes, prejudices and folklore.[4] The entrepreneurship seminar course focuses on providing ASEAN university students with skills to set up SMEs in the urban and rural communities of ASEAN states through group work in coming up with a unique business plan in manufacturing, services, energy or agricultural sectors alongside mentors on-site to provide coaching and advice to the students.[5] The course will then have a final one-day Student Business Plan Competition with awards given out by the private sector for top business plans. The winners will then move on to compete regionally with other ASEAN teams.[6]

The Venture Capital/Corporate Finance 3 course covers equity capital in the venture capital industry, including subtopics like performance metrics, partnership structure, fund economics, entrepreneurial character, business models, due diligence, negotiation, managing investment portfolios, etc. from the lens of the principals who manage equity funds, limited partner investors who fund venture capitalists and entrepreneurs who take on venture financing.[7] The course examines the role of venture capitalist in selecting new firms for funding through risk–reward determinations, gauging new start-ups and investment growth, working with management teams to augment their businesses, exit strategies and will include invited entrepreneurs and venture capitalists in their academic activities.[8]

Upskilling

In Southeast Asia individually, things are moving fast on the entrepreneurial front as well. The Kingdom of Thailand's authorities is emphasizing mentorship and business skills with an "Entrepreneurship University" for staff and students to upgrade their skills in business development, mobilizing 30 000 individuals in over 30 universities across the country for training in 2017.[9] Besides institutional training, some countries are

---

[4] *Ibid*, p. 7.
[5] *Ibid*, p. 18.
[6] *Ibid*, p. 19.
[7] *Ibid*, pp. 19–20.
[8] *Ibid*, p. 20.
[9] Xu, Haoliang, "Asia's young entrepreneurs need help with the hustle" dated 10 August 2018 in World Economic Forum (WEF) [downloaded on 10 August 2018], available at

tapping into their top performers as entrepreneurial inspirations for the younger counterparts.

Mentoring

Mentoring schemes are also found in individual ASEAN countries. One Singaporean example stands out. Forrest Li is the founder, chairperson and Chief Executive Officer (CEO) of Singapore-based Sea and Garena (a video game distribution firm established in 2009) and "Businessman of the Year for 2019/2020" in the Singapore Business Awards. In the era of the pandemic, he is adapting to uncertainties by shaping his Shopee outfit to become an essential service in the pandemic and converting its search engine for older Chinese language users in Singapore, creating an e-wallet and accelerating Garena accessibility to keep up with customer demand during the lockdown.[10] Forrest Li (founder of successful company Sea) became a board member of Singapore's Economic Development Board (EDB) in February 2020 and served on the Singapore Committee on the Future Economy from 2016 to 2017:

> I would love to find other ways to use my own experience as an entre-
> preneur, and pass (it on) to the younger generations. Eventually, we need
> an ecosystem here. ... A lot of people say, why do you do this? Why do
> you bother yourself? If you look (at it) on paper, the failure rate could
> be super high [He had previously taken a healthy dose of calculated risks
> in establishing Shopee in 2015, entering a risk-laden industry when his
> core gaming business was performing optimally].[11]

By sharing his experiences through a state appointment, Li's personal objective is to inspire future Southeast Asian tech founders towards the bigger goal of digitalizing Southeast Asia to beef up connectivity between Asian countries to the advantage of small businesses and the individual

---

https://www.weforum.org/agenda/2018/08/asias-young-entrepreneurs-need-help-with-the-hustle/.

[10] Pillai, Sharanya, "Don't miss forrest for the trees" dated 25 November 2020 in *Business Times* [downloaded on 25 November 2020], available at https://www.businesstimes.com.sg/garage/news/singapore-business-awards-2020/dont-miss-forrest-for-the-trees.

[11] *Ibid.*

entrepreneurs within the region.[12] The state committee appointment can be useful in other ways too. Tristan Ace (Head, British Council's social enterprise program) and Alfie Othman (Head, Singapore Centre for Social Enterprise providing training/resources for ethical entrepreneurship) both argue that recognition by government institutions and committees send an important signal to the market that entrepreneurship is important and the state can help develop talents for the social enterprise sector and widen access to finance.[13]

ASEAN countries are also designing mentoring programs for youths who are interested in entrepreneurial pursuits. Since 2007, Indonesia's Bank Mandiri has trained university students and youngsters through the Mandiri Young Entrepreneur Program (WMM), organized public talks on leadership/entrepreneurship to change their mindsets to engage in entrepreneurial activities while its Mandiri Institute researches on national entrepreneurship for policy suggestions for the government to support those starting/upgrading businesses.[14] All these are done to gear them up for engagement with the ASEAN Economic Community (AEC) with its integrated market and possibility of niches for Indonesian products. The next section looks at a case study of entrepreneurship education in Singapore through a selected case study.

A Case Study of Entrepreneurship Education in Singapore

Introduction

With 14,000 students, Singapore University of Social Sciences (SUSS) is the newest of Singapore's six autonomous universities providing lifelong education that equips learners to serve society and offers applied learning

---

[12] *Ibid.*

[13] Chandran, Rina, "Regulation can hinder not help Asia's social enterprises, analysts say" dated 7 March 2019 in *Reuters* [downloaded on 7 March 2019], available at https://www.reuters.com/article/us-thailand-lawmaking-socialenterprise/regulation-can-hinder-not-help-asias-social-enterprises-analysts-say-idUSKCN1QO0TU.

[14] Carolina, Elisabeth, "Analysis: ASEAN economic community for entrepreneurs" dated 13 January 2016 in *The Jakarta Post* [downloaded on 13 January 2016], available at https://www.thejakartapost.com/news/2016/01/13/analysis-asean-economic-community-entrepreneurs.html.

for undergrads and mature students. It has a flexible and practice-focused pedagogy with more than 60 undergraduate degree courses across a spectrum of disciplines.[15] According to the research by GoDaddy (a webhosting provider), approximately 66.6% of Singaporean millennials in Singapore want to be entrepreneurs within the coming decade but some may be aware of the risk of failure and an entrepreneur's role is not clearly delineated.[16] Other than coming up with a clear vision to build the venture, would-be entrepreneurs need to have the appropriate skills and/or employ staff to work towards the objective together while developing resilience to overcome challenges and improve the business approach.[17]

More companies (including accounting companies) are considering blockchain business, which are likely to take over record maintenance functions, including how transactions are started, processed, authenticated and reported.[18] Financial education (knowledge of critical financial statements like balance sheet and profit/loss statements) is crucial for entrepreneurs as it represents the extent of their control over their businesses, the ability to track business well-being and growth projections and make decisions, etc.[19]

Entrepreneurs have to assume a spectrum of roles and functions to build their businesses (including managing the technologies or business development by themselves), particularly the early stages of their career and there is no cookie cutter approach to entrepreneurship, given that every firm and process differ, although reading up beforehand, mentors and accumulating experience help.[20] Well-laid out education policies and curriculums are important in influencing would-be entrepreneurs, as they

---

[15] Alibaba Cloud, "SUSS and Alibaba cloud to spur entrepreneurship with new accredited program" dated 6 September 2017 in Alibaba Cloud website [downloaded on 6 September 2017], available at https://www.alibabacloud.com/de/press-room/suss-and-alibaba-cloud-to-spur-entrepreneurship-with-new-accredited.

[16] Singapore University of Social Sciences (SUSS), "Ingredients for building successful companies" dated 1 November 2019 in the SUSS website [downloaded on 1 January 2021], available at https://www.suss.edu.sg/blog/detail/ingredients-for-building-successful-companies.

[17] *Ibid.*

[18] *Ibid.*

[19] *Ibid.*

[20] Tech in Asia and Singapore University of Social Sciences (SUSS), "Becoming a chameleon entrepreneur" dated 6 April 2020 in the SUSS website [downloaded on 6 April 2020], available at https://www.suss.edu.sg/blog/detail/becoming-a-chameleon-entrepreneur.

assist individuals to have an open-mind, exhibit flexibility and nimbleness to take on a variety of career and skills-enhancing opportunities, take on personalized approaches to learning/development and plan ahead.[21]

In the SUSS dialogue session between Singapore Prime Minister (PM) Lee Hsien Loong and approximately 500 students from the Singapore University of Social Sciences (SUSS) on 4 September 2019, the PM was asked a question.[22] He was asked about whether Singapore's societal culture is "forgiving enough" to accommodate Singaporeans failing and how institutes of higher learning can assist students to develop strong grit and courage to take the plunge.[23] PM Lee noted in reply that a number of people are already doing that, organizing the start-ups themselves and being willing to try again and he does not think there is stigma or shame to abandon an idea that did not work to try an alternative one.[24] He believes that Singapore youth have this attitude given that it is natural that the first good idea is not likely to work and cited his experience in searching for candidates for the People's Action Party (PAP) and not disqualifying any candidates simply because the venture she/he has started no longer exists.[25] Instead, PM Lee would probe further about the candidate's motivations for starting the company and, if the candidate continues to have the commitment and belief in the project, PM Lee would still consider accepting the candidate given that it is impossible for anyone to have a perfect record in creating unicorns in all ventures attempted.[26]

The essence of entrepreneurship are ideational innovations, adapting services or technology to tackle current or new needs that were insufficiently managed, producing new enhanced products/services, create new markets, generate wealth, create jobs, and re-energize economies.[27] These

---

[21] *Ibid.*

[22] Mokhtar, Faris, "S'pore culture allows young entrepreneurs to fail with no shame, then succeed: PM Lee" dated 5 September 2019 in *TodayOnline* [downloaded on 5 September 2019], available at https://www.todayonline.com/singapore/spore-culture-allows-young-entrepreneurs-fail-no-shame-then-succeed-pm-lee.

[23] *Ibid.*

[24] *Ibid.*

[25] *Ibid.*

[26] *Ibid.*

[27] Singapore University of Social Sciences (SUSS), "Entrepreneurship: A light in the dark?" dated 26 August 2020 in the SUSS website [downloaded on 26 August 2020], available at https://www.suss.edu.sg/blog/detail/entrepreneurship-a-light-in-the-dark.

qualities were highlighted in the SUSS Venture Builder which is an immersive training programme to transform mindsets and convert ideas into profits to help graduates start new ventures with students crafting problem statements in their domain knowledge while taking up a rigorous three or nine months of hands-on training to establish a firm.[28] The Venture Builder Co-Founder and Lead helps to enhance the success of each team and put in place personal goal-setting checks to assist trainees in the optimal direction of setting up their firm.[29] They can tap into domain experts who are industry practitioners and academic faculty members armed with industry contents knowledge and perspectives in the areas of early childhood, gerontology, mental health, education technology, fintech or blockchain, e-commerce, social services and SME digital transformation.[30]

COVID-19 Pandemic

Indeed, some see 2020 as both a crisis as well as opportunity for entrepreneurs since the COVID-19 pandemic has disrupted traditional business models and has compelled individuals to get used to new modes of conduct business as people in general are forced to cope with the changes. The SUSS blog site indicated worries about COVID-19's impact on the global economy in the form of a post-pandemic economic crisis but noted the strength of Singaporeans have led the way to manage the crises and catalyzed an uptake in entrepreneurial activities throughout Singapore.[31]

To continue knowledge acquisition during the pandemic, SUSS also offers specialized courses for would-be entrepreneurs who want to manage the legal protection of their inventions and innovative new products. IPOS International and the SUSS offered free access to a nine-hour internet-based training course on managing a company's intellectual property (IP) assets for business growth from 13 April 2020 to 4 May 2020.

---

[28] Singapore University of Social Sciences (SUSS), "Venture builder traineeship programme" undated in the Singapore University of Social Sciences (SUSS) website [downloaded on 1 January 2021], available at https://www.suss.edu.sg/experience-at-suss/entrepreneurship/venture-builder-traineeship-programme.

[29] *Ibid.*

[30] *Ibid.*

[31] Singapore University of Social Sciences (SUSS), "Entrepreneurship: A light in the dark?" dated 26 August 2020 in the SUSS website [downloaded on 26 August 2020], available at https://www.suss.edu.sg/blog/detail/entrepreneurship-a-light-in-the-dark.

This course was taught during Singapore's COVID-19 "Circuit Breaker" home confinement period so that they can continue learning IP and intangible assets (IA) and their basic concepts such as brands, technologies, design, creations and data.[32] It was created for existing and would-be entrepreneurs and business proprietors to teach them how to pick out the IP and IA that generate value-add for their companies, legally own their unique and idiosyncratic features while participating in actual applied learning in simulated real-world case scenarios and tests.[33] The course titled "Intellectual Property Essentials for Business" assist students to identify value-added IP and IA and use them to enhance business resilience in the post-COVID-19 period by familiarizing the students with the basic topics of IP management, law, brands, technologies, design, creations and data.[34] Participants participate in real-life, applied learning through actual case studies and tests.[35]

The pandemic also unleashed tech start-ups, home retailers (selling artisanal trinkets) and internet-based sales of confectionery, leading to the possibility of home-centred entrepreneurship as an alternative for job applicants to survive though the pandemic period (especially during circuit breakers).[36] They are also given the tools to drive up entrepreneurship. The tools include government/private grants, digital apps platforms like Shopee, Qoo10, Lazada and Carousell while the pandemic has given Singaporeans more time at home to take up entrepreneurship or sell items to eke a living in the hard times (and some unexpectedly thrived instead).[37]

---

[32] Singapore University of Social Sciences (SUSS) "Business owners and entrepreneurs to gain access to IP course" dated 13 April 2020 in SUSS Media Releases [downloaded on 13 April 2020], available at https://www.suss.edu.sg/news-and-events/media-resources/media-releases/business-owners-and-entrepreneurs-to-gain-access-to-ip-course.
[33] *Ibid.*
[34] de Leon, Espie Angelica A., "IPOS, SG university offering online IP course for entrepreneurs, business owners" dated 14 April 2020 in the Asia IP Law website [downloaded on 14 April 2020], available at https://asiaiplaw.com/article/ipos-sg-university-offering-online-ip-course-for-entrepreneurs-business-owners.
[35] *Ibid.*
[36] Singapore University of Social Sciences (SUSS), "Entrepreneurship: A light in the dark?" dated 26 August 2020 in the SUSS website [downloaded on 26 August 2020], available at https://www.suss.edu.sg/blog/detail/entrepreneurship-a-light-in-the-dark.
[37] *Ibid.*

In a user behavior study surveyed by Carousell (which was an entrepreneurial start-up and now a major e-commerce outfit), the average Singaporean made S$2,200 on Carousell during the Circuit Breaker period (7 April to 1 June 2020) and, due to more home-bound businesses retailing baked confectionaries, there was a five times surge in searches for baking items and materials.[38] The Singaporean government is supporting this surge in public interest in home entrepreneurship with initiatives like Startup SG (discussed in the section below), the Productivity Solutions Grant, Specialized Cleaning Programme (defraying disinfection) and the Local Enterprise and Association Development (LEAD) Programme to support Singaporeans start-ups.[39] For would-be entrepreneurs, the Start-up SG Programme provides state funding of up to S$150 million to boost Singapore start-ups with the complementary combination of grant capital and mentorship (established in 2017 to support new entrepreneurial ventures).[40]

In August 2020, to re-energize Singapore's economy in the pandemic-era downturn, Start-up SG Founders was augmented to encompass venture-building and the start-up capital grant (increased from S$30,000 to S$50,000 with two tracks: "Start" track and the "Train" track (a newer track).[41] The Start-up SG Founders Grant "Start" Track (implemented from 25 September 2020) is meant for entrepreneurs on the verge of working on a start-up with a workable business plan, offering a grant capital up to S$50,000 for groups of minimally three Singapore citizens (SC) or Singapore permanent residents (SPRs) as the main applicants of the grant.[42] Minimally two of the three applicants are first-time entrepreneurs having at least 30% equity in the start-up, minimally 51% SC/PR shareholdings, not incorporated for more than half a year when submitting application and the main applicant(s) should not be fully employed

---

[38] *Ibid.*

[39] *Ibid.*

[40] Koo, Angela, "Guide to start-up SG founders grant and how aspiring entrepreneurs can receive government support to start a business" dated 25 September 2020 in DollarsAndSense Business and OCBC Business Banking [downloaded on 25 September 2020], available at https://dollarsandsense.sg/business/guide-startup-sg-founders-grant-how-entrepreneurs-can-receive-government-support-start-business/.

[41] *Ibid.*

[42] *Ibid.*

by others or receive funding from others, and must be a key decision maker(s) in the start-up.[43]

Other conditions include: the venture proposal cannot be in the sectors of: cafes, restaurants, night clubs, lounges, bars, foot reflexology, massage parlors, gambling, prostitution, social escort services, employment agencies (including recruiting foreign work permit holders and workers/support staff, relocation services, and manpower services) and geomancy.[44] An Accredited Mentor Partners (AMP) will lead the would-be entrepreneur through the application up to the approving authority of Enterprise Singapore (ESG) and such AMPs include educational institutes (c.g. SUSS), venture capital, incubators and accelerators and co-working spaces (i.e. Found8 and WeWork), all of whom have different strengths and can take up equity in the start-up.[45]

Because Start-up SG Founders Grant "Train" Track is meant for would-be entrepreneurs who do not have entrepreneurial skills or viable business plans, applicants will go through a three-month venture building programme with Accredited Mentor Partners Venture Builders ("AMP-VB") while having a S$1,500 monthly stipend in the process of searching for co-founders and are guided through business development.[46] The applicable conditions are SC)/PR, commitment to 100% attendance and one does not need to be a university student or an alumnus to apply and mid-career professionals, managers, executives and technicians (PMETs) are also eligible.[47] The "Train" track motivates entrepreneurs to turn ideas into reality with a stipend for daily expenses and the participants identify business ideas, carry out product development, test market validation and search for capital before applying for the "Start" track with the identified co-founders.[48] In the Singapore University of Social Sciences (SUSS), it has a duration of half a year (including 3 months of venture-building and incubation support for remaining 3 months). The "Start" track complements those who are ready to plunge into the process with a business idea and offers more AMP mentors, along with an enhancement of grant capital from S$30,000 to S$50,000 but need some

---

[43] *Ibid.*
[44] *Ibid.*
[45] *Ibid.*
[46] *Ibid.*
[47] *Ibid.*
[48] *Ibid.*

time/efforts to search for appropriate co-founders (especially for first-time entrepreneurs) and the program accommodates applications of second-time co-founders individually.[49]

Case Study of Singapore University of Social Sciences

In encouraging entrepreneurship, SUSS is offering alternative job pathways like the Alibaba Cloud-SUSS Entrepreneurship incubation programme (in place since 2017) and the programme has churned out 35 student start-ups (14 generated funding up to S$8 million).[50] In 2017, SUSS and Alibaba Cloud (cloud computing division of Alibaba Group) started an entrepreneurship program to assist university students scale up their start-ups in a pioneering tie-up between Alibaba Cloud and a Singaporean institute of higher learning (IHL) with regards to a university-accredited program.[51] The program is made up of three required components: (1) a two-day Alibaba Cloud Certified Professional ("ACP") certification, (2) pitching sessions to investors organized by Alibaba Cloud/SUSS and (3) securing of finances; as well as taking any of the 500 SUSS modular courses (without exams) relevant to them.[52]

During the course, they will be under the mentorship of Alibaba executives as well as C-level industry experts with entrepreneurship experience and, once the entire course is completed, successful students will be given a Minor in Entrepreneurship (40 credit units) while non-SUSS students gains a certificate credit recognition for future SUSS degree programs.[53] Students who cannot get funding at the end of the maximum duration will receive a certificate of participation with no credits and, so long as the students do not go beyond the programme's maximum dura-

---

[49] *Ibid.*
[50] Singapore University of Social Sciences (SUSS), "Entrepreneurship: A light in the dark?" dated 26 August 2020 in the SUSS website [downloaded on 26 August 2020], available at https://www.suss.edu.sg/blog/detail/entrepreneurship-a-light-in-the-dark.
[51] Alibaba Cloud, "SUSS and Alibaba cloud to spur entrepreneurship with new accredited program" dated 6 September 2017 in Alibaba Cloud website [downloaded on 6 September 2017], available at https://www.alibabacloud.com/de/press-room/suss-and-alibaba-cloud-to-spur-entrepreneurship-with-new-accredited.
[52] *Ibid.*
[53] *Ibid.*

tion of the program, they can continue to seek funding.[54] The entrepreneurship program prioritizes existing start-ups that are scalable, can expand beyond Singapore or contribute to urgent social challenges and, to encourage entrepreneurship, SUSS and Alibaba Cloud are offering free courses as well.[55] The entrepreneurship program is Alibaba Cloud's contribution to enable start-ups and enhance talent development in ASEAN and, in July 2017, 15 start-ups from ASEAN competed in the Create@ Alibaba Cloud Start-up Contest for empowering start-ups with best-in-class cloud technology as well as access to a global cloud network.[56]

Joey Tan, Head of Global Strategic Initiatives Alibaba Cloud, expressed her excited about working with SUSS: "We are very excited to work with SUSS, who share our vision of developing the next generation of outstanding entrepreneurs. This program is another example of our commitment to provide the exciting drivers of change to start-ups with Alibaba Cloud's advanced technology as well as Alibaba Group's global resources".[57] Established in 2009, Alibaba Cloud is China's biggest public cloud services firm in terms of revenue and offers a whole spectrum of cloud computing services to companies internationally and e-merchants conduct trade on Alibaba Group marketplaces, start-ups, companies and state organizations.[58] SUSS also offers programmes in entrepreneurship and the gig economy, Venture Builder programme for training entrepreneurs and 100 traineeship positions in departments such as Business Intelligence and Analytics, Human Resources as well as Communications and Marketing as components of the Government's SGUnited Traineeships Programme for newer graduates.[59]

The SUSS Impact Start-up Challenge (CDO303) bootcamp aimed at would-be entrepreneurs (18 years and older) can be taken in Singapore and abroad to challenge their ideas and write up a business proposal while forming teams, participate in brainstorming, actualize their ideas, come up

---

[54] *Ibid.*

[55] *Ibid.*

[56] *Ibid.*

[57] *Ibid.*

[58] *Ibid.*

[59] Singapore University of Social Sciences (SUSS), "Entrepreneurship: A light in the dark?" dated 26 August 2020 in the SUSS website [downloaded on 26 August 2020], available at https://www.suss.edu.sg/blog/detail/entrepreneurship-a-light-in-the-dark.

with prototypes, and pitch them before a panel of evaluators.[60] Some participants interact with their business co-founders, others will establish a company and in the process pick up new knowledge, challenge their ideas to the maximum and convert them into value-added businesses.[61] Students learn to construct results-oriented branding and expand firms while learning from less successful ventures through linking up with diverse groups of experts (an ecosystem of potential co-founders) in the start-up communities during study excursions.[62]

In the SUSS School of Business, the course "Entrepreneurial Management" is targeted at individuals who are starting their own businesses and for managers to gain the skills and mindset of an entrepreneur to carry out their activities with flexibility, innovation and responsiveness for value-adding to her/his corporation.[63] It prods the participants to respond to questions concerning business objectives, customer attraction, provision of products/services, competition, awareness of applicable laws and regulations, venture funding, break-even point and payback.[64] The theoretical aspects of the course centred on strategy, innovation and entrepreneurial management teaches participants to come up with a business idea, manage its growth and cultivate small and medium size enterprises (SMEs).[65]

Another module (also a Lifelong Learning Credit, L2C) from the SUSS School of Business is "BUS357 Starting & Managing a Business" that provides basic ideas of entrepreneurship and its value to society, markets and innovative individuals for the successful implementation, entrepreneurial decision-making and strategic skills.[66] Class participants learn

---

[60] Singapore University of Social Sciences (SUSS), "Impact start-up challenge" in the SUSS website [downloaded on 1 January 2021], available at https://www.suss.edu.sg/experience-at-suss/entrepreneurship/impact-startup-challenge?utm_source=suss_website&utm_medium=entrepreneur_landing&utm_campaign=entrep_our_prog_4&utm_content=impact_startup_challenge.

[61] *Ibid.*

[62] *Ibid.*

[63] Singapore University of Social Sciences (SUSS), "Entrepreneurial management (BUS553)" undated in the SUSS website [downloaded on 1 January 2021], available at https://www.suss.edu.sg/courses/detail/bus553.

[64] *Ibid.*

[65] *Ibid.*

[66] Singapore University of Social Sciences (SUSS), "Starting and managing a business (BUS357)" undated in the SUSS website [downloaded on 1 January 2021], available at https://www.suss.edu.sg/courses/detail/bus357.

to mitigate the common challenges with tested ways to increase business successes, develop the entrepreneurial mindset that motivate success, assist entrepreneurs to locate and capitalize on opportunities, construct strategic, financial, legal, and business frameworks and yield value from the entrepreneur-built businesses.[67]

Overseas

Some of the modules outreaches to overseas destinations as well. OEL333 provides students an in-depth comprehension of Israel's entrepreneurial, politico-cultural background through experiential learning, e-learning, in-class contents and a trip to Israel to countenance first-hand the idiosyncratic approach to lifelong learning and critical thinking.[68] In the post-trip segment, then Minister Ng Chee Meng inspired the participants on preparing for life and noted that in Israel:

> "Questioning is learning and no questions is considered silly. Students are encouraged to ask questions in class and outside of class. Concepts were debated and not taken as cast in stone. A level of messiness was tolerated. We were told that when the students returned home, their parents do not ask them about homework, test scores, or even about what they had learnt. Instead, they asked their children, 'What questions did you ask in school today?' Learning was not only about results, but having the sense of joy to explore, ask questions, discover and find out answers".[69]

Israel provides the space for SUSS students to expand their worldviews culturally and technologically situated in a different cultural-economical regional space and, with excursions to the holy sites, interacting with firms/locals, SUSS students can visualize how three global religions co-exist together, countenance dynamic innovation at

---

[67] *Ibid.*

[68] Singapore University of Social Sciences (SUSS), "Entrepreneurial spirit in Israel (OEL333)" undated in the SUSS website [downloaded on 1 January 2021], available at https://www.suss.edu.sg/courses/detail/oel333?urlname=bachelor-of-science-in-finance-with-minor-ftfnce.

[69] *Ibid.*

play beyond its small size and how Israel embrace life despite geopolitical environmental risks.[70]

Redeemable as Lifelong Learning Credit (L2C), the SUSS Centre for Continuing and Professional Education runs a SUSS Entrepreneurship Bootcamp to generate ideas, test, validate and pivot their business proposals and apply them in Singapore's start-up scene to link up with co-founders, advisors and extract lessons from the entrepreneurship ecosystem.[71] The goal is to convert ideas into value-added businesses and let class participants obtain a more detailed comprehension of the issue they are trying to resolve, test their ideas and tinker with them after receiving feedback and evaluations of their viabilities before coming up with the initial prototype.[72] Would-be entrepreneurs can better succeed if they are part of an entrepreneurship ecosystem, emulating the successful business founders and failures, linking up with domain experts, interacting with Singapore's start-up community in events like Fuckup Nights, Impact Hub, JTC Launchpad @ One North and Echelon, interact with potential co-founders and experience teamwork.[73]

Entrepreneurship education at SUSS appears to have paid off as new start-ups in a variety of industries have emerged. They include the following setups. The one-stop platform genre includes: CombineSell is a software as a service (SaaS) platform that makes it easy for multichannel e-commerce retail by aggregating well-visited internet-based marketplaces into a one-stop site and Orama, a company that makes it easy to come up with shipping solutions using blockchain technology.[74] There are also education-related outfits. For example, LightBeijing offers easily accessible Chinese language lessons and work opportunities in China in the form of a one-to-one Mandarin e-learning service available to regional Asian students and the Institute of Blockchain Singapore (established January 2018), a blockchain private school offering blockchain and

---

[70] *Ibid.*

[71] Singapore University of Social Sciences (SUSS), "SUSS entrepreneurship bootcamp (Shenzhen) (GSP303SZX)" undated in the SUSS website [downloaded on 1 January 2021], available at https://www.suss.edu.sg/courses/detail/gsp303szx.

[72] *Ibid.*

[73] *Ibid.*

[74] Singapore University of Social Sciences (SUSS), "Start-ups" undated in the SUSS website [downloaded on 1 January 2021], available at https://www.suss.edu.sg/experience-at-suss/entrepreneurship/startups.

cryptocurrency education for enhancing public knowledge of the digital ledger of economic transactions.[75]

Amongst the start-ups created, there are also those with social conscience and ethical concerns. Lumitics (former name "Good For Food") assists food and beverage (F&B) industry and conserve food for those who need it while Wanderer International (a non-profit organization [NPO]) brings socio-financial benefits to underprivileged global communities through voluntary educational and collaborative initiatives as content creation platform that advocates positive media activism among young people.[76] Retro Gate retails used textiles/clothing in the Japanese vintage streetwear and urban American wear genres at accessible prices, revolutionizing the concept of a mall-based brick and mortar store into a broad collaborative space for users to feature fashion items drawn from global cultures.[77]

Concluding Remarks

There is a prize at the end of the academic process too. The SUSS–EMP Alumni Entrepreneurship Award awards SUSS graduating students with praiseworthy entrepreneurial features like leadership qualities, taking initiative, self-motivation, energy, possessing confidence/courage and resilience after experiencing setbacks and have high potential for making a positive social impact.[78] Every year, one to three prizes (adding up to S$5000 each) are awarded to graduating entrepreneurial SUSS, nominated by SUSS faculty, staff members, students and investors/partners of students for interview and adjudication by a committee made up of faculty/staff and winners have to carry out the responsibilities of entrepreneurship advocacy and supporting the SUSS Entrepreneurship programme.[79]

---

[75] *Ibid.*

[76] *Ibid.*

[77] *Ibid.*

[78] Singapore University of Social Sciences (SUSS), "SUSS–EMP alumni entrepreneurship award" undated in the SUSS website [downloaded on 24 July 2020], available at https://suss.edu.sg/experience-at-suss/entrepreneurship/suss-emp-alumni-entrepreneurship-awards.

[79] *Ibid.*

SUSS keeps in close touch with its alumni members. SUSS Alumni Relations organized the first SUSS Entrepreneur Par-tee 2019 for alumni entrepreneurs at the mini golf course Holey Moley at Clarke Quay where Director Evelyn Chong (Office of Student and Alumni Relations) connected with participants to find out more about their ventures and link them up with those in the similar or related industries for possible cooperation.[80] The participants were organized into four-member groups to tee off at the course before gathering to listen to James Chia (founder of ArcLab, an edu-tech company established in 2012 and now a significant industry player) who shared his struggles in the building his start-up such as retrenching staff members because of funding deficiency, work-life balance and the rewards.[81] Ellen Goel (Head of Entrepreneurship Programme at the Centre of Experiential Learning) also shared SUSS entrepreneurship activities with the participants and emphasized the Alibaba Cloud-SUSS Certificate that attracted immediate sign-ups.[82]

---

[80]Lee, Nicole, "SUSS entrepreneur Par-Tee 2019" dated 2020 in SUSScribe Issue 52 in SUSScribe.com website [downloaded on 31 December 2020], available at https://susscribe.com/suss-entrepreneur-par-tee-2019/.
[81]*Ibid.*
[82]*Ibid.*

Chapter 5

A History of Attracting Talented Foreign Entrepreneurs: The Southeast Asia Case Study

History

Southeast Asia is embedded geographically in both East Asian and Western maritime trade routes, and the trading activities that come with this favorable location honed the foreign and indigenous entrepreneurs' business acumen and lowered the costs of goods transportation and logistics. In this intersection of the Maritime Silk Road (MSR), the Southeast Asian region attracted talented foreign entrepreneurs and traders plying through or settling down permanently in the region for trade. Located at the intersection between the Indian Ocean, the South China Sea and the Pacific Ocean routes, the Southeast Asian spice trade attracted talented Arab, Indian and Chinese traders and entrepreneurs to this region.

Many arrived by 600 A.D., and this spurred the Maritime Silk Road trade to expand significantly by 1000 A.D., especially with Chinese and Indian traders calling at port cities from Malacca (also spelt Melaka) to Kerala in the 1300s–1600s and trading with indigenous entrepreneurs made up of indigenous Malays, Sulus, Javanese and others.[1] The foreign

---

[1] Bräutigam, Deborah, "Local entrepreneurship in Southeast Asia and Subsaharan Africa: Networks and linkages to the global economy" dated 14 July 1998 in United Nations University [downloaded on 1 January 2021], available at https://archive.unu.edu/hq/academic/Pg_area4/Brautigam.html.

traders, native retailers and settler-entrepreneurs all contributed to business activities in the region. There were other textile traders/entrepreneurs who settled down in the Malay Peninsula and North Sumatra (Indonesia) from West India's Gujarat, leaving behind archaeological material evidence in Thai historic sites like Khao sam Kaeo/Phu Kaho where excavations uncovered sizable yields of glassware and precious stone beads imported from India (these products were later manufactured locally in the region).[2]

An important group of talented foreign entrepreneurs that arrived on the shores of Southeast Asia were the overseas ethnic Chinese. Historically, Chinese migration displayed a feature characterized by some observers as "maritime mobility" where generations of Chinese migrants arrived in Southeast Asia in waves and became closely related to the region's economic development.[3] The first overseas ethnic Chinese trading post in Southeast Asia was in the Filipino island of Luzon, 340 miles from Swatow (Shantou in Hanyu Pinyin), a distance reachable within three days with strong winds propelling a junk; eventually, Chinese Admiral Cheng Ho (Zheng He in Hanyu Pinyin) sailed there with an ambassadorial official in 1405.[4] In terms of macro migratory patterns, Chinese/Indian traders and entrepreneurs have been in Southeast Asia for more than a millennium with increasing numbers found among the Southeast Asian populations (33% of Malaysians, 13% of Thais and 3% of Indonesians)

---

[2]Bhattacharya, Jayati, "Ties that bind: India and Southeast Asia connectivities" dated Winter 2020 in Education about Asia: Online Archives — Ties that Bind: India and Southeast Asia Connectivities Teaching Asia's Giants: India, Vol. 25, p. 3 (Winter 2020) [downloaded on 1 January 2021], available at https://www.asianstudies.org/publications/eaa/archives/ties-that-bind-india-and-southeast-asia-connectivities/.

[3]Bräutigam, Deborah, "Local entrepreneurship in Southeast Asia and Subsaharan Africa: Networks and linkages to the global economy" dated 14 July 1998 in United Nations University [downloaded on 1 January 2021], available at https://archive.unu.edu/hq/academic/Pg_area4/Brautigam.html.

[4]Gambe, Annabelle, "Overseas entrepreneurship in Southeast Asia" dated November 1996 in the Thammasat University website Nr. 14, p. 10 [downloaded on 1 January 2021], available at http://econ.tu.ac.th/archan/rangsun/MB%20663/MB%20663%20Readings/%E0%B9%95.%20%E0%B8%A3%E0%B8%B0%E0%B8%9A%E0%B8%9A%E0%B8%97%E0%B8%B8%E0%B8%99%E0%B8%99%E0%B8%B4%E0%B8%A2%E0%B8%A1%E0%B9%84%E0%B8%97%E0%B8%A2/Overseas%20Chinese%20Capitalism/Overseas%20Entrepreneurship%20in%20SE%20Asia.pdf.

and welcomed by local rulers for several hundred years.[5] The Chinese added on to the numbers of Indians and Arab merchants/traders/entrepreneurs. Business and economic interactions in the Malay Archipelago connected with an Arab-Persian maritime trade route resulted in the emergence of a pan-Asian "Indo-Islamic trading world –Al-bahr al-Hindi" emerging from the 7th to the 8th centuries with intellectual historian and Sanskrit scholar Sheldon Pollock characterizing this development in the following manner:

> … a Sanskrit cosmopolis for much of the first millennium CE [in spite of the inevitable impact of Indian culture, the extent, means, and homogeneity of Indian influence in Southeast Asia].[6]

Indigenous ruling elites made pragmatic arrangements with Chinese entrepreneurs in facilitating and complementing their business activities with Chinese entrepreneurs. For example, in Malaysia, the rulers "tax farmed" Chinese entrepreneurs for their state revenues while retaining their political power even as the Chinese entrepreneurs zeroed in on an industry or commodity for monopolization (either in output or distribution) by paying a predetermined rent to the sovereign while lucratively pocketing any surplus profits.[7] Many overseas Chinese entrepreneurs became wealthy in this manner. In the Philippines, they worked closely with the locals, transferring valuable skills and know-how. The overseas ethnic Chinese entrepreneurs even introduced proto-industrialization to the indigenous Southeast Asians. For example, Chinese traders and entre-

---

[5]Bräutigam, Deborah, "Local entrepreneurship in Southeast Asia and Subsaharan Africa: Networks and linkages to the global economy" dated 14 July 1998 in United Nations University [downloaded on 1 January 2021], available at https://archive.unu.edu/hq/academic/Pg_area4/Brautigam.html.
[6]Bhattacharya, Jayati, "Ties that bind: India and Southeast Asia connectivities" dated Winter 2020 in Education about Asia: Online Archives — Ties that Bind: India and Southeast Asia Connectivities Teaching Asia's Giants: India, Vol. 25, p. 3 (Winter 2020) [downloaded on 1 January 2021], available at https://www.asianstudies.org/publications/eaa/archives/ties-that-bind-india-and-southeast-asia-connectivities/.
[7]Bräutigam, Deborah, "Local entrepreneurship in Southeast Asia and Subsaharan Africa: Networks and linkages to the global economy" dated 14 July 1998 in United Nations University [downloaded on 1 January 2021], available at https://archive.unu.edu/hq/academic/Pg_area4/Brautigam.html.

preneurs who became residents in Spain's Philippines brought along basic food processing know-how in extracting sugar from sugar cane, sugar refinement through claying, fruit tree cultivation, truck gardening (systematic cultivation of vegetables as commodified crop) and plough-training the junk-transported *carabao* (Chinese water buffalo).[8]

Modern Era

Entrepreneurs generally start off as small-time artisans/craftsmen/traders before entering manufacturing activities as trade facilitates capital accumulation and absorption of new innovative ideas, and promotes the knowledge of markets and familiarity with distribution channels (especially those embedded in an ethnic network), a point articulated by the Bamboo network (overseas Chinese business network) scholar Murray Weidenbaum:

> … in a region where capital markets are rudimentary, financial disclosure is limited, and contract law very weak, interpersonal networks are critical to moving economic resources across political boundaries.[9]

The Chinese migrant entrepreneurs were located in unfamiliar territories and sometimes hostile environments. Marginalized in their host societies, they needed each other's support and resources to overcome the difficulties. Scholar Bert Hoselitz argued as follows:

> … marginal men [e.g. Jews, Greeks in medieval Europe, Lebanese in West Africa, Chinese in Southeast Asia, Indians in East Africa], because

---

[8]Gambe, Annabelle, "Overseas entrepreneurship in Southeast Asia" dated November 1996 in the Thammasat University website Nr. 14, p. 11 [downloaded on 1 January 2021], available at http://econ.tu.ac.th/archan/rangsun/MB%20663/MB%20663%20Readings/ %E0%B9%95.%20%E0%B8%A3%E0%B8%B0%E0%B8%9A%E0%B8%9A%E0%B8 %97%E0%B8%B8%E0%B8%99%E0%B8%99%E0%B8%B4%E0%B8%A2%E0%B8 %A1%E0%B9%84%E0%B8%97%E0%B8%A2/Overseas%20Chinese%20Capitalism/ Overseas%20Entrepreneurship%20in%20SE%20Asia.pdf.

[9]Bräutigam, Deborah, "Local entrepreneurship in Southeast Asia and Subsaharan Africa: Networks and linkages to the global economy" dated 14 July 1998 in United Nations University [downloaded on 1 January 2021], available at https://archive.unu.edu/hq/ academic/Pg_area4/Brautigam.html.

of their ambiguous position from a cultural or social standpoint, are peculiarly suited to make creative adjustments in situations of change and, in the course of this adjustment process, to develop genuine innovations in social behavior.[10]

Some 15th century writings recorded the important historical roles played by two southern Indian merchant communities, Chulias (Tamil Muslim merchants) and Kelings/Klings (Chetti, Tamil, Telugu, Kannada Hindu merchants), in the trading emporium of Melaka (also spelt Malacca, in contemporary Malaysia).[11] The Sultanate of Melaka or Malacca was the seat of Malay civilization where cosmopolitan trading activities took place in a city replete with Ming Chinese warehouses, Arab trading groups, Javanese communities, Turkish mercenaries and vassal state protection from Ming Dynasty China against the Siamese Kingdom.

Existing literature suggests that Southeast Asia's blend of capitalism and entrepreneurship shows the features of tapping both indigenous and non-indigenous entrepreneurs and the experiences they accumulated from the pre- and post-colonial era and the business networks formed during this period.[12] The Chinese and Indian entrepreneurs were particularly crucial in servicing urban business, retail and service sector needs. Historian Jean Taylor highlighted in her Indonesian study that most participants in the Southeast Asian Muslim trading network were localized in port cities where "opportunities in the ports were disproportionately enjoyed by

---

[10] Gambe, Annabelle, "Overseas entrepreneurship in Southeast Asia" dated November 1996 in the Thammasat University website Nr. 14, p. 5 [downloaded on 1 January 2021], available at http://econ.tu.ac.th/archan/rangsun/MB%20663/MB%20663%20Readings/ %E0%B9%95.%20%E0%B8%A3%E0%B8%B0%E0%B8%9A%E0%B8%9A%E0%B8 %97%E0%B8%B8%E0%B8%99%E0%B8%99%E0%B8%B4%E0%B8%A2%E0%B8 %A1%E0%B9%84%E0%B8%97%E0%B8%A2/Overseas%20Chinese%20Capitalism/ Overseas%20Entrepreneurship%20in%20SE%20Asia.pdf.

[11] Bhattacharya, Jayati, "Ties that bind: India and Southeast Asia connectivities" dated Winter 2020 in Education about Asia: Online Archives — Ties that Bind: India and Southeast Asia Connectivities Teaching Asia's Giants: India, Vol. 25, p. 3 (Winter 2020) [downloaded on 1 January 2021], available at https://www.asianstudies.org/publications/ eaa/archives/ties-that-bind-india-and-southeast-asia-connectivities/.

[12] Bräutigam, Deborah, "Local entrepreneurship in Southeast Asia and Subsaharan Africa: Networks and linkages to the global economy" dated 14 July 1998 in United Nations University [downloaded on 1 January 2021], available at https://archive.unu.edu/hq/ academic/Pg_area4/Brautigam.html.

foreigners" because indigenous political elites tapped the urban skills of foreign entrepreneurs like the Chinese, Arabs or Indians for business activities, management and administration.[13] Entrepreneurs need to overcome high transactional, initial start-up risks and learning curve costs through business networks that would eventually expand to a global marketplace where they can absorb investments, ideas, experiences and catalysts for business projects.[14] [This applies even to the contemporary situation. In fact, these very reasons appealed to 21st century Indian entrepreneurs when looking eastward as Southeast Asian start-ups and ecosystems show powerful economic growth, attracting Indian entrepreneurs to the region through its large economic community market, business-friendly environment and potential for IT growth due to absent local know-how].[15]

But, before the contemporary Indian entrepreneurs came to the region, the Southeast Asia business sector was already dominated by the overseas Chinese entrepreneurs from the late pre-modern period onward due to their ability to form strong informal business networks. The early overseas ethnic Chinese (and to a lesser extent Indian entrepreneurs) in Southeast Asia depended on informal networks for raising capital, usually relying on family clans, hometown association ties and/or artificial brotherhoods based on familiarity with each other and long-term friendship. Even the Southeast Asian women entrepreneurs who came much later started off the same way. Marginalized by traditional banking institutions and small capital options, these female entrepreneurs depended on informal sources like family, friends, colleagues and, much

---

[13] Bhattacharya, Jayati, "Ties that bind: India and Southeast Asia connectivities" dated Winter 2020 in Education about Asia: Online Archives — Ties that Bind: India and Southeast Asia Connectivities Teaching Asia's Giants: India, Vol. 25, p. 3 (Winter 2020) [downloaded on 1 January 2021], available at https://www.asianstudies.org/publications/eaa/archives/ties-that-bind-india-and-southeast-asia-connectivities/.

[14] Bräutigam, Deborah, "Local entrepreneurship in Southeast Asia and Subsaharan Africa: Networks and linkages to the global economy" dated 14 July 1998 in United Nations University [downloaded on 1 January 2021], available at https://archive.unu.edu/hq/academic/Pg_area4/Brautigam.html.

[15] Fok, Evelyn, "Why Southeast Asia is a magnet for ambitious Indian entrepreneurs" dated 20 February 2015 in the *Economic Times* [downloaded on 20 February 2015], available at https://economictimes.indiatimes.com/small-biz/entrepreneurship/why-southeast-asia-is-a-magnet-for-ambitious-indian-entrepreneurs/articleshow/46307256.cms?from=mdr.

later in the contemporary era, angel investors (who were likely to be females as well).[16]

The European Age of Commerce

The arrival of the Europeans or the age of commerce introduced changes to the business landscape with the Portuguese and the Dutch reconfiguring the Southeast Asian local trading circuits in the 17th century by encouraging Chinese/Indian immigrants to attract their compatriots from their hometowns, and such workforce expansion efforts bolstered the development of colonial economic systems.[17] When the Philippines came under Spanish control, the Spaniards encouraged the Chinese to settle in the Philippines permanently and carry on with their entrepreneurial and business activities. Spanish Governor-General Legazpi set up a Chinese trading post, the Alcayceria, in 1580 and allowed the Chinese to settle permanently in that outpost where more than 400 shops with 8,000 employees traded in goods and produced metal works.[18]

These early residents were mostly men. But, as time progress, the Chinese male entrepreneurs and business owners either intermarried with the locals or migrated with their families to Southeast Asia. Others returned back to China to be buried there. Local or migrant women, however, did not necessarily tap into the entrepreneurial network because Southeast Asian women did not have sufficient entrepreneurial time, energy, flexibility and focus as the primary caregivers of their kids, senior

---

[16]Seno-Alday, Sandra, "Quiet achievers: How women are changing regional business" undated in Asia Society [downloaded on 1 August 2021], available at https://asiasociety. org/australia/quiet-achievers-how-women-are-changing-regional-business.

[17]Bräutigam, Deborah, "Local entrepreneurship in Southeast Asia and Subsaharan Africa: Networks and linkages to the global economy" dated 14 July 1998 in United Nations University [downloaded on 1 January 2021], available at https://archive.unu.edu/hq/academic/Pg_area4/Brautigam.html.

[18]Gambe, Annabelle, "Overseas entrepreneurship in Southeast Asia" dated November 1996 in the Thammasat University website Nr. 14, p. 11 [downloaded on 1 January 2021], available at http://econ.tu.ac.th/archan/rangsun/MB%20663/MB%20663%20Readings/%E0%B9%95.%20%E0%B8%A3%E0%B8%B0%E0%B8%9A%E0%B8%9A%E0%B8%97%E0%B8%B8%E0%B8%99%E0%B8%99%E0%B8%B4%E0%B8%A2%E0%B8%A1%E0%B9%84%E0%B8%97%E0%B8%A2/Overseas%20Chinese%20Capitalism/Overseas%20Entrepreneurship%20in%20SE%20Asia.pdf.

family members, siblings and extended family members, and such perceived gender roles did not get help as childcare and elderly care facilities were nonexistent.[19] This remained the case right up to the contemporary era; therefore, the business networks were predominantly male. Throughout Southeast Asia, Western observers noted the emergence of "guild-like dialect organizations" in the mid-19th century that shaped Chinese business and commerce in terms of business partnerships, patronage alliances, political connections, single-family firm structures and trade associations.[20] Sometimes, the alliances and connections were established transactionally with Western powers during the colonial era. For example, while the retail sector in Java was dominated by the overseas ethnic Chinese, foreign trade was a monopoly of the Dutch East Indies Company, which was reliant on the ethnic Chinese middlemen for the distribution of their imported goods, and this was the symbiotic arrangement since the days of the early Dutch colonial rule of Indonesia.[21]

Based on kinship and dialects, overseas Chinese networks provided credit, preferential distribution pacts, business advice, market intelligence and networking among themselves in the 18th and 19th centuries, thereby reducing the costs of doing business, providing trustworthy business partners across generations and buffering the risks needed to go into the manufacturing sector.[22] Sometimes, the colonial powers worked closely

---

[19] Seno-Alday, Sandra, "Quiet achievers: How women are changing regional business" undated in Asia Society [downloaded on 1 August 2021], available at https://asiasociety. org/australia/quiet-achievers-how-women-are-changing-regional-business.

[20] Bräutigam, Deborah, "Local entrepreneurship in Southeast Asia and Subsaharan Africa: Networks and linkages to the global economy" dated 14 July 1998 in United Nations University [downloaded on 1 January 2021], available at https://archive.unu.edu/hq/ academic/Pg_area4/Brautigam.html.

[21] Gambe, Annabelle, "Overseas entrepreneurship in Southeast Asia" dated November 1996 in the Thammasat University website Nr. 14, p. 51 [downloaded on 1 January 2021], available at http://econ.tu.ac.th/archan/rangsun/MB%20663/MB%20663%20Readings/ %E0%B9%95.%20%E0%B8%A3%E0%B8%B0%E0%B8%9A%E0%B8%9A%E0%B8 %97%E0%B8%B8%E0%B8%99%E0%B8%99%E0%B8%B4%E0%B8%A2%E0%B8 %A1%E0%B9%84%E0%B8%97%E0%B8%A2/Overseas%20Chinese%20Capitalism/ Overseas%20Entrepreneurship%20in%20SE%20Asia.pdf.

[22] Bräutigam, Deborah, "Local entrepreneurship in Southeast Asia and Subsaharan Africa: Networks and linkages to the global economy" dated 14 July 1998 in United Nations University [downloaded on 1 January 2021], available at https://archive.unu.edu/hq/ academic/Pg_area4/Brautigam.html.

with the Chinese entrepreneurs based on a practical arrangement. For example, when business capital/funding was hard to come by in the Filipino Chinese community before 1900, Chinese businesses were funded by sources within the British Empire (then the largest trading entity in the world) though provision of credit, capital or as guarantors of Chinese notes held by Spanish banks, eventually leading some to call this an "Anglo-Chinese alliance".[23]

Some consider the human resource of the entrepreneur as "the only resource that takes risks and marshals other financial, physical, technological, and intangible resources for creative, productive and profitable use".[24] Indeed, the Chinese or Indian entrepreneurs in Southeast Asia working alongside European companies began to transition the region toward modern manufacturing sectors. By the late 19th century, Southeast Asia started an early modern manufacturing economy with almost entirely foreign (e.g. Western), ethnic Chinese or Indian investments in Southeast Asia cement, food canning, beer, soap/biscuit production and rubber processing sectors between 1870 and 1914 before moving on to manufacturing chemicals, refined sugar, light machinery, cycles, paper, textiles, etc., by 1930.[25] [In the 21st century, John Lee argues that Southeast Asian overseas ethnic Chinese continue to dominate the regional economy. He says they are dominant in the private sectors of every Southeast Asian country and, like the Europeans of yore, they are significant investors in China and pathfinders for Southeast Asian/China businesses; for example, 90% of Sino-Indonesia's commerce is intermediated by

---

[23] Gambe, Annabelle, "Overseas entrepreneurship in Southeast Asia" dated November 1996 in the Thammasat University website Nr. 14, pp. 15–16 [downloaded on 1 January 2021], available at http://econ.tu.ac.th/archan/rangsun/MB%20663/MB%20663%20 Readings/%E0%B9%95.%20%E0%B8%A3%E0%B8%B0%E0%B8%9A%E0%B8%9A %E0%B8%97%E0%B8%B8%E0%B8%99%E0%B8%99%E0%B8%B4%E0%B8%A2 %E0%B8%A1%E0%B9%84%E0%B8%97%E0%B8%A2/Overseas%20Chinese%20 Capitalism/Overseas%20Entrepreneurship%20in%20SE%20Asia.pdf.

[24] Seno-Alday, Sandra, "Quiet achievers: How women are changing regional business" undated in Asia Society [downloaded on 1 August 2021], available at https://asiasociety. org/australia/quiet-achievers-how-women-are-changing-regional-business.

[25] Bräutigam, Deborah, "Local entrepreneurship in Southeast Asia and Subsaharan Africa: Networks and linkages to the global economy" dated 14 July 1998 in United Nations University [downloaded on 1 January 2021], available at https://archive.unu.edu/hq/ academic/Pg_area4/Brautigam.html.

Chinese-Indonesians even though they are not majority shareholders of those infrastructural and natural resources assets].[26]

By the early 20th century, Southeast Asia had major Chinese family-run companies in a range of business activities; for example, the Khaw family started their wealth-building in the 19th century as tax farmers in Hong Kong and Southeast Asia and then insurance, shipping, and tin mining and smelting in Siam (Thailand), Burma and the Malay States in the early 20th century.[27] From such humble origins, overseas ethnic Chinese business networks accumulated wealth and economic power that became a dominant pan-Southeast Asian economic force half a century later. In 1995, Australia's Department of Foreign Affairs and Trade (DFAT) published a 350-page report on the 50 million-strong overseas ethnic Chinese business networks located predominantly in Taiwan, Hong Kong, Macau and Southeast Asia, describing it as "one of the main forces driving the dynamic growth that characterises the region".[28]

Modern Origins

Southeast Asian Chinese firms started strong in small and medium-sized (SME) industrial sectors in the 1930s and 1940s before taking on larger-scale manufacturing activities in the 1950s in more rudimentary technological sectors like garments, molded plastics, wood products and paper; for example, Khaw family business operations included joint ventures (JVs) with Australian companies, Chettiar groups and other Chinese outfits.[29] Two decades later, such family operations would turn their sights to

---

[26]Lee, John, "The Chinese diaspora's role in the rise of China" dated 14 September 2016 in East Asia Forum [downloaded on 1 January 2020], available at https://www.eastasiaforum.org/2016/09/14/the-chinese-diasporas-role-in-the-rise-of-china/.

[27]Bräutigam, Deborah, "Local entrepreneurship in Southeast Asia and Subsaharan Africa: Networks and linkages to the global economy" dated 14 July 1998 in United Nations University [downloaded on 1 January 2021], available at https://archive.unu.edu/hq/academic/Pg_area4/Brautigam.html.

[28]Lee, John, "The Chinese diaspora's role in the rise of China" dated 14 September 2016 in East Asia Forum [downloaded on 1 January 2020], available at https://www.eastasiaforum.org/2016/09/14/the-chinese-diasporas-role-in-the-rise-of-china/.

[29]Bräutigam, Deborah, "Local entrepreneurship in Southeast Asia and Subsaharan Africa: Networks and linkages to the global economy" dated 14 July 1998 in United Nations University [downloaded on 1 January 2021], available at https://archive.unu.edu/hq/academic/Pg_area4/Brautigam.html.

investing in mainland China when the economic reforms started in 1978 under Chinese paramount leader Deng Xiaoping. In China, just as they were in Southeast Asia, the ethnic Chinese diasporic entrepreneurs were highly competitive. More than other non-Chinese competitors in China, they utilized cultural-ancestral ties to manage political risks and even participated in the economic reform process as representatives in the Chinese People's Political Consultative Conference (CPPCC) and the National People's Congress (NPC) (both are sometimes dubbed as China's "twin parliaments") and building their *guanxi* connections right up to paramount leader Deng Xiaoping himself.[30]

Chinese and Indian investments/trading networks grew to compete with their European counterparts and some wealthy Chinese entrepreneurs even lent credit to European merchants. The European colonial authorities like the Indonesian Dutch administration introduced quotas on textiles in the 1930s to steer local capital (mainly Chinese) and foreign capital into the manufacturing sector.[31] Besides the symbiotic relationship between the European colonials and overseas ethnic Chinese, the latter intermarried with the elite local indigenous Southeast Asia class as well. Though difficult to quantify, some observers like John Lee argued that contemporary China would eventually seek to leverage Southeast Asian opinions by tapping into the high degree of Chinese ancestry in some ASEAN elites like the Thai royal family.[32]

In the 1930s, Chinese investments in Southeast Asia were similar in scale to Western investments in the region, and in Southeast Asia, the non-indigenous entrepreneurs who had accumulated the networks, funding and business know-how tapped into an international network to transition

---

[30]Lee, John, "The Chinese diaspora's role in the rise of China" dated 14 September 2016 in East Asia Forum [downloaded on 1 January 2020], available at https://www. eastasiaforum.org/2016/09/14/the-chinese-diasporas-role-in-the-rise-of-china/.

[31]Bräutigam, Deborah, "Local entrepreneurship in Southeast Asia and Subsaharan Africa: Networks and linkages to the global economy" dated 14 July 1998 in United Nations University [downloaded on 1 January 2021], available at https://archive.unu.edu/hq/academic/Pg_area4/Brautigam.html.

[32]Lee, John, "The Chinese diaspora's role in the rise of China" dated 14 September 2016 in East Asia Forum [downloaded on 1 January 2020], available at https://www. eastasiaforum.org/2016/09/14/the-chinese-diasporas-role-in-the-rise-of-china/.

from purely trading/commercial activities to modern manufacturing.[33] These very same capabilities forged and honed in modern industries would later serve the infant People's Republic of China (PRC) very well as it embarked on its own program of modernization and industrialization, especially during the economic reform period from 1978 onward. Overseas ethnic Chinese business networks played an important part in developing China's export industries, its regional economic integration and their market experimentation with the Southeast Asian regional export market while keeping China's socialist political system intact, retaining key features of its pre-1979 centralized socialist political system and this was a valuable resource not found in other rising powers.[34]

The decade of the 1940s was perhaps a golden era of Southeast Asian industrialization, not only for the overseas ethnic Chinese entrepreneurs but also for the entire region as a whole. By 1941, Southeast Asian industrialization was led by Chinese, Indian, European and Japanese entrepreneurs' investments operating from their trading bases to expand their presence in the domestic market before progressing on to a pan-Asian market portfolio through cartel-like formation (effectively encouraging Southeast Asian intra-regional trade and investments).[35] Some tycoon entrepreneurs were careful not to ruffle socio-political sensitivities even as they accumulated immense wealth. For example, despite assimilation into Filipino society, Chinese-Filipino tycoons witnessed the animosities toward their counterparts in Indonesia and Malaysia and decided to open up their closed family networks to public stockholders through the stock markets to dispel any negative images of their businesses and share their

---

[33] Bräutigam, Deborah, "Local entrepreneurship in Southeast Asia and Subsaharan Africa: Networks and linkages to the global economy" dated 14 July 1998 in United Nations University [downloaded on 1 January 2021], available at https://archive.unu.edu/hq/academic/Pg_area4/Brautigam.html.

[34] Lee, John, "The Chinese diaspora's role in the rise of China" dated 14 September 2016 in East Asia Forum [downloaded on 1 January 2020], available at https://www.eastasiaforum.org/2016/09/14/the-chinese-diasporas-role-in-the-rise-of-china/.

[35] Bräutigam, Deborah, "Local entrepreneurship in Southeast Asia and Subsaharan Africa: Networks and linkages to the global economy" dated 14 July 1998 in United Nations University [downloaded on 1 January 2021], available at https://archive.unu.edu/hq/academic/Pg_area4/Brautigam.html.

wealth through company stock options with a bigger percentage of the Filipino population.[36]

Post-War Era

Entrepreneurship in Southeast Asia could only take off with the inflow of foreign technologies. Indian traders, merchants and entrepreneurs facilitated one of the earliest technological transfers in the Southeast Asia region in the midst of operating their business activities. Imported and later locally manufactured Indic textiles and potteries highlighted how Indian craftsmen/artisans facilitated technology transfers from India to Southeast Asia through trans-oceanic exchanges across the eastern Indian Ocean.[37] Overseas ethnic Chinese retail/service middlemen/small-time entrepreneurs contributed to Spanish Philippines through the China trade and in the professions of carpenters, tailors, cobblers, locksmiths, masons, weavers and bakers.[38] In the modern era, the post-Industrial Revolution Europeans would take over the role of providing modern technologies to the Southeast Asians.

After World War II, Japan, which was the first country in East Asia to modernize successfully, rose out of the ashes of the Pacific War like a

---

[36]Gambe, Annabelle, "Overseas entrepreneurship in Southeast Asia" dated November 1996 in the Thammasat University website Nr. 14, pp. 39–40 [downloaded on 1 January 2021], available at http://econ.tu.ac.th/archan/rangsun/MB%20663/MB%20663%20 Readings/%E0%B9%95.%20%E0%B8%A3%E0%B8%B0%E0%B8%9A%E0%B8%9A %E0%B8%97%E0%B8%B8%E0%B8%99%E0%B8%99%E0%B8%B4%E0%B8%A2 %E0%B8%A1%E0%B9%84%E0%B8%97%E0%B8%A2/Overseas%20Chinese%20 Capitalism/Overseas%20Entrepreneurship%20in%20SE%20Asia.pdf.

[37]Bhattacharya, Jayati, "Ties that bind: India and Southeast Asia connectivities" dated Winter 2020 in Education about Asia: Online Archives — Ties that Bind: India and Southeast Asia Connectivities Teaching Asia's Giants: India, Vol. 25, p. 3 (Winter 2020) [downloaded on 1 January 2021], available at https://www.asianstudies.org/publications/ eaa/archives/ties-that-bind-india-and-southeast-asia-connectivities/.

[38]Gambe, Annabelle, "Overseas entrepreneurship in Southeast Asia" dated November 1996 in the Thammasat University website Nr. 14, p. 11 [downloaded on 1 January 2021], available at http://econ.tu.ac.th/archan/rangsun/MB%20663/MB%20663%20 Readings/%E0%B9%95.%20%E0%B8%A3%E0%B8%B0%E0%B8%9A%E0%B8%9A %E0%B8%97%E0%B8%B8%E0%B8%99%E0%B8%99%E0%B8%B4%E0%B8%A2 %E0%B8%A1%E0%B9%84%E0%B8%97%E0%B8%A2/Overseas%20Chinese%20 Capitalism/Overseas%20Entrepreneurship%20in%20SE%20Asia.pdf.

phoenix and rapidly re-industrialized. With rapid recovery, Japan was now in a position to be a source of advanced industrial technologies. Japanese firms through their joint ventures (JVs) transferred technologies and skills to their Southeast Asian partners who were usually Chinese business entrepreneurs who had established local distribution networks, and they had a long history of doing so; for example, Mitsubishi trading company already had a foothold in Southeast Asia by 1917.[39] After World War II and the decolonization phase, the emergence of Japanese know-how, investments, technologies and aid further stimulated the rise of entrepreneurial firms in Southeast Asia. This process allowed the entrepreneurs to accumulate capital; especially in the post-war period, Japanese firms operated in joint ventures with Southeast Asian companies transferring technologies to the local entrepreneurs and companies and this enabled the Southeast Asian entrepreneurs to graduate from working only in commodity-based industries.[40]

The Japanese role in facilitating technological advancements and profit-making would continue into the 21st century, especially in enabling Southeast Asia to develop as a high-technology center to facilitate regional companies in implementing industrial technologies and prepping their infrastructure for regional growth, upgrading tech services and delivering cutting-edge products. This kind of regional drive, ambition and production networking blueprint was lagging in its nearest regional competitors, like India, as Japanese companies like Softbank partnered with Indonesia's telecom giant Indosat to form a US$50-million (Rs. 310 crore) fund with investments made in the Philippines as well.[41] Such blueprints and plans were only possible with a long history of state policy

---

[39] Bräutigam, Deborah, "Local entrepreneurship in Southeast Asia and Subsaharan Africa: Networks and linkages to the global economy" dated 14 July 1998 in United Nations University [downloaded on 1 January 2021], available at https://archive.unu.edu/hq/academic/Pg_area4/Brautigam.html.

[40] Bräutigam, Deborah, "Local entrepreneurship in Southeast Asia and Subsaharan Africa: Networks and linkages to the global economy" dated 14 July 1998 in United Nations University [downloaded on 1 January 2021], available at https://archive.unu.edu/hq/academic/Pg_area4/Brautigam.html.

[41] Fok, Evelyn, "Why Southeast Asia is a magnet for ambitious Indian entrepreneurs" dated 20 February 2015 in the *Economic Times* [downloaded on 20 February 2015], available at https://economictimes.indiatimes.com/small-biz/entrepreneurship/why-southeast-asia-is-a-magnet-for-ambitious-indian-entrepreneurs/articleshow/46307256.cms?from=mdr.

formulation and a state-led role in the economy, a political-economic feature that East Asian countries are known for.

Policy changes have also helped with encouraging entrepreneurship in Southeast Asia during the nation-building days right after decolonization. Some of these policy changes in Southeast Asia were considered progressive. For example, in Indonesia and the Philippines, commercial banks provided business loans for female-led enterprises, facilitated by streamlined application processes and prerequisites, flexible collaterals and customized repayment periods.[42] But, most of the state's policy attention was focused on creating favorable conditions for economic growth. Some argue that entrepreneurs require a stable and predictable political-economic environment and the absence of strong disincentives (conversely, preferably with strong incentives) to encourage their growth; for example, a 1955 World Bank report urged Malaysia to increase tariffs on manufactured goods to jump-start import-substitution-based industrialization.[43] The importance of entrepreneurship in the Southeast Asian region is underlined by the fact that all its individual countries' economies are mostly driven by the micro, small and medium enterprises (MSMEs), which had become the engine of Southeast Asian economic growth.[44]

All entrepreneurs in East Asia were boosted by the state's role in the economy. The World Bank's study on the East Asian "miracle" attributed Thailand, Indonesia and Malaysia's successes in economic development in the 1980s and 1990s to their government's value-added consultations and guidance with their entrepreneurs (a feature that originated from Northeast Asia); for example, Malaysia institutionalized such consultations in 1991.[45] As the foreign migrant entrepreneurs attained successes in

[42] Seno-Alday, Sandra, "Quiet achievers: How women are changing regional business" undated in Asia Society [downloaded on 1 August 2021], available at https://asiasociety. org/australia/quiet-achievers-how-women-are-changing-regional-business.

[43] Bräutigam, Deborah, "Local entrepreneurship in Southeast Asia and Subsaharan Africa: Networks and linkages to the global economy" dated 14 July 1998 in United Nations University [downloaded on 1 January 2021], available at https://archive.unu.edu/hq/ academic/Pg_area4/Brautigam.html.

[44] Seno-Alday, Sandra, "Quiet achievers: How women are changing regional business" undated in Asia Society [downloaded on 1 August 2021], available at https://asiasociety. org/australia/quiet-achievers-how-women-are-changing-regional-business.

[45] Bräutigam, Deborah, "Local entrepreneurship in Southeast Asia and Subsaharan Africa: Networks and linkages to the global economy" dated 14 July 1998 in United Nations University [downloaded on 1 January 2021], available at https://archive.unu.edu/hq/ academic/Pg_area4/Brautigam.html.

their businesses, local indigenous native entrepreneurs could then emulate these early movers and leaders from the diasporic group (in the process diluting/neutralizing their economic power) and such emulation incrementally spread throughout the entire host society over time.[46] Malaysia promoted Malay-owned businesses, and strengthened small and medium-sized entrepreneurs (many were ethnic Chinese) in subcontracting; Thailand gradually transitioned its Japanese textile factories from the mid-1960s to indigenous Thai ownership by the 1980s; and indigenous Indonesian entrepreneurs engaged in more joint ventures (JVs) with foreign firms in "textiles, electronics, glass manufacture, pharmaceuticals, and finance" by the 1990s.[47]

Challenges

There are some political dangers and risks faced by overseas Chinese or Indian entrepreneurs based in Southeast Asia. By the mid-1990s, the size of the Chinese diaspora had grown to an estimated 17–40 million overseas Chinese globally and many of them resided in Southeast Asia.[48] In the early 1990s, the overseas ethnic Chinese diaspora competed with Japan for business influence in East Asia, with a total wealth value similar to

---

[46]Gambe, Annabelle, "Overseas entrepreneurship in Southeast Asia" dated November 1996 in the Thammasat University website Nr. 14, pp. 5–6 [downloaded on 1 January 2021], available at http://econ.tu.ac.th/archan/rangsun/MB%20663/MB%20663%20 Readings/%E0%B9%95.%20%E0%B8%A3%E0%B8%B0%E0%B8%9A%E0%B8%9A %E0%B8%97%E0%B8%B8%E0%B8%99%E0%B8%99%E0%B8%B4%E0%B8%A2 %E0%B8%A1%E0%B9%84%E0%B8%97%E0%B8%A2/Overseas%20Chinese%20 Capitalism/Overseas%20Entrepreneurship%20in%20SE%20Asia.pdf.

[47]Bräutigam, Deborah, "Local entrepreneurship in Southeast Asia and Subsaharan Africa: Networks and linkages to the global economy" dated 14 July 1998 in United Nations University [downloaded on 1 January 2021], available at https://archive.unu.edu/hq/academic/Pg_area4/Brautigam.html.

[48]Gambe, Annabelle, "Overseas entrepreneurship in Southeast Asia" dated November 1996 in the Thammasat University website Nr. 14, p. 9 [downloaded on 1 January 2021], available at http://econ.tu.ac.th/archan/rangsun/MB%20663/MB%20663%20 Readings/%E0%B9%95.%20%E0%B8%A3%E0%B8%B0%E0%B8%9A%E0%B8%9A %E0%B8%97%E0%B8%B8%E0%B8%99%E0%B8%99%E0%B8%B4%E0%B8%A2 %E0%B8%A1%E0%B9%84%E0%B8%97%E0%B8%A2/Overseas%20Chinese%20 Capitalism/Overseas%20Entrepreneurship%20in%20SE%20Asia.pdf.

China's then Gross Domestic Product (GDP).[49] In 1998, overseas Chinese Indonesians contributed some 70% to the domestic investment but they were scapegoated in the 1997 Asian Financial Crisis (AFC) as a cause of the economic problems, and approximately 1000 Chinese were murdered (and 87 women raped) in the anti-Chinese riots to protest against state price hikes to mitigate the crisis.[50] In contrast, Thailand went in the opposite way in removing state policies of ethnic discrimination dating back to the late 1950s; consequently, "there has been virtually no significant indigenous business class in Thailand in competition with the Chinese".[51]

As a coping mechanism to let off some pent-up pressure on overseas Chinese entrepreneurs from the indigenous population, governments sometimes do intervene to level the playing field for the indigenous entrepreneurs, multinational firms or government players. For example, President Ramos removed the Filipino telecommunications monopoly that was under the control of a Chinese-Filipino in 1994 to liberalize that economic sector.[52] By the 21st century, the overseas ethnic Chinese diaspora had added more first-generation mainland Chinese migrants to their numbers as China transitioned toward a knowledge-based economy (KBE) accompanied by more intense cross-boundary business activities/interactions, thereby shaping the role and nature of overseas ethnic

---

[49]Lee, John, "The Chinese diaspora's role in the rise of China" dated 14 September 2016 in East Asia Forum [downloaded on 1 January 2020], available at https://www.eastasiaforum.org/2016/09/14/the-chinese-diasporas-role-in-the-rise-of-china/.

[50]Glionna, John M., "In Indonesia, 1998 violence against ethnic Chinese remains unaddressed" dated 4 July 2010 in *LA Times (LOS Angeles Times)* [downloaded on 4 July 2021], available at https://www.latimes.com/archives/la-xpm-2010-jul-04-la-fg-indonesia-chinese-20100704-story.html.

[51]Bräutigam, Deborah, "Local Entrepreneurship entrepreneurship in Southeast Asia and Subsaharan Africa: Networks and Linkages linkages to the Global global Economyeconomy" dated 14 July 1998 in United Nations University [downloaded on 1 January 2021], available at https://archive.unu.edu/hq/academic/Pg_area4/Brautigam.html.

[52]Gambe, Annabelle, "Overseas entrepreneurship in Southeast Asia" dated November 1996 in the Thammasat University website Nr. 14, p. 28 [downloaded on 1 January 2021], available at http://econ.tu.ac.th/archan/rangsun/MB%20663/MB%20663%20Readings/%E0%B9%95.%20%E0%B8%A3%E0%B8%B0%E0%B8%9A%E0%B8%9A%E0%B8%97%E0%B8%B8%E0%B8%99%E0%B8%99%E0%B8%B4%E0%B8%A2%E0%B8%A1%E0%B9%84%E0%B8%97%E0%B8%A2/Overseas%20Chinese%20Capitalism/Overseas%20Entrepreneurship%20in%20SE%20Asia.pdf.

Chinese communities and their relationship with mainland China with growing political significance.[53]

With growing scale and sophistication, Southeast Asian businesses started to exhibit changes. These contemporary categories of entrepreneur businesses became more diversified, professional and acquired greenfield investments by relying on external finance, such as stock issues and bank borrowing, facilitated by the establishment of stock markets (Kuala Lumpur Stock Exchange in 1973, Thailand in 1975, Indonesian take-off in the late 1980s), to raise capital (through reputation and not traditional networks).[54] Southeast Asian entrepreneurs started to shift away from dependence on traditional networks in favor of institutionalized banking systems, trade fairs and trade promotion activities as they globalized, listed on stock exchanges and integrated modern/Western management methodologies; as Ruth McVey points out, "The need to act in an increasingly internationalized business world imposes forms and behavior which erode Chinese exclusivity."[55]

Many would also go on to acquire Western business education. For example, despite achieving entrepreneurial success, Filipino tycoon Gokongwei insisted on acquiring Western management/skills by participating in a Harvard Business School Advanced Management Program (his brother Johnson Robert followed suit), while his youngest sibling went to the Massachusetts Institute of Technology, his son Lance graduated from Wharton Business School and even his management team has degrees from New York University.[56] Opportunities made possible by education were not restricted only to male entrepreneurs. Another visible change by

---

[53] Lee, John, "The Chinese diaspora's role in the rise of China" dated 14 September 2016 in East Asia Forum [downloaded on 1 January 2020], available at https://www.eastasiaforum.org/2016/09/14/the-chinese-diasporas-role-in-the-rise-of-china/.

[54] Bräutigam, Deborah, "Local entrepreneurship in Southeast Asia and Subsaharan Africa: Networks and linkages to the global economy" dated 14 July 1998 in United Nations University [downloaded on 1 January 2021], available at https://archive.unu.edu/hq/academic/Pg_area4/Brautigam.html.

[55] *Ibid.*

[56] Gambe, Annabelle, "Overseas entrepreneurship in Southeast Asia" dated November 1996 in the Thammasat University website Nr. 14, pp. 38–39 [downloaded on 1 January 2021], available at http://econ.tu.ac.th/archan/rangsun/MB%20663/MB%20663%20 Readings/%E0%B9%95.%20%E0%B8%A3%E0%B8%B0%E0%B8%9A%E0%B8%9A %E0%B8%97%E0%B8%B8%E0%B8%99%E0%B8%99%E0%B8%B4%E0%B8%A2 %E0%B8%A1%E0%B9%84%E0%B8%97%E0%B8%A2/Overseas%20Chinese%20 Capitalism/Overseas%20Entrepreneurship%20in%20SE%20Asia.pdf.

the mid-2010s was that more women were also participating in the Southeast Asian entrepreneurial landscape. By 2015, female entrepreneurial activity in the Philippines, Thailand, Indonesia and Vietnam (averaging at around 17%) doubled that of India (8%) and China (9%) despite the challenges and obstacles in the field of entrepreneurship traditionally dominated by men.[57]

---

[57] Seno-Alday, Sandra, "Quiet achievers: How women are changing regional business" undated in Asia Society [downloaded on 1 August 2021], available at https://asiasociety.org/australia/quiet-achievers-how-women-are-changing-regional-business.

Chapter 6

Family Ownership in Southeast Asia: Case Study of Overseas Ethnic Chinese Businesses

Another unique Southeast Asian entrepreneurial feature is the family-based variety found amongst overseas Chinese firms. Unlike state-based entrepreneurship education initiatives and its cultivation of entrepreneurial mindsets, overseas Chinese firms often succeed due to reliance on family bonds, family-oriented succession and networking through blood ties, ethnic ties and community solidarity. This is an organic, random and non-systematic solution. Deloitte recommended that Asian business families may need to overcome challenges of business succession, find enthusiastic and committed successive managers by providing entrepreneurial training for business development and succession plans to receptive family businesses.[1] Structurally, family ownership can be a plus point. The official youth unemployment rate in Asia is relatively low, at under 10% and up to 65% of entrepreneurs borrow seed money from family, and a further 21% from friends or neighbors.[2]

---

[1] SMU and Deloitte, "Asian Business Families Succession Going the Distance with the Next Generation" in Deloitte website [downloaded on 1 Dec 2020], (Singapore: SMU and Deloitte), available at https://www2.deloitte.com/content/dam/Deloitte/sg/Documents/finance/sg-fas-bfi-smu-deloitte-report.pdf, p. 44.

[2] Xu, Haoliang, "Asia's young entrepreneurs need help with the hustle" dated 10 Aug 2018 in World Economic Forum (WEF) [downloaded on 10 August 2018], available at

Entrepreneurial Ethics, Mindsets, Value Systems and Education: A Case Study of Overseas Chinese Entrepreneurs in Southeast Asia

Introduction and Literature Review

The willingness to pick up entrepreneurial and other business skills appears to be very strong amongst one group of Southeast Asians — the overseas ethnic Chinese. Existing literatures have attributed this to the status of education in their culture. Due to the cultural feature of groupism and collectivism in Confucian societies, cultural traits are often highly socialized amongst the population and homogenized in their beliefs. Cooperation behavior is said to be one of the trademark features of Confucian values and related to the concept of collectivism.[3] Thus, this leads to the dissemination of ideas of upskilling or reskilling amongst sections of the population quite easily, including the entrepreneurial class, eager to harness the benefits of education as a form of human capital.

Environmental factors have compelled the overseas ethnic Chinese entrepreneurs to develop survival instincts in overcoming a foreign and sometimes hostile environment to succeed in their businesses. Historically, shut out from colonial-era civil service and marginalized in localized business networks, they were compelled to form their own businesses. Some scholars have termed this as a "refugee mentality", akin to refugees escaping from their homelands and sinking roots in a foreign region. This has led to a mindset of constant sniffing out of business opportunities and niches for economic survival.

Due to their response to marginalization, they built their organizations on family, dialect, hometown, racial, ethnic, linguistic and sub-ethnic ties. Consequently, these close bonds then turned around to make the inclusion of outsiders difficult. The do-or-die attitude in a perceived hostile environment created the mindset and determination for success. Uncertainty avoidance was downplayed since they had very little to lose amongst the

---

https://www.weforum.org/agenda/2018/08/asias-young-entrepreneurs-need-help-with-the-hustle/.

[3] Chuah, Swee Hoon, Robert Hoffmann, Bala Ramasamy and Jonathan HW Tan, "Is there a Spirit of Overseas Chinese Capitalism?" dated 4 June 2016 in *Small Business Economics* (2016) 47 [downloaded on 26 Jan 2021], (Singapore: Springer), available at https://link.springer.com/article/10.1007/s11187-016-9746-5, p. 1102.

pioneering generations of overseas ethnic Chinese entrepreneurs. The risk-taking mindset is also prominent amongst mainland Chinese who took a risk to migrate to other countries for their livelihoods and this enterprising spirit has been passed on to the younger generations.[4]

Cultural factors are also strongly influential on the mindsets of overseas ethnic Chinese entrepreneurs. Chuah, Hoffman, Ramasamy and Tan argued that "cultural innovation and change were necessary for the survival of the [overseas ethnic Chinese immigrants," so "traditional Chinese heritage of folklores and Confucian thought was therefore merged with a 'refugee mentality' that arose from the immigrant experience and exposure to Western culture in the colonised settlement nations."[5] The overseas ethnic Chinese were very adaptable to the dynamically changing external environment. They often hybridized traditions and old ways of doing things with the progressive rational and scientific forms of management that they observed in the Western colonies in Southeast Asia during the late pre-modern to early modern period. Combined with the survival instincts, it became a very powerful form of entrepreneurial mindset.

Traditional Confucian ethics were selectively adapted and hybridized with modern ways of management to mitigate a foreign, unstable and sometimes hostile environment in Southeast Asia. The process forced the early overseas ethnic Chinese entrepreneurs to discard some old ways of thinking (hitherto fossilized in ancient Chinese culture). These discarded features of their mindsets included the low status of merchants in the Confucian order. According to ancient Confucian doctrines, individuals with the highest statuses in a hierarchical Confucian order were the scholar gentry mandarins due to their meritocratic attainment of position through rigorous examination systems. The second ranked were the farmers toiling hard on the lands as they were the food producers and the fruits of their labor is needed by all to survive.

The third ranking occupation was that of the artisans who were also productive in making tools that were necessary for all in society to enjoy the comforts of life. The tools helped to increase the efficiency of many human functions (construction, harvesting, ploughing the fields, cooking,

---

[4]Chuah, Swee Hoon, Robert Hoffmann, Bala Ramasamy and Jonathan HW Tan, "Is there a Spirit of Overseas Chinese Capitalism?" dated 4 June 2016 in *Small Business Economics* (2016) 47 [downloaded on 26 Jan 2021], (Singapore: Springer), available at https://link.springer.com/article/10.1007/s11187-016-9746-5, p. 1113.

[5]*Ibid*, p. 1110.

etc.). And the last in the pecking order were the merchants, traders and business people as they were seen as profiteers, leaching parasitically on the hard work of others. So powerful was this Confucian order that it was exported to China's peripheral countries like Korea, Vietnam and Japan. In Japan, the hierarchical order at the top replaced the mandarins with the warrior class (or the samurais) who were seen as able administrators and security guarantors as they were the only individuals authorized to wield swords.

The rapid adoption of Western language and education known as "rationalistic traditionalism" inherently had contradictions and tensions in reconciling traditions with modernity.[6] This contradiction did not result in a dichotomy, but the emergence of "a new kind of Chinese" with an "amazing willingness to split their personalities" and a "remarkable ability to move in and out of the two traditions."[7] This mindset navigated between scientific/modern rationality (defined as beliefs, progress and modernization[8]) and time-honored traditionalism (e.g. hardworking ethics) that socializes mindsets of its adherents and practitioners. The latter is conducive to facilitating overseas ethnic Chinese in the rapid mobilization of their resources. The hybridization of East–West thoughts also breaks the orthodoxy and particularism of Chinese Confucian mindset so that it can interact with other cultural mindsets (Southeast Asian or/and Western thinking) for business efficacy.

For example, in the linguistics field, overseas ethnic Chinese entrepreneurs, business people, compradors, traders and middlemen were able to effectively code-switch between native tongues and working European languages during the colonial era. This remains the case even today. In terms of lifestyle, they were also able to demonstrate an understanding of Western cultural nuances and modern/Western civilizational understanding. They also demonstrated legal minds with a modern understanding of the rule of law, contract laws, articles of incorporation, criminal and civil codes. All these convinced Westerners to feel safe and secure in conducting business relationships with overseas ethnic Chinese businesses during the colonial era and some aspects of such complementarities remain in place today.

---

[6] *Ibid*, p. 1110.

[7] *Ibid*, p. 1110.

[8] *Ibid*, p. 1105.

History

The modern history of Chinese outbound migration from China really started in the late Qing dynasty period, as they travelled to many regions of the world, including Southeast Asia. They settled down in their host societies and sank their roots in their areas over generations. Being foreigners and cut off from state support, many turned to entrepreneurship to make a living and to survive. Some of these host societies excluded them from job opportunities or were downright hostile, compelling them to rely on starting businesses in order to survive. In many host societies, they were also cut off from serving in the public service. In a few of these societies like Thailand, they sought actively to integrate overseas Chinese communities.

Based on hardworking ethics and strong family-based ties that bind, they accumulated capital and started businesses in areas where they spotted opportunities. Therefore, very often, their successes are attributed to cultural reasons. Sometimes, research on overseas Chinese associate overseas Chinese entrepreneurship with Confucian traditions. Guanxi relationships based on blood ties, ethnic identification, cultural bonds are another good example of cultural explanations for the successes of overseas Chinese entrepreneurs. Because of these ethnic ties that bind or family relations, the overseas Chinese are tied tightly with their business partners, allies, relatives' businesses and businesses run by compatriots from the same hometown. In the overseas Chinese entrepreneurial mindset, the senior–junior relationship based on traditional Confucian values like benevolence shown by seniors to loyal juniors comes into place. A senior (sometimes former employers) is obliged to support an entrepreneurial junior to set up his/her own company, a mindset considered by some to be an unwritten "cultural rule".[9]

These mindsets and values of Confucian ethics, hardworking ethos, frugality, loyalty, etc. tend to dilute with time and over generations. With each successive generation, the overseas ethnic Chinese identification with their ancestral lands becomes more distant as they localize and

---

[9]Yeung, Henry Wai-chung and Olds, Kris, "Globalizing Chinese business firms: where are they coming from, where are they heading?" dated 2000 in The Globalisation of Chinese Business Firms Henry Wai-chung Yeung and Kris Olds (eds.), (London: Macmillan), [downloaded on 1 Jan 2020], available at https://courses.nus.edu.sg/course/geoywc/publication/Macmillan.PDF, p.17 [online edition].

indigenize with time. When this happens, the mindsets may evolve into a hybridized form of value system that integrates Western education with local host societies' ethics and remnants of Confucian values. Some may, however, completely remove traces of Chinese Confucian ethics after many generations of localization.

One such example is the Peranakans who may lose linguistic and cultural affinities with traditional mindsets completely. Peranakans have ethnic Chinese ancestors who inter-married with Malay families and/or have adapted Malay traditional value systems and/or colonial education (and/or Western mindsets). Renowned sociologist/anthropologist William Skinner defined Indonesian Peranakans as ethnic Chinese who have a creolized or mestizo culture with strong Indonesian features and they married local Indonesians, speak Bahasa Indonesia at home while Chinese language (written, spoken and read) and cultural proficiency have eroded and dissipated over time.[10]

Mindsets and value system

Cooperative behavior is cited as the foundation of the bamboo network formation amongst ethnic Chinese businesses in Southeast Asia for interconnecting financial, informational and investment opportunities based on ethnicity and cultural affiliations.[11] Some of these networks based on family or hometown ties may trade across borders with other hometown groups (e.g. Teochew merchants in Southeast Asia trading with their counterparts in China) and form their own transboundary networks. The diasporic Chinese community is about 30 million-strong dispersed in more than 136 different countries in the furthest corners of the Earth,

---

[10] Jacobsen, Michael, "Living in the Shadow of Mainland China: On Delineating Social and Political Constraints Among Southeast Asian Chinese Entrepreneurs" dated 2007 in *The Copenhagen Journal of Asian Studies* 25 [downloaded on available at file:///E:/2021% 20Soka/Article%202021/Submit%20Entrepreneur%20190121/Mat%20280121%201428-Article%20Text-4993-1-10-20080116.pdf, p. 35.

[11] Chuah, Swee Hoon, Robert Hoffmann, Bala Ramasamy and Jonathan HW Tan, "Is there a Spirit of Overseas Chinese Capitalism?" dated 4 June 2016 in *Small Business Economics* (2016) 47 [downloaded on 26 Jan 2021], (Singapore: Springer), available at https://link. springer.com/article/10.1007/s11187-016-9746-5, pp. 1102–1103.

far more than any other diasporas and holding cash and assets of a few trillion USD.[12]

Cooperative behavior began to be harnessed by mainland China to build its own entrepreneur network for investing in China when Chinese paramount leader Deng Xiaoping came into power and launched the economic reforms in 1978–1979. Deng saw the clusters of dialect and sub-ethnic cultures amongst overseas ethnic Chinese business networks that he could tap into. For example, when he decided to launch the market economy experimental zones, Special Economic Zones (SEZs) were created to attract investments by overseas ethnic Chinese businesses and entrepreneurs.

Noticing that the value systems, dialects and mindsets of overseas ethnic Chinese entrepreneurs had similarities with their kinsfolk from the ancestral hometown, Beijing's leadership set up Shenzhen and Guangdong to attract Cantonese entrepreneurs and their investments from Hong Kong, Malaysia and Singapore. Fujian and Xiamen were then primed to attract investments from Hokkien (also known as Fukien, Fujian and Minnanese) and Teochew (also known as Chaozhou or Chiu Chow) entrepreneurs' investments from Taiwan, Thailand, Singapore and Malaysia. Later on, Hainandao (Hainan Island) was added into to the free market zones as well. Amongst the pioneering overseas Hainanese entrepreneurs from Southeast Asia, Singaporean Hainanese business people invested in Hainandao (Hainan Island) with investment starting points often based on social and ethnic ties with their ancestral villages in China.[13] Their entry strategies often depend on cooperative relationships with their Hainanese relatives or networked partners, with the company generally starting out as a local operation focusing on local consumers.[14]

---

[12]Ohio University Libraries, "The Importance of the Overseas Chinese" undated in the Ohio University Archives & Special Collections Digital Archives Overseas Chinese Collection Shao Center [downloaded on 26 Jan 2021], available at https://www.ohio.edu/library/collections/international/overseas-chinese-collection/importance-overseas-chinese.

[13]Yeung, Henry Wai-chung and Olds, Kris, "Globalizing Chinese business firms: where are they coming from, where are they heading?" dated 2000 in The Globalisation of Chinese Business Firms Henry Wai-chung Yeung and Kris Olds (eds.), (London: Macmillan), [downloaded on 1 Jan 2020], available at https://courses.nus.edu.sg/course/geoywc/publication/Macmillan.PDF, p. 27 [online edition].

[14]*Ibid.*

The Southern Chinese and overseas ethnic Chinese whose ancestors came from southern China shared some broad commonalities when it comes to value systems. In general, family orientation, paternalism, hardworking ethics, *guanxi* connections, loyalty, informal sources when it comes to raising money, and tackling risk adversity into industries that they are unfamiliar with were some of the characteristics amongst the earlier generations of overseas ethnic Chinese businesses. These value systems conjured up some popular stereotypes and lingo for describing the typical overseas ethnic Chinese entrepreneurs, calling them *towkays*, *sengleys*, *laoban*, *loban*, etc. in various parts of Southeast Asia. The words and phrases were drawn from the Hokkien, Mandarin and Cantonese dialect languages. These terminologies assume that the general values and mindsets described above were stereotypically embodied in overseas ethnic Chinese entrepreneurs and their business practices.

These free market zones had dialect compositions that matched the major dialect groups found in Southeast Asia. For example, the Hokkiens were the largest dialect group in Singapore, followed by the Teochews and the Cantonese. In Thailand, particularly clustered around the capital city of Bangkok, the Teochews formed the main dialect group. Thailand has one of the most well-integrated overseas ethnic Chinese communities in Southeast Asia. Many Hokkien merchants and businessmen/women were found in southern Malaysia near Johor while Cantonese entrepreneurs were from the Kuala Lumpur greater area. Other southern Chinese dialect overseas ethnic Chinese entrepreneurs drew from Southeast Asian states like Indonesia.

The close dialect ties and linguistic familiarity that the overseas ethnic Chinese had with counterparts in their ancestral hometowns facilitated business connections and communications. The overseas ethnic Chinese entrepreneurs introduced modern Western management techniques, scientific rationality, technologies, Western legal systems, business networks, overseas market knowhow, government connections, marketing methodologies, foreign language training, lifestyle patterns, consumption trends, and other new business knowhow they have hybridized in running businesses outside China for generations.

Upskilling

Interestingly, the Confucian accent on learning and education may have compelled many of these overseas Chinese entrepreneurs to focus on building schools for their communities, forming an organic and community-driven form of upskilling programs. One of the ways in which overseas Chinese entrepreneurs contributed back to society is to set up schools for those societies. Singapore businessman Tan Kah Kee (Chen Jiageng in Hanyu Pinyin) is an example of an overseas Chinese entrepreneur who eventually contributed to establishing one of the most well-known universities in China, Xiamen University in Xiamen (Amoy). Many overseas Chinese entrepreneurs tried to use their newfound wealth to contribute to society.

The premium status of education amongst overseas ethnic Chinese communities is argued in Chuah, Hoffman, Ramasamy and Tan's paper that noted overseas Chinese parents in Singapore have the traditional Chinese beliefs in education and Confucian values.[15] While the values promoting the idea of education as human capital are based on traditional cultural foundations, overseas ethnic Chinese communities actually hybridize the educational contents by integrating Western education into the training programs and academic curriculum. The educators see the benefits of European and American theories of modern management, scientific rationality and technological embrace for business modernization. Western business management and entrepreneurial education have a powerful influence over the evolution of overseas ethnic Chinese businesses. It has become more commonplace for younger generations of overseas ethnic Chinese business entrepreneurs and managers to study in the West, especially North America, and the graduates then return back to Southeast Asian with a heightened sense of professionalism and enthusiasm for Western management techniques.[16]

---

[15]Chuah, Swee Hoon, Robert Hoffmann, Bala Ramasamy and Jonathan HW Tan, "Is there a Spirit of Overseas Chinese Capitalism?" dated 4 June 2016 in *Small Business Economics* (2016) 47 [downloaded on 26 Jan 2021], (Singapore: Springer), available at https://link.springer.com/article/10.1007/s11187-016-9746-5, p. 1101.

[16]Po, Gerley Q., "A Comparative Analysis of the Entrepreneurial Styles of Second, Third, and Fourth Generation Overseas Chinese and Filipinos in the Philippines" dated 2010 in DLSU (De La Salle University) *Business & Economics Review* 19.2 [downloaded on 1 Jan 2021], available at https://www.dlsu.edu.ph/wp-content/uploads/2019/10/AComparativeAnalysisoftheEntrepreneurialStylesofSecondThirdandFourthGeneration OverseasChineseandFilipinosinthePhilippines.pdf, p. 17.

Concluding Remarks

Some of these overseas Chinese entrepreneurs are tapped on by the Chinese government for working on the Belt and Road Initiative (BRI, formerly known as One Belt One Road or OBOR), since these entrepreneurs understand the local conditions of their host societies better. At the same time, overseas ethnic Chinese must conduct any interactions and relations with mainland Chinese authorities carefully, as they do not want to be perceived as Beijing's conduits in exercising economic soft power or even be accused of being Trojan horses. They are also aware of historical animosities and local sentiments towards the overseas Chinese communities in Southeast Asia if they gravitate too close to China and its political–economic diplomatic schemes like BRI. Therefore, they adopt a host society-centric approach in maximizing national interests and economic benefits of their host societies while establishing goodwill and bridges between their national governments and China's state/private sector. The overseas ethnic Chinese, particularly those who have sunk their roots into host societies over generations, are essentially keen to help their government tap into China's newfound economic superpower status.

The following chapter will examine how indigenous host societies and governments in Southeast Asia are also encouraging and facilitating entrepreneurship through policy instruments as well.

Chapter 7

Case Study of Hong Kong Entrepreneurs in Southeast Asia

Historical Background

By the end of the 20th century, the overseas ethnic Chinese diaspora with its 55 million individuals could have been equated to a medium-sized country or economy with a GDP close to US$600 billion and a major source of capital and entrepreneurship in Singapore, Thailand, Malaysia, Indonesia, Taiwan, Hong Kong, the Philippines, Vietnam and China.[1] The overseas ethnic Chinese diaspora in pre-1997 Hong Kong and Southeast Asian economies actively carry out trade and commerce within a regional Bamboo Network (an informal overseas Chinese business network). These two entities also have complementary attributes as many Southeast Asia countries like Thailand are rich in natural resources that are useful for Hong Kong-based or Hong Kong-capitalized factories and industries in the Greater Bay Area (GBA) region. Based on these attributes, there appears to be much to leverage off each other. Some ASEAN countries can even provide access to economic sub-regions like Thailand's central core location as a possible gateway to ASEAN, and access to the Ayeyawady Chao Phraya Mekong Economic Cooperation Strategy

---

[1] Weidenbaum, Murray, "The bamboo network: Asia's family-run conglomerates" dated 1 January 1998 in PWC Strategy+Business [downloaded on 1 January 2020], available at https://www.strategy-business.com/article/9702.

(ACMECS) bloc comprising Cambodia, Laos, Myanmar, Thailand and Vietnam.[2]

Some observers dubbed Hong Kong's investments and entrepreneurial role in Southeast Asia as part of a "Chinese commonwealth" with an "open architecture" providing entry to local resources like information, business connections, raw materials, low labor costs and a diversity of business practices in different business environments, and it is an "interconnected yet potentially open system".[3] Such open architectures are still drawing in Bamboo network–Western company collaborations today. For example, Hong Kong companies owned by top entrepreneurs like tycoon Li Ka-shing are teaming up with Western multinational firms to invest in Southeast Asia. In 2020, the Li Ka-shing-owned Horizon Ventures and Alpha JWC (which manages US$200 million funds with investments in 40 start-ups) invested in Indonesian online stock brokerage Ajaib, expanding coffee chain Kopi Kenangan and capsule hotel group Bobobox.[4]

Overall, economic relations between ASEAN and Hong Kong have boomed and have been flourishing between 2011 and 2021 with ASEAN becoming Hong Kong's second largest trading partner in merchandise trade (Thailand, Singapore and Vietnam were Hong Kong's highest ranking trading partners at US$13.4 billion, US$12.3 billion, and US$10.7 billion, respectively, in 2018).[5] HKTDC (Hong Kong Trade Development Council) Deputy Executive Director Patrick Lau highlighted the longstanding bilateral trading relationship between Hong Kong and ASEAN economies like Thailand:

---

[2]Hong Kong Trade Development Council (HKTDC), "Thailand beckons Hong Kong entrepreneurs" dated 4 August 2020 in HKTDC [downloaded on 4 August 2020], available at https://hkmb.hktdc.com/en/1X0AKRED/market-spotlight/Thailand-beckons-Hong-Kong-entrepreneurs.

[3]Kao, John, "The Worldwide Web of Chinese Business" dated April 1993 in the Harvard Business Review (HBR) from the Magazine (March–April 1993) [downloaded on 1 January 2020], available at https://hbr.org/1993/03/the-worldwide-web-of-chinese-business.

[4]Bloomberg, "Tycoon Li Ka-shing bets on South-east Asia's tech startups" dated 7 May 2021 in *Business Times (BT)* [downloaded 7 May 2021], available at https://www.businesstimes.com.sg/garage/tycoon-li-ka-shing-bets-on-south-east-asias-tech-startups.

[5]BlackStorm Consulting, "BlackStorm consulting to bridge Hong Kong based companies to Southeast Asia in 2021" dated 17 January 2021 [downloaded on 17 January 2021], available at https://medium.com/blackstorm-consulting/blackstorm-consulting-to-bridge-hong-kong-based-companies-to-southeast-asia-in-2021-12679a5b3de4.

Thailand and Hong Kong have long been close trading partners, and our ties have further strengthened in recent years with growth in two-way investment and new cooperation agreements such as our free trade agreement (FTA) and investment agreement [The FTA and investment agreement have been effective since June 2019].[6]

In the reverse direction, Southeast Asian tycoons have always been active in Hong Kong in terms of their business operations. In 1993, Robert Kuok officially retired from the daily operations of his Kuok Group and apportioned the Hong Kong and Singapore/Malaysian operations between his two sons, with the elder one placed in charge of the Hong Kong operations while Kuok kept tabs on the Group's business activities and sometimes placed his imprint on the Group's major business decisions.[7] The Malaysian entrepreneur-tycoon owned important assets in Hong Kong as well. The Kuok family used to own the influential South China Morning Post (SCMP) before selling it to Jack Ma of Alibaba quite recently. Complementing Thailand or other Southeast Asian states' gateway function, Hong Kong is one of the Chinese Belt and Road Initiative's (BRI, formerly known as One Belt One Road OBOR initiative), as well as the Guangdong–Hong Kong–Macao Greater Bay Area development plan's, financial nucleus.[8]

The Kingdom of Thailand

Thailand has had a special relationship with Hong Kong through both Thai companies as well as the Hong Kong business sector's entrepreneurial energies in Southeast Asia. Historically, after Hong Kong's return to

---

[6]Hong Kong Trade Development Council (HKTDC), "Thailand beckons Hong Kong entrepreneurs" dated 4 August 2020 in HKTDC [downloaded on 4 August 2020], available at https://hkmb.hktdc.com/en/1X0AKRED/market-spotlight/Thailand-beckons-Hong-Kong-entrepreneurs.

[7]Weidenbaum, Murray, "The bamboo network: Asia's family-run conglomerates" dated 1 January 1998 in PWC Strategy+Business [downloaded on 1 January 2020], available at https://www.strategy-business.com/article/9702.

[8]Hong Kong Trade Development Council (HKTDC), "Thailand beckons Hong Kong entrepreneurs" dated 4 August 2020 in HKTDC [downloaded on 4 August 2020], available at https://hkmb.hktdc.com/en/1X0AKRED/market-spotlight/Thailand-beckons-Hong-Kong-entrepreneurs.

the sovereignty of the People's Republic of China (PRC), Southeast Asian entrepreneurial interest in Hong Kong has remained unwavering. For example, the Charoen Pokphand Group, one of the largest conglomerates in Thailand, made investments in mainland China in the late 1990s from its subsidiary in Hong Kong that owned a controlling stake in the umbrella corporation which actually invests in China.[9] With the rise of China, Thailand is now interested to engage Hong Kong as a gateway to the burgeoning mainland Chinese market.

Tull Traisorat, Royal Thai Consul-General in Hong Kong, shared the following with a group of Hong Kong SME (Small and Medium-Sized Enterprises) business owners in 2020: "Thailand is in the heart of the ASEAN [Association of Southeast Asian Nations] region. It's strategically located in the market of 650 million people. Connecting Hong Kong to Thailand means opening up opportunities to ASEAN".[10] Indeed, the current trend appears to corroborate Consul-General Traisorat's views. Demographically, Southeast Asia appears to be in line to benefit from the demographic dividend, making up 8.58% of the global population, expanding faster than the populations of the United States, the United Kingdom and China and doing well with robust economic indicators like a stable Gross Domestic Product (GDP) growth and strong consumer confidence.[11]

Trade between the two economies is no longer restricted to low value-added products and commodities. Within ASEAN countries, Thailand is the fourth largest source of imports for HK (according to HK's Census and Statistics Department), while HK imported US$4.3 billion in products (semi-conductors, electronic valves/tubes, computers, fruits and nuts) from Thailand and Thailand is HK's third biggest ASEAN export market

---

[9]Weidenbaum, Murray, "The bamboo network: Asia's family-run conglomerates" dated 1 January 1998 in PWC Strategy+Business [downloaded on 1 January 2020], available at https://www.strategy-business.com/article/9702.

[10]Hong Kong Trade Development Council (HKTDC), "Thailand beckons Hong Kong entrepreneurs" dated 4 August 2020 in HKTDC [downloaded on 4 August 2020], available at https://hkmb.hktdc.com/en/1X0AKRED/market-spotlight/Thailand-beckons-Hong-Kong-entrepreneurs.

[11]BlackStorm Consulting, "BlackStorm consulting to bridge Hong Kong based companies to Southeast Asia in 2021" dated 17 January 2021 [downloaded on 17 January 2021], available at https://medium.com/blackstorm-consulting/blackstorm-consulting-to-bridge-hong-kong-based-companies-to-southeast-asia-in-2021-12679a5b3de4.

worth US$2.7 billion in goods from January–May 2020.[12] Both economies have had ample opportunities to invest in each other's financial markets and entrepreneurial activities. In the 1990s, for example, the head of the Lippo Group in Hong Kong had his head start with the Salim Group of Indonesia whose boss in turn obtained the initial tranche of funding from the Sophonpanich family that operated the Bank of Bangkok.[13] In 2020, within ASEAN, Thailand is Hong Kong's second biggest foreign direct investment (FDI) originating source (with an FDI stock of US$24.4 billion in HK in end-2018), while Hong Kong is Thailand's third largest FDI source with an FDI stock of US$22.5 billion at the end of 2019 (according to Bank of Thailand).[14]

Southeast Asia's rapid digitization and regional online economy is estimated in a Temasek, Google and Bain & Company report to be valued at US$100 billion in 2019 and is projected to cross US$300 billion by 2025.[15] Individually, Thailand is interested in inviting entrepreneurs and businesses to invest in priority sectors in the Eastern Economic Corridor (EEC, southeast of Bangkok), an important investment destination in ASEAN with opportunities in the digital industry, automation and robotics, smart electronics, next-generation automobiles, medical and comprehensive healthcare and future food, with Tull Traisorat, Royal Thai Consul-General in Hong Kong, articulating the following:

> The Consulate-General in Hong Kong will help not only connect business to business, but also to the right agencies in Thailand… We offer

---

[12]Hong Kong Trade Development Council (HKTDC), "Thailand beckons Hong Kong entrepreneurs" dated 4 August 2020 in HKTDC [downloaded on 4 August 2020], available at https://hkmb.hktdc.com/en/1X0AKRED/market-spotlight/Thailand-beckons-Hong-Kong-entrepreneurs.

[13]Weidenbaum, Murray, "The bamboo network: Asia's family-run conglomerates" dated 1 January 1998 in PWC Strategy+Business [downloaded on 1 January 2020], available at https://www.strategy-business.com/article/9702.

[14]Hong Kong Trade Development Council (HKTDC), "Thailand beckons Hong Kong entrepreneurs" dated 4 August 2020 in HKTDC [downloaded on 4 August 2020], available at https://hkmb.hktdc.com/en/1X0AKRED/market-spotlight/Thailand-beckons-Hong-Kong-entrepreneurs.

[15]BlackStorm Consulting, "BlackStorm consulting to bridge Hong Kong based companies to Southeast Asia in 2021" dated 17 January 2021 [downloaded on 17 January 2021], available at https://medium.com/blackstorm-consulting/blackstorm-consulting-to-bridge-hong-kong-based-companies-to-southeast-asia-in-2021-12679a5b3de4.

one-stop services to SMEs in Hong Kong, from recommending investment incentive programmes to finding the right partners in Thailand.[16]

Indeed, investment firms owned by Hong Kong entrepreneur-tycoon Li Ka-shing are already looking into tech investments in Southeast Asian economies. With new Internet users quadrupling year on year (y-o-y) and reaching 40 million in 2020 in Southeast Asia's six largest economies, pulling 70% of their populations into the digital age (according to yearly research by Google, Bain & Co and Singapore's Temasek Holdings), Director Frances Kang of Horizons Ventures articulated the following:

> In the past, we felt more innovation, opportunities and founders with science and technology background in the US, Europe and Israel, but now we are seeing Indonesia and broader South-east Asia really going through a very critical juncture...[The company] will only deploy more capital [into the region and has set up a team looking into opportunities there].[17]

Indonesia

The business network links established by the overseas ethnic Chinese networks are not exclusive only to them. Both Hong Kong and Singapore do not have capital gains tax or estate tax, another plus point for wealthy retirees, and taxes are low for any company/individual, paying a 17% flat tax in Singapore and 16.5% in Hong Kong as even the very wealthiest of people in either city will pay no more than 20% in taxes.[18] Outsiders may be able to access Southeast Asian markets through the Hong Kong and Singaporean business communities and take advantage of economic

---

[16]Hong Kong Trade Development Council (HKTDC), "Thailand beckons Hong Kong entrepreneurs" dated 4 August 2020 in HKTDC [downloaded on 4 August 2020], available at https://hkmb.hktdc.com/en/1X0AKRED/market-spotlight/Thailand-beckons-Hong-Kong-entrepreneurs.

[17]Bloomberg, "Tycoon Li Ka-shing bets on South-east Asia's tech startups" dated 7 May 2021 in *Business Times (BT)* [downloaded 7 May 2021], available at https://www.businesstimes.com.sg/garage/tycoon-li-ka-shing-bets-on-south-east-asias-tech-startups.

[18]Kirchenbauer, Reid, "Hong Kong and Singapore: Hubs for investors and entrepreneurs" dated 7 February 2020 in the Nomad Capitalist [downloaded on 7 February 2020], available at https://nomadcapitalist.com/finance/investing/hong-kong-and-singapore-010/.

opportunities presented by them in the regions.[19] These two city-economies are natural choices for such purposes because, in the annual World Bank's Ease of Doing Business Index, Hong Kong and Singapore often switch positions as the world's first and second ranked locations.[20]

Besides common perceptions of Singapore and Hong Kong as financial hubs for their businesses, there are also other common features characterizing East Asian entrepreneurs. Some argue that there is a feature of dynastic "succession" in the overseas ethnic Chinese businesses in both Hong Kong as well as Southeast Asia; for example, Wee Cho Yaw, the founder of Singapore's United Overseas Bank, passed the baton to his son Wee Te Cheong as deputy president, and Hong Kong's Li Ka-shing of Cheung Kong Holdings, Malaysia's Robert Kuok of the Shangri-La Hotel group and Indonesia's Liem Sioe Liong of the Salim Group all witnessed family successions as well in favor of their sons.[21] The Salim Group is a good case study of the economic connections between Hong Kong and Indonesian ethnic Chinese businesses. For example, at the end of the 1990s, the Salim Group established by Indonesian Liem Sioe Liong operated more than 60 enterprises in Hong Kong and Singapore, in addition to Indonesia's then blue chip companies: Indocement, Indosteel and Indomilk.[22] On top of stable banking facilities and a transparent rule of law, as two of the lowest taxation systems in the world, foreign capital from wealthy entrepreneurs (including those from Southeast Asia) and businesses finds its way to Hong Kong or Singapore with de facto zero

---

[19]Kao, John, "The Worldwide Web of Chinese business" dated April 1993 in the Harvard Business Review (HBR) from the Magazine (March–April 1993) [downloaded on 1 January 2020], available at https://hbr.org/1993/03/the-worldwide-web-of-chinese-business.

[20]Kirchenbauer, Reid, "Hong Kong and Singapore: Hubs for investors and entrepreneurs" dated 7 February 2020 in the Nomad Capitalist [downloaded on 7 February 2020], available at https://nomadcapitalist.com/finance/investing/hong-kong-and-singapore-010/.

[21]Kao, John, "The Worldwide Web of Chinese business" dated April 1993 in the Harvard Business Review (HBR) from the Magazine (March–April 1993) [downloaded on 1 January 2020], available at https://hbr.org/1993/03/the-worldwide-web-of-chinese-business.

[22]Weidenbaum, Murray, "The bamboo network: Asia's family-run conglomerates" dated 1 January 1998 in PWC Strategy+Business [downloaded on 1 January 2020], available at https://www.strategy-business.com/article/9702.

taxation for non-local customers, making them ideal locations for internet-based businesses.[23]

Salim operated two Chinese ports in the late 1990s in a joint venture (JV) managed by the Dutch-based Hagemeyer Group owned by a Hong Kong-listed entity that is part of the Salim Group in Indonesia.[24] When it comes to the informal capital markets of overseas ethnic Chinese businesses, financial resources are targeted for new venture activities without exclusively involving and relying only on commercial banks, venture companies or government investment agencies.[25] They started out by tapping into informal networks to raise funds. After attaining success as their companies institutionalized and grew into large multinational organizations, the same business networks can then raise funds for growth through the stock market.

In this manner, after achieving success through initial networked sources of funding, the Salim Group proceeded to list on the stock market. Its First Pacific Company Hong Kong subsidiary was listed on the Hong Kong Stock Exchange, its Pacific Link Communications is based in Hong Kong and the flagships in Hong Kong and Singapore carry out business operations in 25 countries in Asia, North America and Europe in sectors like distribution, property management, financial services and telecommunications.[26] In this example, Hong Kong plays an important role in the process of capitalizing promising firms before they list on the stock exchange. In the near future, Hong Kong tycoon Li Ka-shing's private investment firm Horizons Ventures will focus on Indonesia (Southeast Asia's largest economy) by teaming up with Jakarta's Alpha JWC

---

[23] Kirchenbauer, Reid, "Hong Kong and Singapore: Hubs for investors and entrepreneurs" dated 7 February 2020 in the Nomad Capitalist [downloaded on 7 February 2020], available at https://nomadcapitalist.com/finance/investing/hong-kong-and-singapore-010/.

[24] Weidenbaum, Murray, "The bamboo network: Asia's family-run conglomerates" dated 1 January 1998 in PWC Strategy+Business [downloaded on 1 January 2020], available at https://www.strategy-business.com/article/9702.

[25] Kao, John, "The Worldwide Web of Chinese business" dated April 1993 in the Harvard Business Review (HBR) from the Magazine (March–April 1993) [downloaded on 1 January 2020], available at https://hbr.org/1993/03/the-worldwide-web-of-chinese-business.

[26] Weidenbaum, Murray, "The bamboo network: Asia's family-run conglomerates" dated 1 January 1998 in PWC Strategy+Business [downloaded on 1 January 2020], available at https://www.strategy-business.com/article/9702.

Ventures (one of Southeast Asia's largest venture capitalists) to detect start-up companies that could become East Asia's upcoming star companies.[27]

The "Brain" of ASEAN — Singapore

In terms of business-friendly, capitalist and financially sound economies in East Asia, Hong Kong and Singapore are ranked near the highest positions.[28] Singapore is often nicknamed the "brain of ASEAN". Many business intellectual ideas flow out of Singapore for the region. It is also Southeast Asia's high-tech hub (along with the large market of Indonesia), and its large tech Southeast Asian deals have attracted news headlines in East Asia. Examples of such deals include the US$40 billion listing of Singapore's start-up Grab, a cab-sharing app firm (Japanese tech giant SoftBank Group and billionaire Mohamed Mansour are investors in Southeast Asia's "most valuable startup"), which is now a tech giant, and Indonesian online ticketing/travel firm Traveloka, potentially worth US$5 billion.[29] Singapore is the first choice that comes to mind when many Hong Kong business owners come up with plans to enter the rapidly developing Southeast Asian market. Some private sector analysts like Eddie Lin, Partner of BlackStorm Consulting, have opined as follows:

> There is an overwhelming response for businesses in Hong Kong to explore operations in Southeast Asia, therein lies great opportunities for sustainable growth and diversification for these companies.[30]

---

[27] Bloomberg, "Tycoon Li Ka-shing bets on South-east Asia's tech startups" dated 7 May 2021 in *Business Times (BT)* [downloaded 7 May 2021], available at https://www.businesstimes.com.sg/garage/tycoon-li-ka-shing-bets-on-south-east-asias-tech-startups.
[28] Kirchenbauer, Reid, "Hong Kong and Singapore: Hubs for investors and entrepreneurs" dated 7 February 2020 in the Nomad Capitalist [downloaded on 7 February 2020], available at https://nomadcapitalist.com/finance/investing/hong-kong-and-singapore-010/.
[29] Bloomberg, "Tycoon Li Ka-shing bets on South-east Asia's tech startups" dated 7 May 2021 in *Business Times (BT)* [downloaded 7 May 2021], available at https://www.businesstimes.com.sg/garage/tycoon-li-ka-shing-bets-on-south-east-asias-tech-startups.
[30] BlackStorm Consulting, "BlackStorm consulting to bridge Hong Kong based companies to Southeast Asia in 2021" dated 17 January 2021 [downloaded on 17 January 2021], available at https://medium.com/blackstorm-consulting/blackstorm-consulting-to-bridge-hong-kong-based-companies-to-southeast-asia-in-2021-12679a5b3de4.

Both city-economies are well known for their financial hub status. According to a Bloomberg report, Singapore and Hong Kong made up only 0.5% of the global population, but their banks have taken up two spots each to make up four out of the top 10 global banks, more than the European continent.[31] Besides the financial firms, Hong Kong has also been a vehicle in the past for Singapore firms to set up operational headquarters. Singapore has also had a long history of local entrepreneurs setting up offices in Hong Kong to manage East Asian or Chinese market operations. For example, Ong Beng Seng, a prominent hotelier-entrepreneur based in Singapore, owned Planet Hollywood Holdings in the late 1990s and had a 30% stake in Planet Hollywood based in Hong Kong.[32] Ultimately, some argue that Singapore and Hong Kong are specialized in different areas; for example, Singapore is a hub for venture capital and entrepreneurship with its transparent legal system and English language use, while Hong Kong is a good connection with financial markets in mainland China.[33] They have their respective strengths and are complementary in many ways.

Greater Interdependence

According to Kao, the Confucian tradition is intact in the overseas ethnic Chinese business networks despite Westernized features as entrepreneurial business remains a way to maintain control in a disorderly world as entrepreneurs work hard, long hours to build up capital in an unsafe world, motivated by a survivor mentality.[34] This has led to some observers

---

[31] Kirchenbauer, Reid, "Hong Kong and Singapore: Hubs for investors and entrepreneurs" dated 7 February 2020 in the Nomad Capitalist [downloaded on 7 February 2020], available at https://nomadcapitalist.com/finance/investing/hong-kong-and-singapore-010/.

[32] Weidenbaum, Murray, "The bamboo network: Asia's family-run conglomerates" dated 1 January 1998 in PWC Strategy+Business [downloaded on 1 January 2020], available at https://www.strategy-business.com/article/9702.

[33] Kirchenbauer, Reid, "Hong Kong and Singapore: Hubs for investors and entrepreneurs" dated 7 February 2020 in the Nomad Capitalist [downloaded on 7 February 2020], available at https://nomadcapitalist.com/finance/investing/hong-kong-and-singapore-010/.

[34] Kao, John, "The Worldwide Web of Chinese business" dated April 1993 in the Harvard Business Review (HBR) from the Magazine (March–April 1993) [downloaded on 1 January 2020], available at https://hbr.org/1993/03/the-worldwide-web-of-chinese-business.

visualizing Southeast Asia's market as an important additional market in face of global challenges. Southeast Asia's importance to Hong Kong has increased significantly. Due to challenges from the COVID-19 coronavirus pandemic and the Sino-US trade tensions affecting traditional sources of revenue and income for Hong Kong small and medium-sized enterprises (SMEs), Hong Kong entrepreneurs are looking toward emerging Southeast Asia as an option for the diversification of sources of income and investment destination.[35] [Some would apply this observation to China itself, calling the Southeast Asian region China's own "Plus One" strategy to avoid overdependence on traditional developed markets in the West and developed economies].

When starting out, Hong Kong entrepreneurs who were first-generation overseas ethnic Chinese entrepreneurs showed a preference for certain archetypal business choices like real estate, shipping and import–export companies.[36] In the year 1998 in Hong Kong, HK tycoon "Superman" Li Ka-shing (now already 92 years old[37]) owned 12% of the listed stocks.[38] As both Southeast Asia and Hong Kong move up the value chain, they (as well as Hong Kong's hinterland of China) are heading in the high-tech direction. Hong Kong investment firms owned by entrepreneur extraordinaire Li Ka-shing are making changes to their portfolio. He is focusing on developing Southeast Asian economies after emphasizing North America, Europe and Israel in his portfolio in the recent past, capitalizing on how the COVID-19 coronavirus pandemic is powering accelerated digitalization and the growing emerging start-up scene in Southeast Asia as more users tap into digital services and apps resulting in the

---

[35] Hong Kong Trade Development Council (HKTDC), "Thailand beckons Hong Kong entrepreneurs" dated 4 August 2020 in HKTDC [downloaded on 4 August 2020], available at https://hkmb.hktdc.com/en/1X0AKRED/market-spotlight/Thailand-beckons-Hong-Kong-entrepreneurs.

[36] Kao, John, "The Worldwide Web of Chinese business" dated April 1993 in the Harvard Business Review (HBR) from the Magazine (March–April 1993) [downloaded on 1 January 2020], available at https://hbr.org/1993/03/the-worldwide-web-of-chinese-business.

[37] Bloomberg, "Tycoon Li Ka-shing bets on South-east Asia's tech startups" dated 7 May 2021 in *Business Times (BT)* [downloaded 7 May 2021], available at https://www.businesstimes.com.sg/garage/tycoon-li-ka-shing-bets-on-south-east-asias-tech-startups.

[38] Weidenbaum, Murray, "The bamboo network: Asia's family-run conglomerates" dated 1 January 1998 in PWC Strategy+Business [downloaded on 1 January 2020], available at https://www.strategy-business.com/article/9702.

region's major listings.[39] With an alluring regional economy attracting tech start-ups, Southeast Asian implementation of digital services has been accelerated by the COVID-19 coronavirus pandemic compelling Southeast Asians to revert to net-based tech for virtual connectivity and to carry on with everyday life. With 40 million more digital users, the total number of internet users in Southeast Asia is nearing 400 million (70% of the total population in the region), leading industry watchers like Ryan Wong, Partner of BlackStorm Consulting, to argue as follows:

> The economic stability in Southeast Asia, coupled with the large consumer market and increasing adoption of technologies, shows huge economic growth potential in this region.[40]

In May 2021, Li Ka-shing's private investment firm Horizons Ventures designated Southeast Asia a priority in his investment portfolio, given the region's surging digitalized economy as the pandemic motivates more Southeast Asians to use the Internet and its online applications.[41] It is no surprise that both Hong Kong and Singaporean investors are keen to be the conduits for tech sector investments in Southeast Asia. The ease of carrying out business activities in a transparent, efficient and speedy manner in Hong Kong and Singapore is a major draw for entrepreneurs and investors as they enjoy registering businesses to paying taxes without red tape, excessive litigation, vague laws and legal loopholes.[42] With such favorable conditions, the next generation of scion-entrepreneurs is ready to take over and make waves in the business world. For example, "Superman" Li Ka-shing's son, Richard Li, chairperson of Hong Kong's

[39]Bloomberg, "Tycoon Li Ka-shing bets on South-east Asia's tech startups" dated 7 May 2021 in *Business Times (BT)* [downloaded 7 May 2021], available at https://www.businesstimes.com.sg/garage/tycoon-li-ka-shing-bets-on-south-east-asias-tech-startups.

[40]BlackStorm Consulting, "BlackStorm consulting to bridge Hong Kong based companies to Southeast Asia in 2021" dated 17 January 2021 [downloaded on 17 January 2021], available at https://medium.com/blackstorm-consulting/blackstorm-consulting-to-bridge-hong-kong-based-companies-to-southeast-asia-in-2021-12679a5b3de4.

[41]Bloomberg, "Tycoon Li Ka-shing bets on South-east Asia's tech startups" dated 7 May 2021 in *Business Times (BT)* [downloaded 7 May 2021], available at https://www.businesstimes.com.sg/garage/tycoon-li-ka-shing-bets-on-south-east-asias-tech-startups.

[42]Kirchenbauer, Reid, "Hong Kong and Singapore: Hubs for investors and entrepreneurs" dated 7 February 2020 in the Nomad Capitalist [downloaded on 7 February 2020], available at https://nomadcapitalist.com/finance/investing/hong-kong-and-singapore-010/.

Pacific Century Group, has cooperated with iconic Silicon Valley American tech investor Peter Thiel to establish two "blank-cheque" firms to scout for merger and acquisition (M & As) in Southeast Asia.[43] It seems the second and subsequent waves of Hong Kong entrepreneurs are keen to pave the way for future investments in Southeast Asia, especially in the tech sector.

---

[43] Bloomberg, "Tycoon Li Ka-shing bets on South-east Asia's tech startups" dated 7 May 2021 in *Business Times (BT)* [downloaded 7 May 2021], available at https://www. businesstimes.com.sg/garage/tycoon-li-ka-shing-bets-on-south-east-asias-tech-startups.

Chapter 8

Regional Organization/State Help and Entrepreneurship

The Indonesian government has also prepared five major state policies for preparing Indonesia's foray into the ASEAN Economic Community (AEC). They did so by: (1) instituting Aku Cinta Indonesia (I love Indonesia) national branding drive promoting local products (garments, accessories, entertainment, tourism, etc.) to Indonesian consumers and (2) augmenting the micro, small and medium enterprises (MSMEs) sector and their entrepreneurial activities through encouraging ambition, manufacturing efficiency, good management, supporting purchases of local MSMEs products and fostering optimal business conditions.[1] Other schemes include: (3) providing infrastructure upgrades in land/sea/air transportations, communication/information systems and energy supply, (4) upgrading quality of human resources through education and (5) national reforms to stop and eliminate corruption.[2]

---

[1] Carolina, Elisabeth, "Analysis: ASEAN Economic Community for entrepreneurs" dated 13 January 2016 in *The Jakarta Post* [downloaded on 13 January 2016], available at https://www.thejakartapost.com/news/2016/01/13/analysis-asean-economic-community-entrepreneurs.html.

[2] *Ibid.*

ASEAN and Regional Initiatives

Xu Haoliang, Assistant Secretary General United Nations, stressed the importance of providing support and help as well in a World Economic Forum (WEF) article where he pointed out the United Nations Development Programme (UNDP) report and the Global Entrepreneurship Monitor's suggestions that entrepreneurship must tap into Asian government policy-making to bring about collective benefits/advantage to the region.[3] Xu opines that Asia's young entrepreneurs cannot succeed without state/societal help to augment entrepreneurship skills across age groups to deal with automation, competition and institutionalize the "hustle", with the private sector coming to the forefront to train millions of ASEAN youths to release Asia's digital technological potential.[4]

Young Asians now need to maintain the economic growth started in their parents' generation with the current challenge of automation killing up to 50% the world's occupations and, in this equation, the middle-income average-skilled youngsters are the most vulnerable.[5] In Xu's view, to assist the "hustle" is to support the laggards in overcoming the hindrances of weak skills, construct entrepreneurship and absorb new soft/hard skills needed for coping with disruptions as the Fourth Industrial Revolution, which eliminates labor-intensive manufacture and new jobs are needed to re-hire the younger workers within societies retuning their traditional mindsets to future-proof past economic growth.[6]

ASEAN Institutional Initiatives

ASEAN organized the second ASEAN Lifestyle Week 2019 (ALW2019) at the Kuala Lumpur Convention Centre in Malaysia. The event exhibited outstanding lifestyle products manufactured by ASEAN small and medium enterprises (SMEs) from a spectrum of outfits, along with forums/dialogues/conversations by ASEAN private sector leaders and

---

[3]Xu, Haoliang, "Asia's young entrepreneurs need help with the hustle" dated 10 August 2018 in World Economic Forum (WEF) [downloaded on 10 August 2018], available at https://www.weforum.org/agenda/2018/08/asias-young-entrepreneurs-need-help-with-the-hustle/.

[4]*Ibid.*

[5]*Ibid.*

[6]*Ibid.*

other outstanding speakers, supported by the ASEAN Malaysia National Secretariat and endorsed by the Malaysia External Trade and Development Corporation (MATRADE).[7]

The ASEAN Lifestyle Week is accessible by both mature firms as well as venture companies with the intention of internationalization of transboundary branding in handicrafts (from the Sarawak Craft Council), fashion, souvenirs, food, technology, handmade Batik dresses, Cambodian herbal oils, face masks and Borneo fruit juices/jams (promoted by Tourism Malaysia and the Sarawak Tourism Board).[8] Understanding the lifestyle needs of the future can also benefit from an understanding of heritage products from the past like the Sarawak Craft Council's historically widespread *keringkam* head coverings, with the event emerging as an entrepreneurs' platform to network and promote businesses.[9]

Events like ASEAN Lifestyle Week also put together "Angel Investment in the Lifestyle Sector" seminars hosted by the Malaysian Business Angel Network (MBAN) with entrepreneur panellists and innovative disruptors to share their angel investment experiences in "early-stage investment" for small companies.[10] The angels dispense financial help, mentorship, ideas-pitching, lifestyle trends detection, digital content support and advice for very high-risk business ideas in technology and disruptive solutions.[11]

Individual ASEAN states have also urged their counterparts to augment entrepreneurial efforts. For example, Vietnamese Deputy Prime Minister (DPM) Trương Hòa Bình gave a talk at the 5th ASEAN Young Entrepreneurs Carnival 2020 (themed "Together — We are making differences"), urging ASEAN young entrepreneurs to expand their vision transnationally for collaboration and common wealth creation in going out to attract regional/international customers.[12]

---

[7] Hasnan, Liyana, "Celebrating ASEAN's entrepreneurs" dated 18 September 2019 in *The ASEAN Post* [downloaded on 18 September 2019], available at https://theaseanpost.com/article/celebrating-aseans-entrepreneurs.
[8] *Ibid.*
[9] *Ibid.*
[10] *Ibid.*
[11] *Ibid.*
[12] Viet Nam News, "ASEAN young entrepreneurs urged to promote co-operation" dated 30 November 2020 in Viet Nam News [downloaded on 30 November 2020], available at

DPM Truong Hoa Binh emphasized:

> I suggest young ASEAN entrepreneurs promote their dynamic and creative advantages, focus on highly skilled human resources, apply science and technology, support young people in disadvantaged areas, and develop hi-tech and digital economy regions. I appreciate digital initiatives, building an open ecosystem, and the right supply chain for development. The Government of Viet Nam is committed to always working and supporting to strengthen links and connections among ASEAN young entrepreneurs … In this difficult context, ASEAN must strive to perform at the same time the "dual role", while ensuring community building and coping with the pandemic and working towards a sustainable recovery. The results achieved in ASEAN 2020 so far this year have shown that ASEAN has successfully completed this dual role … Acknowledging this issue, governments of ASEAN countries are promoting comprehensive recovery and sustainable development, in which businesses, especially young entrepreneurs, are the key force. This forum continues to be an opportunity for young businesspeople from ASEAN countries to enhance solidarity, promote creativity, exchange experiences, share initiatives, strengthen alliances, and co-operate in doing business, innovating, making good use of the opportunities and achievements of the Fourth Industrial Revolution brought about for a growing and prosperous ASEAN community.[13]

ASEAN Social Enterprises

Vietnam's DPM Trương Hòa Bình opined that the forum is an example of ASEAN entrepreneurial adaptability to changes in the world, including coping with the COVID-19 pandemic, natural disasters, climate change, encroaching protectionism, digitization, etc. and urged young ASEAN entrepreneurs to be mindful of combining corporate interests with community benefits.[14] Đặng Hồng Anh, Chairperson of Việt Nam Young Entrepreneurs Association (VYEA) and rotating chair for the ASEAN Young Entrepreneurs Council 2020, agreed that the annual carnival linked

https://vietnamnews.vn/economy/816212/asean-young-entrepreneurs-urged-to-promote-co-operation.html.
[13] *Ibid.*
[14] *Ibid.*

and inspired ASEAN young entrepreneurs to exchange best practices in business, social responsibilities and ASEAN contributions to the ASEAN Economic Community (AEC).[15]

Like Vietnam, Thailand is also emphasizing socially conscious enterprises. Thailand has a long history of social enterprises, for example, the profitable Cabbages and Condoms restaurant, established in 1975 to finance AIDS projects and sex education programs, has become a restaurant chain and resorts in Thailand (and beyond) with its founder Mechai Viravaidya nicknamed as the "godfather" of Thai social enterprises and an advocate of awareness/education of social causes.[16] In 2019, Thailand legislated a social enterprise act to provide tax breaks and other perks for registered profitable social enterprises ventures that generate 50% of their revenues from businesses and reinvest 70% of the profits, which can help to meet social, economic/environmental challenges like inequity and job creation in Thai society.[17]

Mohit Mehrotra, a Deloitte's Asia-Pacific region expert, opined young ASEAN firms must tap into the ASEAN network and ecosystems (consumer/connectivity ecosystems like food, transportation, healthcare, banking, entertainment, schools and 5G) as a product platform building markets and linking companies to the platform for capitalizing on opportunities, breakthroughs, resilience augmentation, particularly for a rapid recovery.[18]

ASEAN is also working with their Northeast Asian counterparts like Republic of Korea (ROK or South Korea) in the annual ASEAN Entrepreneur Award hosted by the ASEAN Korea Centre and Maekyung Media Group to promote outstanding ASEAN businesses, increase profile of the region as an investment hub and strengthen more economic

---

[15] *Ibid.*

[16] Chandran, Rina, "Regulation can hinder not help Asia's social enterprises, analysts say" dated 7 March 2019 in *Reuters* [downloaded on 7 March 2019], available at https://www.reuters.com/article/us-thailand-lawmaking-socialenterprise/regulation-can-hinder-not-help-asias-social-enterprises-analysts-say-idUSKCN1QO0TU.

[17] *Ibid.*

[18] Viet Nam News, "ASEAN young entrepreneurs urged to promote co-operation" dated 30 November 2020 in *Viet Nam News* [downloaded on 30 November 2020], available at https://vietnamnews.vn/economy/816212/asean-young-entrepreneurs-urged-to-promote-co-operation.html.

collaborations between ROK businesses and ASEAN.[19] The criteria used for evaluating the winners are highly progressive in nature and enhance entrepreneurship potential of young business owners. The judging categories include: building regional champion and giants with a robust presence in more than three ASEAN countries for transboundary trade and raising ASEAN profile, rewarding innovative solutions with smart tech and life quality improvements.[20] Other criteria include: empowering women who are role models, rewarding innovative and novel business models, support potential unicorn, for a panel of evaluators drawn from organizers and the South Korean mission to ASEAN.[21]

Case Study on Social Enterprises in Singapore by Kenneth Wong (Institute of Technical Education (ITE), Singapore)

While many of us are familiar with the usual commercial model of for-profit businesses or companies, also commonly known simply as enterprises, not many lay observers or untrained individuals can differentiate it unambiguously from social enterprises which can with its own set of characteristics. Even for those who are engaged in the industry, due to the dynamic nature of the concept for social enterprise, which has always been constantly changing and evolving, it is very challenging to define exactly the role and meaning of social enterprise due to the blurring of the lines between the traditional for-profit businesses and not-for-profit businesses.[22]

Though there may have different definitions or interpretation of social enterprises, one factor that remains constant is that social enterprises are set up to address to a satiate an unmet basic need or to solve specific social, environmental, economic problems through an enterprise model.

---

[19] Biz Brunei, "DARe inviting businesses to apply for ASEAN Entrepreneur Award" dated 26 April 2020 in Biz Brunei [downloaded on 26 April 2020], available at https://www.bizbrunei.com/2020/04/dare-inviting-businesses-to-apply-for-asean-entrepreneur-award/.

[20] *Ibid.*

[21] *Ibid.*

[22] Johnson. S. "Literature Review of Social Enterprise" dated on November 2000 in the Research Gate [downloaded on 11 March 2021], available at https://www.researchgate.net/publication/246704544_Literature_Review_Of_Social_Entrepreneurship

Hence, social enterprises have both business and social goals weaved into their business model, which differentiate them from other for-profit organisations and corporations. Many Singaporeans have turned to social enterprises to address to some of the most pressing issues and needs faced by the society and to rally people to do their parts for the lesser-fortunate community.[23]

Having said that, social enterprise itself is not a silver bullet in fulfilling all unmet social needs in the society. It can be a good additional avenue for addressing these unmet needs, together within the existing multipronged approaches put together by the government, social service agencies (SSAs) and public and private agencies. In the recent years, social enterprises have gained more emphasis from increasing awareness on social issues among the community and the public over the years – gaining more tractions from various stakeholders, such as investors, consumers, universities, media and policymakers, in the community.

In Singapore, the Singapore Centre for Social Enterprise (raiSE) was set up to raise awareness on social entrepreneurship and support for social enterprises in Singapore. raiSE hopes to strengthen the social enterprise sector in Singapore and encourage the growth of social enterprises as a sustainable way to address social needs.[24] According to the "State of Social Enterprise" report published by raiSE in 2017, it highlighted that, among the various social enterprises set up, the top three industries sectors were education, training and health and wellness.[25] Interestingly, 66% of the social enterprises in Singapore are still in the seeding and early stages of development while only 34 % of the social enterprises are in the growth and mature stages.[26] raiSE is currently supporting over 350 social enterprises on their journeys from set-up to growth and expansion.[27] It is also worth noting that the most urgent challenges faced by social enterprises in

---

[23] Jonathan C. "Commentary: The power of Singapore's social entrepreneurs in a profit-driven world" dated on 9 August 2017 in the Channel News Asia, [downloaded on 28 March 2021], available at https://www.channelnewsasia.com/news/singapore/commentary-the-power-of-singapore-s-social-entrepreneurs-in-a-9085494.
[24] raiSE Ltd. "The State of Social Enterprise in Singapore" dated on May 2017 in the raiSE Singapore [downloaded on 21 March 2021], available at: https://www.raise.sg/images/resources/pdf-files/raiSE---State-of-Social-Enterprise-in-Singapore-2017-Report.pdf.
[25] *Ibid.*
[26] *Ibid.*
[27] *Ibid.*

Singapore are customer acquisition and market development, lack of public awareness and access to financial support.[28]

Below are some case studies of noteworthy social enterprises with interesting projects that were set up by Singaporeans to serve the larger community in various socio-economic contexts: (Sources for the information are also provided below through indication of the websites of the respective social enterprises)

hello flowers!

hello flowers! is a social enterprise in the form of a floral studio specialising in rustic-style bouquets. Some of the social initiatives that hello flowers! have been involved in include collaborating with Yong En Care Centre to conduct regular food distributions to residents staying in the aging and lower income flats of the Chin Swee estate, conducting pro bono floral therapy workshops and initiating Handpicked!, a floral repurposing initiative to give 'used' fresh flowers (e.g. post wedding flowers) a second life.[29]

Inclus

Inclus Pte Ltd was set up in hope of creating an inclusive society for people with disabilities (PwD) through helping PwD to reach their maximum potential in life through gainful employment, social integration and independent living through gainful employment and supported living via job training, job placement and job support. PwD candidates will go through a suitability assessment prior to joining the one-month "InclusIVE Train and Place Programme" - supported and partially funded by SG Enable Singapore. The programme consists of two weeks of internal assessment and classroom training and another two weeks of on-site practical on-the-job training.[30] Once the training is completed, Inclus will create individual business profiles for them and place them with suitable

---

[28] *Ibid.*

[29] Helloflowers.sg, "Our Social Initiatives" undated in Helloflowers.sg [downloaded on 14 June 2021], available at https://helloflowers.sg/

[30] Inclus, "About Us" dated 2019 in Inclus [downloaded on 14 June 2021], available at https://www.inclus.sg/about.html

employer.[31] Once they started their employment, a dedicated life skills coach will be assigned to the PwD candidates to support them at their workplace to ensure PwD candidates do well at work and also to understand some of the challenges which may arise in the workplace and to work together with the PwD candidate to come out with a feasible solution to keep their employment with the employers.[32]

UglyFood

UglyFood was set up with the aim to eliminate food waste and revamp the food ecosystem by recycling aesthetically "ugly" or unsold fresh produce that are in good edible conditions to encourage Singaporeans to eat healthily while wasting less food.[33] UglyFood prevents fresh produce from becoming trash and reclassify into delicious and nutritious products or resell the good quality ones at better prices. By doing so, they have saved more than 2,800 tonnes of food![34]

Seastainable Co.

Seastainable Co. is a social enterprise that contributes towards environmental conservation efforts using a two-pronged approach - by selling reusable metal straws at wallet-friendly prices, to reduce the usage of single-use plastics and to donate 50% of business's profits towards marine conservation efforts.[35] Since the inception of the business, Seastainable Co. contributed over S$30,000 to over 33 conversation projects, impacted over 5,200 individuals.[36] Besides raising awareness, Seastainable Co. also put words into actions through events, workshops and talks to encourage individuals to rethink and relive a more sustainable living by providing sustainable alternatives to everyday disposable items. Seastainable Co.

[31] *Ibid.*
[32] *Ibid.*
[33] UglyFood, "About Us" dated 2021 in UglyFood [downloaded on 14 June 2021], available at https://www.uglyfood.com.sg/about/
[34] *Ibid.*
[35] Seastainable.Co, "About Seastainable" dated 2021 in Seastainable.Co [downloaded on 14 June 2021], available at https://www.seastainable.co/pages/about-seastainable-co
[36] *Ibid.*

also aims to ensure that minimal waste is generated throughout the entire operational processes (procurement, manufacturing, to shipping), and Seastainable's initiatives are carefully tailored to minimise our impact on the environment and guarantee a zero plastic packaging shipment process.[37]

anothersole

Besides providing good quality footwear, through their business model, anothersole hopes to contribute to the cause against child hunger. To achieve the mission, anothersole launched their "Buy1Feed1" initiative whereby 10% of the business's profits will be donated to charity to buy food supplies and fund sustainability efforts for orphanages.[38] At the current moment, anothersole partner with World Vision International in Vietnam to support the local non-governmental organisations (NGOs) to fight against child hunger.[39]

The Animal Project

The Animal Project is a social enterprise set up to celebrate the artistic abilities of creative artists with special needs. As the name of the social enterprise spelt out, The Animal Project's sales of lifestyle products revolve around the design theme of animals, featuring the unique talent and designs of the artists, whose illustrated animal motifs are printed onto fashion pieces, art, gift items, homeware and stationery.[40] The Animal Project seeks to raise awareness and contribute artistically and commercially to people with special needs. For every item sold, artists will earn royalties from the sales as part of their income and, in addition, The Animal Project also pledges 50% of their business profits to be donated to their partner charities.[41]

---

[37] *Ibid.*

[38] anothersole, "About" dated 2021 in anothersole [downloaded on 14 June 2021], available at https://sg.anothersole.com/pages/about-us

[39] *Ibid.*

[40] The Animal Project, "About Us" dated 2021 in The Animal Project [downloaded on 14 June 2021], available at https://theanimalproject.sg/pages/about-us

[41] *Ibid.*

Bloomback

Bloomback, a social enterprise that specialises in gift sets that features the use of dried/ preserved/ fresh flowers, speakers, plushies and terrariums, have associated their craft-making with social empowerment through using sales proceeds for training and hiring marginalised individuals, in particular, underprivileged women.[42] Bloomback also gave out scholarships for creative workshops to equip learners with skillsets and knowledge such as floral arrangement, gift wrapping and entrepreneurship. It is also worth noting that BloomBack is supporting 4 out of the 17 UN Global Sustainability Goals, mainly Goal 3 - Promoting Good Health and Well-Being through flower therapy workshops; Goal 5 – Promoting Gender Equality through giving opportunities and empowering women; Goal 8 - Promoting Decent Work and Economic Growth through hiring and training people with special needs and; Goal 12 - Promoting Responsible Consumption and Production through using eco-friendly flowers and reducing products wastage.[43]

In conclusion, this article does not pretend to cover the wide spectrum and diversity of social enterprises based in Singapore. It provides a selective focus on social enterprises set up by Singaporeans, serving wide-ranging unmet social needs like supporting low-income communities, employment opportunities for people with special needs, marginalised communities, environmental conversation, child poverty and food wastage.

Help from States, Regional Organizations (ROs) and Governments

The ASEAN Women Entrepreneurs' Network (AWEN) AWEN links businesswomen together in Southeast Asia to exchange knowledge, experience, develop/propose initiatives for economic and trade activities to improve gender equality, augment entrepreneurship skills for ASEAN women and foster advantageous conditions for women business leaders

---

[42]Bloomback, "About Bloomback" dated 2017 in Bloomback [downloaded on 14 June 2021], available at https://bloomback.org/about-bloomback/
[43]*Ibid.*

and their businesses.[44] The network led by rotational chairmanship was unfurled by Vietnam at the 6th ASEAN Committee on Women (ACW) Meeting on 7–8 November 2007 in Chiang Mai as a component of the poverty alleviation collaboration between the ASEAN Committee on Women (ACW) and the ASEAN Confederation of Women's Organizations (ACWO).[45]

The ASEAN Women Entrepreneurs Network (AWEN) advocates gender business mainstreaming in ASEAN, empower women entrepreneurs in the region, creates a structural umbrella for women's organizations drawn from all ASEAN economic sectors, foster a supportive environment for women-led enterprises and has a motto of leaving no one behind.[46] For women entrepreneurs, ASEAN intends to improve their digitalization of market access, improve financial literacy, re-skilling MSMEs (Micro, Small Medium Sized Enterprises), advocate sustainability, meet environmental/climate issues, complement the November 2017 ASEAN Declaration on Innovation in giving opportunities for innovative start-ups and disruptive technologies, equip regional entrepreneurs with skills to manage Industry 4.0.[47] AWEN also showcases high-profile success stories, best business practices in strengthening female entrepreneurs, work with ASEAN/non-ASEAN stakeholders like ASEAN Development Bank Institute, ASEAN-Business Advisory Council, ASEAN Committee on Women, Australia-Department of Foreign Affairs and Trade, Global Affairs Canada, EU, Republic of Korea, UNDP, UNESCAP, UN Women, United States Agency for International Development, US-ASEAN Business Advisory Council and WB.[48]

Unleashing the Power of Women Entrepreneurs

The McKinsey Global Institute projected that if women in Northeast/Southeast Asia were to reach parity with male entrepreneurs in terms of

---

[44]ASEAN Women Entrepreneurs Network (AWEN), "About Us — ASEAN Women Entrepreneurs Network" undated in AWEN ASEAN (Association of Southeast Asian Nations) [downloaded on 1 January 2021], available at http://www.awenasean.org/?page_id=97.

[45]*Ibid.*

[46]*Ibid.*

[47]*Ibid.*

[48]*Ibid.*

economic activity level, they would add US$900 billion to yearly output in 2025, increasing the region's GDP by 8%, so the strategy is to encourage business ambitions among women, currently held back by culture and policy.[49] Centennial Asia Advisors research studies, backed by Mastercard Center for Inclusive Growth, uncovered motivating/demotivating reasons for women to restrict their economic activity within the informal economy, for example, lack of confidence making bigger purchase orders, shortage of funding for raw materials or more staff to satiate demand, not hiring outside family members and permission from spouse for loans and collaterals.[50]

Indonesian female entrepreneurial ventures are frequently seen as supplemental income with household economic contribution centred on "luxury" items (e.g. tuition payments, medical fees and emergency savings) while a disproportionate ratio of unpaid housework and elderly/childcare continues to be undertaken by women.[51] As ASEAN countries advance towards parity in educational levels in both genders, educated young females are waiting to participate more in the economy (a return on educational investments), particularly since ASEAN is young and demographically dynamic (benefitting from the demographic dividends.[52]

Family influences and institutions are well-placed to construct sturdy economic foundations within the household and the Centennial Asia Advisors focus groups indicated that both male and female Indonesian entrepreneurs cited four networking ways for them to unleash the potential of attaining greater productivity.[53] They include having more information on harnessing and accessing market opportunities/access, streamlining the legal registration of companies/firms to join the formal economy, getting hold of quick credit with repayment conditions that commensurate with their cash flow and accessing banks that are willing to lend based on non-traditional kinds of collateral.[54]

Another institution poised to help ASEAN women are the semi-official local promotion boards/agencies and successful social enterprises.

---

[49]Eskesen, Alison, "Here are four ways ASEAN can help entrepreneurs thrive — especially women" dated 31 August 2018 in World Economic Forum (WEF) [downloaded on 31 August 2018], available at https://www.weforum.org/agenda/2018/08/four-ways-asean-entrepreneurs-thrive-economy/.

[50]*Ibid.*

[51]*Ibid.*

[52]*Ibid.*

[53]*Ibid.*

[54]*Ibid.*

The Brunei Malay Chamber of Commerce and Industry (DPPMB) supports Brunei business activities. This industries body helps to display Bruneian products globally and marketing them, like the manually woven songket by Syarikat Daiyu village community company while Sarawak enterprises markets handmade ceramic beads, jewelry and handbags with their artisans making rare appearances (outside their busy schedules in their studios) in DPPMB-organized events supported by Kraftangan Malaysia in terms of facilities and equipment.[55] The Sarawakian firms also assume the role of social enterprises in organizing lessons for jobless mothers and single parents to teach them craft-making, firing ceramic and create their start-ups from ground up.[56]

Coaching or mentoring help provided for entrepreneurs is universally considered important and it emphasizes the importance of increasing skills enhancement to make up for weaker professional networking amongst women, and such training can increase their entrepreneurial ambitions, unfetter economic opportunities, turn women into productive individuals that can mitigate East Asia's ageing population.[57] The 1,200-member Association of Bumiputera Women in Business and Profession in Malaysia or Peniagawati (the oldest Malaysian women entrepreneur association founded in 1980) organizes its members to engage with fashion, beauty, wellness, logistics, food, etc. to market their products and advise them on running businesses by intermediating their needs with the appropriate grantors and advisors.[58]

The next chapter of the volume looks at case studies of condensed practice applied learning courses that are potentially useful for entrepreneurs to build up their skillsets and knowledge base without taking too much of their away from managing businesses.

---

[55] Hasnan, Liyana, "Celebrating ASEAN's entrepreneurs" dated 18 September 2019 in *The ASEAN Post* [downloaded on 18 September 2019], available at https://theaseanpost.com/article/celebrating-aseans-entrepreneurs.

[56] *Ibid.*

[57] Eskesen, Alison, "Here are four ways ASEAN can help entrepreneurs thrive — especially women" dated 31 August 2018 in World Economic Forum (WEF) [downloaded on 31 August 2018], available at https://www.weforum.org/agenda/2018/08/four-ways-asean-entrepreneurs-thrive-economy/.

[58] Hasnan, Liyana, "Celebrating ASEAN's entrepreneurs" dated 18 September 2019 in *The ASEAN Post* [downloaded on 18 September 2019], available at https://theaseanpost.com/article/celebrating-aseans-entrepreneurs.

Chapter 9

Entrepreneurial Training and the Rise of Micro-Credentials

Terminology

Different universities in the world have varying terminologies for micro-credentials. In the UK for example, Coventry University, a leading institution in micro-credentials, defined their ExpertTrack courses as "course certificates" that issue digital certificates. These micro-credentials do not carry any credits.[1] In the case of Australia, Deakin University, a pioneering and leading institute of higher learning (IHL) in micro-credentials in Australia, conceptualizes their micro-credentials as "Professional Practice Credentials" but they do not lead to a micro-degree. Rather, Deakin's professional practice credentials is used as a pathway to postgraduate master's degree (with two credentials equivalent to one credit point into a master's degree in some cases).[2]

Micro degrees are generally offered by private educational institutions in the case of the United States. Currently, one of the leading providers of micro degrees is US-based EdX, which calls these programs

---

[1] Coventry University, "Business strategy and decision making skills" undated in the FutureLearn.com website [downloaded on 31 December 2020], available at https://www.futurelearn.com/experttracks/business-strategy-and-decision-making-skills.

[2] Deakin University, "Professional practice credentials" undated in the Deakin University website [downloaded on 31 December 2020], available at https://credentials.deakin.edu.au/credentials/ and https://credentials.deakin.edu.au/.

"MicroBachelors Programs for Undergraduate Education".[3] The "MicroBachelors Program" typically consists of three courses (e.g. in the case of Introduction to Information Technology MicroBachelor) and they add up to three credits that can be transferable to a full bachelor's program.[4] The evolution of the US EdX private sector model in MicroBachelors is organic and market-based.

Micro-credentials also exist in the form of massive open online courses (MOOCs). According to MoocLab global ranking, the top 10 ranking universities worldwide for MOOC micro-credential courses are the following institutions[5]:

1. Delft University of Technology (Netherlands)
2. University of Pennsylvania (USA)
3. University of Illinois at Urbana-Champaign (USA)
4. Coventry University (UK)
5. University of Michigan (USA)
6. University of Washington (USA)
7. Massachusetts Institute of Technology (USA)
8. Deakin University (Australia)
9. Harvard University (USA)
10. University of California, Berkeley (USA)

Out of the top 10 global rankings for MOOCs, at the point of this writing, only University of Pennsylvania, University of Illinois, Coventry University, University of Michigan and Deakin University offer degrees for the micro-credentials. Even so, most of these degree programs are full-time degree programs and master's programs. Therefore, the field of micro-degrees are still very new amongst the leading university players.

---

[3] EdX, "MicroBachelors® programs for undergraduate education" undated in EdX website [downloaded on 31 December 2020], available at https://www.edx.org/microbachelors.

[4] EdX, "Drive your career forward" dated 2021 in EdX website [downloaded on 1 January 2021], available at https://www.edx.org/microbachelors/wgux-introduction-to-information-technology.

[5] MoocLab, "World University Rankings by MOOC Performance 2020" dated 31 Dec 2021 [downloaded on 31 Dec 2021], available at https://www.mooclab.club/pages/wurmp-full-list/.

Platforms

The platforms for teaching these courses can be in the form of experiential/in-class learning for some courses, digital for others and hybrid mode as well. In the longer term, the eventual aim of the certificate and other micro-credential courses is to make them stackable.

Configurations and Programs

Would-be student entrepreneurs may also be attracted to programs that are flexible and allow them to design their own programs. The world's leading General Studies Programme (GSP) programs can be of useful reference here.

Model A: Columbia University

In the United States, Columbia University's School of General Studies (GS) is probably one of the most developed general studies program in North America. Like the SUSS GSP, Columbia's GS has a core curriculum. But, Columbia GS also offers a concentration to provide in-depth specialization in a secondary field.[6] This allows students to select a secondary field related entrepreneurship for her/his general degree program.

Model B: University of British Columbia

The University of British Columbia allows its students to design their own GSP Program with a defined theme in cognitive science, Latin American studies, and gender and women's studies.[7] A liberal arts education can help train critical minds that can analyze and come up with solutions to cope with dynamically changing environments.

---

[6]Columbia GS School of General Studies, "Undergraduate academics" undated in Columbia GS website [downloaded on 31 December 2020], available at https://gs.columbia.edu/content/general-studies-gs-undergraduates.

[7]University of British Columbia (UBC), "Undergraduate programs and admissions" undated in the UBC website [downloaded on 31 December 2020], available at https://you.ubc.ca/ubc_programs/general-studies/.

Model C: Open University of UK

Out of the 31 UK universities offering general studies program[8], the university with perhaps the most flexible program structure is the Open (Combined Studies) BA/BSc of Open University in the UK. Most of the other UK universities offering General Studies programme are essentially offering liberal arts degrees.

The Open University's Open (Combined Studies) divides its degree programme into three stages: (1) introductory modules; (2) critical thinking and analytical skills modules; (3) specialized topics.[9] These three categories of skills provide higher-level analytical capabilities, basic foundational and contents-based knowledge and specialized topics relevant for entrepreneurship.

The future landscape of entrepreneurial education may depend on lifelong learning, rapid obsolescence of skillsets and the flexibility needed to cope with dynamic economic needs and the gig economy. This applies to the trend of mini-masters as well. UK Open University collaborates with FutureLearn platforms to offer stackable micro credentials but they apply mainly to existing professionals who already have a primary qualification or working experience. Each micro-credential is worth 10 UK credits at the postgraduate level for British Universities for courses like "Teaching Healthcare Professionals"[10].

Model D: Master's Level Exemption

The University of Pittsburgh Joseph M. Katz Graduate School of Business model is instructive here. Their micro-credentials for the business schools are designed for working professionals (or entrepreneurs) through evening/weekend classes or/and blended platforms with course duration

---

[8]WhatUni?, "General studies degrees" undated in WhatUni website [downloaded on 31 December 2020], available at https://www.whatuni.com/degree-courses/search?subject=general-studies&pageno=2.

[9]WhatUni?, "Open (combined studies) BA/BSc" undated at WhatUni? website [downloaded on1 January 2020], available at https://www.whatuni.com/degrees/open-combined-studies-ba-bsc/open-university/cd/57649348/4520/.

[10]FutureLearn.com, "Teaching healthcare professionals" undated at FutureLearn.com website, available at https://www.futurelearn.com/microcredentials/teaching-healthcare-professionals.

ranging from a semester to three years.[11] The target audiences are individuals who are considering taking an MBA program but not ready to commit to the time and yet, if they score 3.25 GPA and above with 9 credit hours of some micro-credential programs, they can apply to the professional MBA course without going through the GMAT or GRE tests.[12] In this model, therefore, micro-credentials become a pathway for students to progress to MBA when they are ready with the time commitment. Many other US universities' business schools like Duquesne University have a similar system.[13]

Model E: Practitioner Level Mutually Exclusive Dual Track System

In the case of Singapore Nanyang Technological University (NTU)'s Nanyang Business School (NBS) has a Nanyang executive education rubric, which differentiates between executive education programmes and academic programmes.[14] Therefore, they were not mutually transferable. The NTU academic track uses the terminology of "mini masters" to describe their micro-credentials that can lead to an academic track-master's program.[15] According to NTU, this dual structure was constructed to take into account disruptions in technology in the world

---

[11]Joseph M. Katz Graduate School of Business University of Pittsburgh, "Micro-credentials" undated in Joseph M. Katz Graduate School of Business University of Pittsburgh website [downloaded on 1 January 2020], available at https://www.katz.business.pitt.edu/academics/micro-credentials.

[12]*Ibid.*

[13]Duquesne University, "Business essentials micro-credential" undated in Duquesne University website [downloaded on 1 January 2020], available at https://www.duq.edu/academics/schools/business/graduate/business-essentials-micro-credential.

[14]Nanyang Technological University Nanyang Business School, "Nanyang business school" undated in Nanyang Technological University Nanyang Business School [downloaded on 1 January 2021], available at https://nbs.ntu.edu.sg/Programmes/NEE/Pages/FAQ.aspx.

[15]Nanyang Technological University Nanyang Business School, "Overview" undated in the Nanyang Technological University Nanyang Business School website [downloaded on 1 December 2020], available at https://nbs.ntu.edu.sg/Programmes/NEE/Pages/MiniMasters.aspx.

economy requiring business professionals, entrepreneurs, mid-career change individuals and business owners to diversify/future-proof skills.[16]

Another example of a local mini master programme in Singapore is the NTU mini-masters (see: https://www.nie.edu.sg/higher-degrees/minimasters). The National Institute of Education (NIE) Singapore and Nanyang Technological University (NTU)'s MiniMasters Modular Graduate Courses (MGCs) represent yet another model for referencing. Designed in a less research-oriented way and more applied skills-oriented, it targets mainly mid-career change, promotion-seeking, professional development and lifelong learner individuals.[17] Those who take the NIE MiniMasters can transfer 16 AUs to a relevant master's programme if they finish all four courses in the MGC with a minimum C+ for each of these courses, leaving them another 16AUs (Autonomous Universities) left to attain a master's degree.[18] Effectively, in this mode, a mini master is half of a regular master programme. Administratively, for NTU mini master's program, their credit transferability are limited to five years after taking them and applies to the NIE or NBS programmes above.

The US Approach

The American approach towards "alternative credentials" is still in a flux at the point of writing. The United States was the first to use this term to contrast such courses with traditional credentials conferred by IHL's associate, bachelor's, master's and doctoral degrees while Europeans prefer to define the same term as credentials that are not autonomous formal educational qualifications from national education agencies.[19] Historically, micro-credentials were initially spotted at a 2010 Mozilla-sponsored event in the form of digital badges associated with non-traditional learning

[16] *Ibid.*

[17] National Institute of Education (NIE) Singapore and Nanyang Technological University (NTU), "MiniMasters" undated in the NIE website [downloaded on 1 December 2020], available at https://www.nie.edu.sg/higher-degrees/minimasters.

[18] *Ibid.*

[19] Kato, Shizuka, Victoria Galán-Muros and Thomas Weko, "The emergence of alternative credentials" dated 10 March 2020 in OECD Education Working Paper No. 216 EDU/WKP(2020)4 (Paris France: Directorate for Education and Skills, OECD Organization for Economic Co-operation and Development) [downloaded on 10 March 2020], available at https://www.oecd.org/officialdocuments/publicdisplaydocumentpdf/?cote=EDU/WKP(2020)4&docLanguage=En, p. 8.

and a focus on individual expertise/skill-building, and they immediately became attractive to the 20 million tech-savvy millennials learners in 2019 in courses offered by 900 IHLs.[20] The awarding of a digital badge is based on the demonstration of a specific niched skill and the certification then becomes a component of the individual's personal digital file.[21] One could acquire new badges anywhere while working and receiving salaries and any prospective employer can scan through the lists of desired badges in their personnel search and pull out a list of potential applicants whose badge list (as well as social/emotional traits) matches their human resource needs.[22]

Bloomboard provides micro-credentials and badge programs for mainly training and professional development for teachers and learners can log into the system to locate the providers and register for online micro-credential mini-courses that they are interested in, instead of attending formal classroom teaching.[23] These qualifications are then stored cumulatively in a depository. Learning Machine is a depository of digital identities on blockchain while PTB Ventures is an investment in the digital identity ecosystem.[24] There is a definition of such digital micro-credentials found in US-based academic literature. The National Education Association (NEA) defines a micro-credential as "… a competency-based … form of certification" typically created with a "digital badge" to denote a skill or behavior that has been obtained and they were created for the online platform which were themselves originally developed for gaming apps before being used for certifications issued by the private sector like Microsoft and Cisco.[25] Digital badges qualifications

[20]University Canada West (UCW), "How micro-credentials can boost your career" dated 16 September 2020 in UCW website [downloaded on 16 September 2020], available at https://www.ucanwest.ca/blog/education-careers-tips/how-micro-credentials-can-boost-your-career.

[21]Greene, Peter, "Education micro-credentials 101: Why do we need badges?" dated 16 February 2019 in Forbes.com [downloaded on 16 February 2019], available at https://www.forbes.com/sites/petergreene/2019/02/16/education-micro-credentials-101-why-do-we-need-badges/?sh=223aa3224190.

[22]*Ibid.*

[23]*Ibid.*

[24]*Ibid.*

[25]Phelan, Steven E. and Caroline E. Glackin, "A cautionary note on microcredentialing in entrepreneurship education" dated 30 January 2020 in SSRN [downloaded on 30 January 2020], available at https://papers.ssrn.com/sol3/papers.cfm?abstract_id=3500880, p. 2.

may also extend to interpersonal skills, volunteerism, and attendance of extra-curricular activities.[26]

The basic principle of micro credentials is developing bite-sized courses leading to a micro-credential (obtainable via online or on-campus study) to complement today's fast changing technological development and knowledge creation. Contemporary work requirements for many to upgrade their skills in a lifelong format piles on pressure for individuals to take time off for lessons can be fulfilled through micro-credentials that can help them upgrade their skills in bite-sized formats without sacrificing time from their careers and family life. The disadvantage of a partial completion of a degree qualification is that the qualifications are often viewed negatively as potential evidence for the lack of resilience and any credits earned towards a degree is not recognized by most employers as a qualification by itself and these credits are sometimes not universally transferable; moreover they come with expiry dates.[27] Micro-credentials that are stand-alone qualifications can help to overcome these issues.

According to the Organization of Economic Co-operation and Development (OECD) study, IHLs have different motivations and encouragement for instituting micro-credentials.[28] They do it for a variety of reasons. They include: increasing global standing and ranking, building global visibility in some subject areas, experimenting/testing/challenging

[26]Kato, Shizuka, Victoria Galán-Muros and Thomas Weko, "The emergence of alternative credentials" dated 10 March 2020 in OECD Education Working Paper No. 216 EDU/WKP(2020)4 (Paris France: Directorate for Education and Skills, OECD Organization for Economic Co-operation and Development) [downloaded on 10 March 2020], available at https://www.oecd.org/officialdocuments/publicdisplaydocumentpdf/?cote=EDU/WKP(2020)4&docLanguage=En, p. 18.

[27]Oliver, Beverly, "Making micro-credentials work for learners, employers and providers" dated August 2019 in Deakin University website [downloaded on 30 August 2019], available at https://dteach.deakin.edu.au/wp-content/uploads/sites/103/2019/08/Making-micro-credentials-work-Oliver-Deakin-2019-full-report.pdf, p. 8.

[28]Kato, Shizuka, Victoria Galán-Muros and Thomas Weko, "The emergence of alternative credentials" dated 10 March 2020 in OECD Education Working Paper No. 216 EDU/WKP(2020)4 (Paris France: Directorate for Education and Skills, OECD Organization for Economic Co-operation and Development) [downloaded on 10 March 2020], available at https://www.oecd.org/officialdocuments/publicdisplaydocumentpdf/?cote=EDU/WKP(2020)4&docLanguage=En, p. 21.

new pedagogies, testing the limits of technologies, generating extra sources of income, cost-cutting and finally, becoming more reactive to student/manpower needs. Institutionally, four major sources of micro-credentials/MOOC dissemination platforms have emerged. They include: platforms created through private sector business initiatives (e.g. Coursera, Udacity, etc.) awarding credentials under the name of a content provider, private sector brands with hired instructors (e.g. LinkedIn Learning and Udacity), governments platform projects (e.g. SWAYAM of India) and non-profit organization (NPOs) platforms founded by IHLs (e.g. edX and Futurelearn).[29]

For practical purposes, training institutions and universities may need to work with other stakeholders like economic agencies, business chambers, investors, lawmakers, foundations and others to endorse, take up or support micro-credentials and its evaluation system as well as benchmarking.[30] Currently, amongst 190 US institutes of higher learning, two-thirds of these institutions award alternative credentials in collaboration with organizations including professional associations (29%), education tech firms (24%) and online learning platforms (10%).[31] For example, Digital Promise authorized by US Congress in 2008 as the National Center for Research in Advanced Information and Digital Technologies provides its own micro-credentials and a platform for other entities (35 organizations by 2019) to offer their micro-credentials (the likes of Arizona State University, Teaching Matters, and National Geographic).[32] In 2017, Digital Promise held a Symposium on the Currency of Micro-credentials

---

[29] *Ibid*, pp. 11–12.

[30] Phelan, Steven E. and Caroline E. Glackin, "A cautionary note on microcredentialing in entrepreneurship education" dated 30 January 2020 in SSRN [downloaded on 30 January 2020], available at https://papers.ssrn.com/sol3/papers.cfm?abstract_id=3500880, p. 14.

[31] Kato, Shizuka, Victoria Galán-Muros and Thomas Weko, "The emergence of alternative credentials" dated 10 March 2020 in OECD Education Working Paper No. 216 EDU/WKP(2020)4 (Paris France: Directorate for Education and Skills, OECD Organization for Economic Co-operation and Development) [downloaded on 10 March 2020], available at https://www.oecd.org/officialdocuments/publicdisplaydocumentpdf/?cote=EDU/WKP(2020)4&docLanguage=En, p. 19.

[32] Greene, Peter, "Education micro-credentials 101: Why do we need badges?" dated 16 February 2019 in Forbes.com [downloaded on 16 February 2019], available at https://www.forbes.com/sites/petergreene/2019/02/16/education-micro-credentials-101-why-do-we-need-badges/?sh=223aa3224190.

that saw more than 100 participants from schools, state departments, Institute for Personalized Learning, Bill and Melinda Gates Foundation, Chan Zuckerberg Initiative, Google, Michael and Susan Dell Foundation and Laurene Jobs' XQ Institute.[33]

The informative OECD document titled "The Emergence of Alternative Credentials" dated 10 March 2020 in OECD Education Working Paper No. 216 EDU/WKP(2020)4 has been unclassified and declassified by Andreas Schleicher, Director of the Directorate for Education and Skills, OECD.[34] It is a detailed and important source of terminological and definitional ideas and concepts in this field. Readers may also refer to this important paper for more detailed information.

How It Can Help Entrepreneurship

Some have recommended that the best way to design credentials for entrepreneurship is to teach start-up principles to budding entrepreneurs and situating contexts for them to have experimentation with solutions and business formation.[35] Universities are not the only ones that can issue micro-credentials in the United States. In the field of entrepreneurship in the United States, professional associations can also provide micro-credentials to members. For example, the United States Association for Small Business and Entrepreneurship (USASBE) runs the Social Entrepreneurship Certificate Program with seven modules with 21 hours of lesson time and the National Association for Community College Entrepreneurship (NACCE)'s Entrepreneurship Specialist Certificate online training has eight modules taken over 8–24 weeks (students

---

[33] *Ibid.*

[34] Kato, Shizuka, Victoria Galán-Muros and Thomas Weko, "The Emergence of Alternative Credentials" dated 10 March 2020 in OECD Education Working Paper No. 216 EDU/WKP(2020)4 (Paris France: Directorate for Education and Skills, OECD Organisation for Economic Co-operation and Development) [downloaded on 10 March 2020], available at https://www.oecd.org/officialdocuments/publicdisplaydocumentpdf/?cote=EDU/WKP(2020)4&docLanguage=En.

[35] Phelan, Steven E. and Caroline E. Glackin, "A cautionary note on microcredentialing in entrepreneurship education" dated 30 January 2020 in SSRN [downloaded on 30 January 2020], available at https://papers.ssrn.com/sol3/papers.cfm?abstract_id=3500880, p. 9.

determine how long they want).[36] In the case of entrepreneurs, signalling in terms of qualifications is targeted more at the entrepreneur itself for her/him to determine and assess his/her business abilities.[37]

How Micro-Credentials Appeal to Students

When it comes to conventional degree qualifications, OECD data appears to show some important trends. Contemporary challenges confronting the format of the conventional undergraduate degree are varied. They include: obstacles preventing learners taking up the programmes, students spending too much time in the classroom, students not finishing their coursework, coursework not matching employer expectations, educational institutions competing to get more local/foreign students for revenues, policymakers battling with high costs of education and economies finding it challenging to meet programme effectiveness indicators.[38]

In 2011, Scott Young challenged himself to graduate with an MIT computer science degree by studying using free MIT online materials without going to the campus and he constructed his own syllabus relying on recorded classes, finished all the homework/tests and simulated actual conditions in MIT.[39] Young built a curriculum using recorded classes, did the necessary assignments and exams mirroring the MIT environment and got his assignments self-graded by utilizing solutions materials and marking rubrics form MIT, eventually successfully completing his degree without paying any tuition fees.[40] Scott Young's example appear to show some characteristics of the contemporary student in America. Some existing literature argue that contemporary students wanted a faster pace of instructions, with more targeted approaches in university education in reaching

---

[36] *Ibid*, p. 5.

[37] *Ibid*, pp. 7–8.

[38] Oliver, Beverly, "Making micro-credentials work for learners, employers and providers" dated August 2019 in Deakin University website [downloaded on 30 August 2019], available at https://dteach.deakin.edu.au/wp-content/uploads/sites/103/2019/08/Making-micro-credentials-work-Oliver-Deakin-2019-full-report.pdf, p. 3.

[39] Horton, Anisa Purbasari, "The future of work" dated 17 February 2020 in *BBC News* [downloaded on 17 February 2020], available at https://www.bbc.com/worklife/article/20200212-could-micro-credentials-compete-with-traditional-degrees.

[40] *Ibid*.

clear objectives to prepare them for future careers.[41] While full degree problems are highly packaged and critiqued as one-size-fits-all, micro-credentials are personalized training, specifically job-embedded and can cover skills gaps.[42] Young's motivation was to study for a degree in business in an "a la carte" manner rather than through a multiple course dinner.[43]

Acquisition/verification of skills are two major drivers for micro-credential students [further dissected into those interested in upskilling (getting new skills) and reskilling (retraining/upgrading)] and Pearson VUE, which surveyed over 10,000 global individuals who attained an IT certificate, noted that about 75% of respondents were self-motivated and 25% obtained their qualifications as part of an enrolled academic program.[44] Among those who were self-motivated to obtain a certificate, the following data applies. One-third of them were motivated to increase their knowledge of a tech/technical area (i.e. acquisition) and upgrade professional standing (i.e. verification) with most studying for career-related objectives; and OECD Survey of Adult Skills indicated approximately 70% of 25- to 65-year-olds took part in non-formal job-related training programmes and about 50% wanted to improve their career performance and/or potential.[45]

Coursera MOOCs study indicated students who completed the course from non-OECD economies and those with lower levels of

[41] Phelan, Steven E. and Caroline E. Glackin, "A cautionary note on microcredentialing in entrepreneurship education" dated 30 January 2020 in SSRN [downloaded on 30 January 2020], available at https://papers.ssrn.com/sol3/papers.cfm?abstract_id=3500880, p. 3.

[42] University Canada West (UCW), "How micro-credentials can boost your career" dated 16 September 2020 in UCW website [downloaded on 16 September 2020], available at https://www.ucanwest.ca/blog/education-careers-tips/how-micro-credentials-can-boost-your-career.

[43] Horton, Anisa Purbasari, "The future of work" dated 17 February 2020 in *BBC News* [downloaded on 17 February 2020], available at https://www.bbc.com/worklife/article/20200212-could-micro-credentials-compete-with-traditional-degrees.

[44] Kato, Shizuka, Victoria Galán-Muros and Thomas Weko, "The emergence of alternative credentials" dated 10 March 2020 in OECD Education Working Paper No. 216 EDU/WKP(2020)4 (Paris France: Directorate for Education and Skills, OECD Organization for Economic Co-operation and Development) [downloaded on 10 March 2020], available at https://www.oecd.org/officialdocuments/publicdisplaydocumentpdf/?cote=EDU/WKP(2020)4&docLanguage=En, p. 25.

[45] *Ibid*, p. 25.

education were more likely to experience tangible career benefits.[46] When there is a need to upgrade or reskill, micro-credentials can facilitate career transitions from one department to another, for example, skilling IT professionals to transition them from the server room to managerial jobs through training soft skills like leadership and communication.[47]

Theoretical Underpinnings

The theoretical underpinning for micro-credentials has been the human capital theory that advocates investments in training that increases human capital productivity, which is directly tied to their salaries and, in this aspect, micro-credentials can overcome human capital deficiencies by overcoming the high costs of education and accommodating non-traditional students.[48] This theory is based on economic rationality with students conceptualized as rational maximizers of earning within the shortest time at the least cost.[49] Some opine that, despite increase in higher education proliferation, employment of graduates did not increase correspondingly and about 30% of graduates were not armed with the necessary literacy and numeracy proficiency skills level to carry out moderately complex information processing assignments in OECD countries.[50] In addition, between 2005 and 2015, student numbers increased by approximately 10% and overall costs of higher education increased by more than 30% with households contributing approximately one-fifth of the costs.[51]

---

[46]*Ibid*, p. 27.

[47]University Canada West (UCW), "How micro-credentials can boost your career" dated 16 September 2020 in UCW website [downloaded on 16 September 2020], available at https://www.ucanwest.ca/blog/education-careers-tips/how-micro-credentials-can-boost-your-career.

[48]Phelan, Steven E. and Caroline E. Glackin, "A cautionary note on microcredentialing in entrepreneurship education" dated 30 January 2020 in SSRN [downloaded on 30 January 2020], available at https://papers.ssrn.com/sol3/papers.cfm?abstract_id=3500880, pp. 6–7.

[49]*Ibid*, p. 7.

[50]Oliver, Beverly, "Making micro-credentials work for learners, employers and providers" dated August 2019 in Deakin University website [downloaded on 30 August 2019], available at https://dteach.deakin.edu.au/wp-content/uploads/sites/103/2019/08/Making-micro-credentials-work-Oliver-Deakin-2019-full-report.pdf, p. 1.

[51]*Ibid*, p. 1.

While the Americans have cited the high costs of education as one of the motivating factors for creating micro-credentials, the Europeans seem to have a different priority. European institutions of higher learning are said to be mostly public while universities in the United States are mixed public–private with high costs all-round and in the case of Europe/ Australia, the priority for using digital platforms appears to be expanding their outreach and encourage more registration of micro-credentials.[52] In June 2020, Australia inaugurated a national platform and marketplace for micro-credentials with a seed state investment, integrating 54 providers and 344 online courses.[53]

Diversity in Utilization

The second theoretical underpinning of micro-credentials is the conceptualization of these qualifications as a tool for employers/companies to sieve out their job candidates through the use of credentials as a proxy for determining desirable attributes from job applicants.[54] The credential theory expounds the need for credentials to act as sieves for companies or employers keen to seek out the best candidates but facing the problem of credential inflation, which has driven more students and employees to continually accumulate qualifications as skillset evidence for their prospective employers.[55] The assumption is that since skills will become obsolete over time, some qualifications will be needed to determine a person's intelligence, conscientiousness and conformity, differentiating between stronger and weaker job applicants/candidates (with the benefits of strong candidates selection more than the costs of the signalling process).[56] When surveyed on what higher education should emphasize, US companies recommended the items of priority in this order: practical

---

[52]European Commission, "A European approach to micro-credentials" dated December 2020 in the European Union website [downloaded on 31 December 2020], available at https://ec.europa.eu/education/sites/default/files/document-library-docs/european-approach-micro-credentials-higher-education-consultation-group-output-final-report.pdf, p. 21.

[53]*Ibid*, p. 21.

[54]Phelan, Steven E. and Caroline E. Glackin, "A cautionary note on microcredentialing in entrepreneurship education" dated 30 January 2020 in SSRN [downloaded on 30 January 2020], available at https://papers.ssrn.com/sol3/papers.cfm?abstract_id=3500880, p. 7.

[55]*Ibid*, p. 8.

[56]*Ibid*, p. 7.

projects/engagements with employers, academic credit for experiential/ on-the-job (OJT) training, industry-validated curriculum with certifications, help to verify credentials' authenticity and quality assurance.[57]

Besides the traditional degree pathways, training institutions and universities in the West may also utilize micro-credentials for skills broadening, stacking of credentials to replace the degree as a more focused pathway to a career.[58] CEO Simon Nelson of UK-based FutureLearn, which offers MOOCs leading to micro-credentials, cited three international trends: demand for high-quality tertiary education in the developing world, growing skills gap that universities are not filling in fast (especially the new skills) and the last trend is the increasing digitization of higher education sector.[59] MOOC-based degrees have been nicknamed as the "second wave" of MOOC and can play the role of "off ramps" to traditional degrees by offering micro-credentials as admission mechanisms or credits usable for applying to postgrad programs.[60] Technology-related and business courses accounted for approximately 20% of MOOCs in 2019 and another 10% of MOOCs were found in social sciences, general sciences and humanities.[61]

Flexible, distance-learning and wide-ranging online alternative credential programmes can be found in the form of MOOCs that are cost-free or highly affordable accessible to all without entry conditionalities

---

[57] Oliver, Beverly, "Making micro-credentials work for learners, employers and providers" dated August 2019 in Deakin University website [downloaded on 30 August 2019], available at https://dteach.deakin.edu.au/wp-content/uploads/sites/103/2019/08/Making-micro-credentials-work-Oliver-Deakin-2019-full-report.pdf, p. 13.

[58] Horton, Anisa Purbasari, "The future of work" dated 17 February 2020 in *BBC News* [downloaded on 17 February 2020], available at https://www.bbc.com/worklife/article/20200212-could-micro-credentials-compete-with-traditional-degrees.

[59] *Ibid.*

[60] Oliver, Beverly, "Making micro-credentials work for learners, employers and providers" dated August 2019 in Deakin University website [downloaded on 30 August 2019], available at https://dteach.deakin.edu.au/wp-content/uploads/sites/103/2019/08/Making-micro-credentials-work-Oliver-Deakin-2019-full-report.pdf, p. 12.

[61] Kato, Shizuka, Victoria Galán-Muros and Thomas Weko, "The emergence of alternative credentials" dated 10 March 2020 in OECD Education Working Paper No. 216 EDU/WKP(2020)4 (Paris France: Directorate for Education and Skills, OECD Organization for Economic Co-operation and Development) [downloaded on 10 March 2020], available at https://www.oecd.org/officialdocuments/publicdisplaydocumentpdf/?cote=EDU/WKP(2020)4&docLanguage=En, p. 14.

(current statistics in 2020 show more than 100 million learners signed up in 11,000 MOOCs).[62] It is also interesting to note the evolution of MOOCs. Initially free and accessible online to all, they have grown in numbers and become increasingly sophisticated. Consequently, they now typically come with fees and entry test also due partly to increasingly high MOOC start-up and maintenance expenditures affected the cost efficiency of IHLs, particularly since course contents/online materials/videos (usually requiring an average of over 100 hours of preparations) add on to costs.[63]

By 2018, 20 million new learners enrolled in at least one MOOC and commercial entities like Coursera are reaching US$140 million record-breaking revenues in 2018 and the top five commercial MOOC provides were: Coursera (37 million), edX (18 million), XuetangX (14 million), Udacity (10 million) and FutureLearn (8.7 million) while 900 universities globally started 114,000 MOOCs by 2018.[64]

The Singapore Case Study

In Singapore, examples of micro-credentials for practical skills include Nitec/Higher Nitec module certificates for Institute of Technical Education (ITE) in hospitality operations, international logistics, engineering, network security and robotics, while polytechnics are offering AI, biotechnology, building information modelling, business analytics, financial accounting and user experience design. Finally, autonomous universities are offering business analytics, communications, digital marketing strategies and gerontology.[65] As further incentives, the ITE and polytechnics offered 2020 graduates two complimentary Certificate of

[62] *Ibid*, p. 10.
[63] *Ibid*, p. 11.
[64] Oliver, Beverly, "Making micro-credentials work for learners, employers and providers" dated August 2019 in Deakin University website [downloaded on 30 August 2019], available at https://dteach.deakin.edu.au/wp-content/uploads/sites/103/2019/08/Making-micro-credentials-work-Oliver-Deakin-2019-full-report.pdf, p. 11.
[65] Staff Writer, Singapore·Editorial Team, "Fresh graduates can apply for short programmes leading to micro-credentials or certifications: MOE" dated 21 July 2020 in Yahoo Singapore [downloaded on 21 July 2020], available at https://sg.news.yahoo.com/fresh-graduates-can-tap-short-programmes-leading-to-microcredentials-or-certifications-moe-074054501.html.

Competency (CET) modules or course credits to use for selecting from approximately 1,000 CET modules with more than 50% stackable into certificates while the six AUs are granted access to four complimentary CET modules each.[66]

The Future?

For Employers

In a CERIC survey conducted in 2019, 70% of Canadian executives had challenges locating skilled employees, including those with expertise in leadership, critical thinking, planning and communication because of the absence of skills development and training in these areas that are crucial components of private sector organizations.[67] If micro-credentials can provide enough content knowledge for companies, they may eventually be accepted as a non-traditional route to landing a job and micro-credentials can also be in the form of boot-camp certificate or apprenticeship from a traditional university, specialized provider of such micro-credential education or online learning platform like Coursera, EdX or Udacity.[68] This may also help to alleviate the challenges of exorbitant school fees.

Some companies are already asking their human resources (HR) department to source for job candidates from non-traditional degree programs. They may even have a first dip at HR talents if they will consider micro-credentials on top of traditional degree holders, particularly those with skills that are not offered by universities, known as "skill-based hiring".[69] IBM dips into community colleges, boot camps, apprenticeships and internal training programs for 15% of its recruitment, Google has self-paced Coursera certification in IT support jobs for entry/middle-skill jobs, Amazon spends US$700 million (2019–2025) to retrain 100,000 employees

[66] *Ibid.*

[67] University Canada West (UCW), "How micro-credentials can boost your career" dated 16 September 2020 in UCW website [downloaded on 16 September 2020], available at https://www.ucanwest.ca/blog/education-careers-tips/how-micro-credentials-can-boost-your-career.

[68] Horton, Anisa Purbasari, "The future of work" dated 17 February 2020 in *BBC News* [downloaded on 17 February 2020], available at https://www.bbc.com/worklife/article/20200212-could-micro-credentials-compete-with-traditional-degrees.

[69] *Ibid.*

and Ernst and Young has the EY Badge system in data visualization, design thinking and cyber security.[70] Forty percent of Canadians opined their companies will emphasize upskilling, for example, the Royal Bank of Canada is projected to invest C$250 million from 2020 to 2030 to create skilled manpower.[71]

[It may, however, be important to understand the following. Apprenticeship work-based learning are occasionally defined as part of alternative credentials in US policies, but they are also sometimes located outside the education system and not recognized by national education agencies and in most OECD countries, they are considered as formal educational programmes rather than alternative credentials (the term that normally includes micro-credentials).]

There are several ways of recognizing the qualifications. First, the embedded model envisions the use of lesson contents and tests for grading alternative credentials in place of locally developed content and tests, or they can act as recognition of prior learning for credit recognition/exemptions, or in the form of autonomous modules with its own qualifications[72] (such as certification or digital badges). Several systems have emerged to manage credential recognition. They include the Credential Transparency Description Language's (CTDL) unified set of terminologies for the Credential Registry, 2019 Credential Engine's Credential Transparency Partner Program that publishes credential data and bridge between data systems, the European Common Micro-credential Framework with its own European Qualification Framework, an assessment for awarding of

[70]Oliver, Beverly, "Making micro-credentials work for learners, employers and providers" dated August 2019 in Deakin University website [downloaded on 30 August 2019], available at https://dteach.deakin.edu.au/wp-content/uploads/sites/103/2019/08/Making-micro-credentials-work-Oliver-Deakin-2019-full-report.pdf, p. 13.

[71]University Canada West (UCW), "How micro-credentials can boost your career" dated 16 September 2020 in UCW website [downloaded on 16 September 2020], available at https://www.ucanwest.ca/blog/education-careers-tips/how-micro-credentials-can-boost-your-career.

[72]Kato, Shizuka, Victoria Galán-Muros and Thomas Weko, "The emergence of alternative credentials" dated 10 March 2020 in OECD Education Working Paper No. 216 EDU/WKP(2020)4 (Paris France: Directorate for Education and Skills, OECD Organization for Economic Co-operation and Development) [downloaded on 10 March 2020], available at https://www.oecd.org/officialdocuments/publicdisplaydocumentpdf/?cote=EDU/WKP(2020)4&docLanguage=En, pp. 17–18.

academic credit and transcript publication.[73] The European approach is based on a common consensus on the future direction of micro-credentials with a shared understanding of its development, ensuring transparency and formulating a common definition of micro-credentials to instil trust in micro-credentials in the institutions and economies across the European region.[74]

With growing sophistication, MOOCs have also evolved into modules that advance to degree programs, for example, Coursera's online master of business administration (iMBA) programme developed by University of Illinois at Urbana-Champaign (costing approximately US$21,000 in school feels with 50 intake in 2019.[75] Even if "skill-based hiring" does not take off or does not become the norm, micro-credential holders can use these qualifications to supplement their main degrees, educators have termed these supplementary qualifications as "post-baccalaureate" qualifications or a shorter version of a masters with the future of micro-credentials pending on the availability of more data for evaluating the utilitarianism of micro-credentials.[76]

Another emerging market trend for micro-credentials is driven by prestigious business schools like Wharton School of the University of Pennsylvania in allowing students to utilize its credits for entry into their institutions, particularly for individuals who otherwise may not be able

---

[73] Oliver, Beverly, "Making micro-credentials work for learners, employers and providers" dated August 2019 in Deakin University website [downloaded on 30 August 2019], available at https://dteach.deakin.edu.au/wp-content/uploads/sites/103/2019/08/Making-micro-credentials-work-Oliver-Deakin-2019-full-report.pdf, p. 15.

[74] European Commission, "A European approach to micro-credentials" dated December 2020 in the European Union website [downloaded on 31 December 2020], available at https://ec.europa.eu/education/sites/default/files/document-library-docs/european-approach-micro-credentials-higher-education-consultation-group-output-final-report.pdf, p. 8.

[75] Kato, Shizuka, Victoria Galán-Muros and Thomas Weko, "The emergence of alternative credentials" dated 10 March 2020 in OECD Education Working Paper No. 216 EDU/WKP(2020)4 (Paris France: Directorate for Education and Skills, OECD Organization for Economic Co-operation and Development) [downloaded on 10 March 2020], available at https://www.oecd.org/officialdocuments/publicdisplaydocumentpdf/?cote=EDU/WKP(2020)4&docLanguage=En, p. 13.

[76] Horton, Anisa Purbasari, "The future of work" dated 17 February 2020 in *BBC News* [downloaded on 17 February 2020], available at https://www.bbc.com/worklife/article/20200212-could-micro-credentials-compete-with-traditional-degrees.

to get a place through conventional selection and admission criteria.[77] In May 2019, the University of Illinois, Urbana-Champaign terminated its on-campus residential MBA program (charging US$80,000 in fees per person) and replaced it with its MOOC-based iMBA (costing US$22,000) in collaboration with Coursera and, since 2015, the program has accelerated applicants from 1,100 to 3,200.[78]

New benchmarks and standards need to be set for transiting micro-credentials to full qualifications and more coordination is needed between IHLs and the private sector so that skillsets are more targeted and precise while some have even suggested integration of on-the-job training into this mix. In Canada, state-funded NPO eCampusOntario is collaborating with universities and colleges to create micro-credentials in collaboration with industry[79] to ensure both academic quality and industrial relevance. In 2018, New Zealand is probably the pioneer in regulating alternative credentials (including micro-credentials) through the New Zealand Qualifications Authority (NZQA), which covers assessments, qualifications, formulating criteria for training schemes and micro-credentials, certifying achievements in acquiring a set of skills/knowledge, evaluating evidence of market demand and avoidance of duplication and execution of annual review.[80]

---

[77] Kato, Shizuka, Victoria Galán-Muros and Thomas Weko, "The emergence of alternative credentials" dated 10 March 2020 in OECD Education Working Paper No. 216 EDU/WKP(2020)4 (Paris France: Directorate for Education and Skills, OECD Organization for Economic Co-operation and Development) [downloaded on 10 March 2020], available at https://www.oecd.org/officialdocuments/publicdisplaydocumentpdf/?cote=EDU/WKP(2020)4&docLanguage=En, p. 27.

[78] Oliver, Beverly, "Making micro-credentials work for learners, employers and providers" dated August 2019 in Deakin University website [downloaded on 30 August 2019], available at https://dteach.deakin.edu.au/wp-content/uploads/sites/103/2019/08/Making-micro-credentials-work-Oliver-Deakin-2019-full-report.pdf, p. 12.

[79] Horton, Anisa Purbasari, "The future of work" dated 17 February 2020 in *BBC News* [downloaded on 17 February 2020], available at https://www.bbc.com/worklife/article/20200212-could-micro-credentials-compete-with-traditional-degrees.

[80] Kato, Shizuka, Victoria Galán-Muros and Thomas Weko, "The emergence of alternative credentials" dated 10 March 2020 in OECD Education Working Paper No. 216 EDU/WKP(2020)4 (Paris France: Directorate for Education and Skills, OECD Organization for Economic Co-operation and Development) [downloaded on 10 March 2020], available at https://www.oecd.org/officialdocuments/publicdisplaydocumentpdf/?cote=EDU/WKP(2020)4&docLanguage=En, pp. 29–30.

One motivation for expanding and popularizing micro-credentials is to standardize the way credentials are expressed and issued by contents/course providers so that learning outcomes, metadata collection can be standardized for machine reading, enabling human resource departments to rapidly sieve out their ideal candidates.[81] Digital badges can also be digitally searched/manipulated by scanning resumés to highlight specific core competencies and evaluating the attractiveness of these candidates in the name of matching job prospects.[82] Micro-credentials can provide granular data points that can highlight expertise to curate skills and achievements across a spectrum of knowledge domains, for example, certification in the field of personal development such as emotional intelligence can integrate psychometric readings as part of larger training packages for professional managers.[83]

The European Union is also considering the need to couple strategic career guidance and counseling with micro-credentials to optimize job prospects, especially for those with lower educational levels and at the greatest risk of losing their occupations due to Industry 4.0.[84] Some examples of possible usable tools are: skills intelligence, vocational training, real time labor market analytics, tracking emerging skills, analysis of job adverts and embedded visualized data that are easy to interpret for end users. Even private sector firms have used these tools.[85] For example,

---

[81] Oliver, Beverly, "Making micro-credentials work for learners, employers and providers" dated August 2019 in Deakin University website [downloaded on 30 August 2019], available at https://dteach.deakin.edu.au/wp-content/uploads/sites/103/2019/08/Making-micro-credentials-work-Oliver-Deakin-2019-full-report.pdf, p. 29.

[82] University Canada West (UCW), "How micro-credentials can boost your career" dated 16 September 2020 in UCW website [downloaded on 16 September 2020], available at https://www.ucanwest.ca/blog/education-careers-tips/how-micro-credentials-can-boost-your-career.

[83] Oliver, Beverly, "Making micro-credentials work for learners, employers and providers" dated August 2019 in Deakin University website [downloaded on 30 August 2019], available at https://dteach.deakin.edu.au/wp-content/uploads/sites/103/2019/08/Making-micro-credentials-work-Oliver-Deakin-2019-full-report.pdf, p. 30.

[84] European Commission, "A European approach to micro-credentials" dated December 2020 in the European Union website [downloaded on 31 December 2020], available at https://ec.europa.eu/education/sites/default/files/document-library-docs/european-approach-micro-credentials-higher-education-consultation-group-output-final-report.pdf, p. 24.

[85] *Ibid*, p. 24

Coursera integrated an AI search function to facilitate course searches that is intuitive to use and based on non-technical terminologies.[86] The next chapter is a case study on China detailing how its policymakers are utilizing lifelong learning as a tool to manage the challenges posed by Industry 4.0 in the near future.

---

[86] *Ibid*, p. 24.

Chapter 10

Lifelong Learning and Entrepreneurship in China

Importance of Human Talents and Skills

A number of factors pose challenges to China's attempts to institute lifelong learning skills amongst its people and to cultivate entrepreneurs at the same time. These challenges include the sheer size of China's population and its workforce, the size of its rural workers' population, the presence of technological tools, the rapidly aging workforce and the fast pace of technological development in China.

There are 903 million people living in China's rural areas, making up 72.1% of the population and its rural work force is 522 million strong, with 274 million in the agricultural sector (approximately 38% of the total work force), presenting challenges for lifelong learning in the context of training/re-training the Chinese peasants.[1] With the proliferation of digitization and automation technologies, millions will need to upgrade their skills and/or change occupations (including becoming entrepreneurs) and,

---

[1] Dahlman, Carl, Douglas Zhihua Zeng and Shuilin Wang, "Enhancing China's competitiveness through lifelong learning", 40525, in the World Bank Institute (WBI) series website (Washington DC: The World Bank), 2019, [downloaded on 1 January 2019], available at https://openknowledge.worldbank.org/bitstream/handle/10986/6702/405250CHA0 Life101OFFICIAL0USE0ONLY1.pdf?sequence=1&isAllowed=y, p. 157.

due to the sheer size of China's population, approximately 33.3% of the global occupational transitions may occur in China.[2]

Such skill upgrading can be paired off with incoming investments from entrepreneurs who are lured to rural villages by the local authorities. Henan lured native entrepreneurs who became successful business owners in the urban cities to set up industries back in their hometowns, luring them with cheaper business costs and incentives from provincial authorities.[3] This was also a popular option with entrepreneurs keen to take care of aging parents. Ren Lianjun shifted his clothing and toy factory from Guangdong to Shangshui Henan to care for his parents.[4]

With growing gaps between the rural and urban populations in different stages of economic development and income brackets, the challenge of the "Three Nongs" (agriculture, peasants and rural society) in terms of income gaps are coming to the forefront.[5] The hybrid model (integrating online/offline lessons) provides access for urban/rural students with internet to high-quality digital contents for acquiring skills (including those needed for entrepreneurship), receive lifelong learning skills and micro-curricula courses (approximately 900 million individuals have access to the internet in China).[6]

---

[2] Woetzel, Jonathan, Jeongmin Seong, Nick Leung, Joe Ngai, Li-Kai Chen, Vera Tang, Shivin Agarwal and Bo Wang, "Reskilling China: Transforming the world's largest workforce into lifelong learners" dated 12 January 2021 in McKinsey Global Institute [downloaded on 12 January 2021], available at https://www.mckinsey.com/featured-insights/china/reskilling-china-transforming-the-worlds-largest-workforce-into-lifelong-learners.

[3] Yuan Quan and Sun Qingqing, "China's youth entrepreneurs go back to countryside" dated 9 January 2018 in *Xinhuanet* [downloaded on 9 January 2018], available at http://www.xinhuanet.com/english/2018-01/09/c_136882824.htm.

[4] *Ibid.*

[5] Dahlman, Carl, Douglas Zhihua Zeng and Shuilin Wang, "Enhancing China's competitiveness through lifelong learning", 40525, in the World Bank Institute (WBI) series website (Washington DC: The World Bank), 2019, [downloaded on 1 January 2019], available at https://openknowledge.worldbank.org/bitstream/handle/10986/6702/405250CHA0Life101OFFICIAL0USE0ONLY1.pdf?sequence=1&isAllowed=y, p. 157.

[6] Woetzel, Jonathan, Jeongmin Seong, Nick Leung, Joe Ngai, Li-Kai Chen, Vera Tang, Shivin Agarwal and Bo Wang, "Reskilling China: Transforming the world's largest workforce into lifelong learners" dated 12 January 2021 in McKinsey Global Institute [downloaded on 12 January 2021], available at https://www.mckinsey.com/featured-insights/china/reskilling-china-transforming-the-worlds-largest-workforce-into-lifelong-learners.

A good example of the transformative power of skills training is Lyu Xiaofang. Lyu was one of millions of young Chinese women known as "migrant girls" who left the countryside to search for work in the urban industrial cities but she returned to Shangshui County village hometown in Henan to run nine factories manufacturing shopping bags, hiring other village women in the process.[7] In 2011, she established the first factory by relying on sewing skills she learned in the eastern Jiangsu Province and now she hires more than 300 young women workers from proximate villages,[8] demonstrating the importance of skills to the rural areas of China.

In instituting lifelong learning skills, China's challenge is modifying education and skills development to develop human talents for the innovation-driven, digitized, post-industrial economy while integrating the national ethos of a lifelong learning system that offers equitable education opportunities for all.[9] Fortunately, for China, the percentage of youths interested in lifelong learning appears to be very high. According to an end-2020 survey conducted by *China Youth Daily*, approximately 94.5% of working youths in China replied they continued the life habit of learning even after graduation with men registering a higher participation percentage in informal learning than Chinese women as 95.3% of young males indicated they have continued to increase their knowledge after finishing formal education.[10]

The central government of China is coming up with nationwide satellite and broadband long-distance learning technologies to pare down education costs, upgrade learning efficiency and facilitate

---

[7] Yuan Quan and Sun Qingqing, "China's youth entrepreneurs go back to countryside" dated 9 January 2018 in *Xinhuanet* [downloaded on 9 January 2018], available at http://www.xinhuanet.com/english/2018-01/09/c_136882824.htm.

[8] *Ibid.*

[9] Woetzel, Jonathan, Jeongmin Seong, Nick Leung, Joe Ngai, Li-Kai Chen, Vera Tang, Shivin Agarwal and Bo Wang, "Reskilling China: Transforming the world's largest workforce into lifelong learners" dated 12 January 2021 in McKinsey Global Institute [downloaded on 12 January 2021], available at https://www.mckinsey.com/featured-insights/china/reskilling-china-transforming-the-worlds-largest-workforce-into-lifelong-learners.

[10] Xinhua, "Most employed youth in China keep learning after graduation: Survey" dated 5 September 2020 in *Xinhuanet* [downloaded on 5 September 2020], available at http://www.xinhuanet.com/english/2020-09/05/c_139345153.htm.

learning opportunities for impoverished remote regions of the country.[11] The lifelong learning system can ensure more social cohesion and mitigate the challenges of unequal access to the benefits of social mobility and distributions of wealth offered by education and economic developments.[12]

One of the main challenges had always been the platform for the dissemination of lifelong learning contents, mass education and skills upgrading. In China, from 1979 to 2004, the Chinese Central Radio and TV University (CCRTVU founded in 1979) set up the first radio and television-based long distance learning campus.[13] It had a main central campus, 44 provincial satellite facilities, 961 prefecture/city-level branches and 2075 county level workstations, with coverage enveloping all provinces, municipalities and autonomous regions and it also joined the International Council for Distance Education and the Asian Association of Open Universities.[14]

As technologies progressed, new digital platforms for teaching/ instruction were used for distance learning and lifelong learning programmes. By the end of 1994, Tsinghua and nine other Chinese universities, funded by the Education Commission of People's Republic of China, finished constructing the China Education and Research Network Pilot Project which is China's pioneering TCP/IP-based public computer network linking more than 31 provinces, 200 cities, 1,000 universities and colleges and more than 1.8 million users.[15] Internet-based courses appear to be very popular. According to end-2020 survey conducted by *China Youth Daily* with 1966 Chinese youths in the workplace (52.9% male and 47.1% female), 64.9% of the respondents registered for internet-based courses or buy on-demand knowledge products, 63.5% participated in

[11] Dahlman, Carl, Douglas Zhihua Zeng and Shuilin Wang, "Enhancing China's competitiveness through lifelong learning", 40525, in the World Bank Institute (WBI) series website (Washington DC: The World Bank), 2019, [downloaded on 1 January 2019], available at https://openknowledge.worldbank.org/bitstream/handle/10986/6702/405250CHA0Life101OFFICIAL0USE0ONLY1.pdf?sequence=1&isAllowed=y, p. xvi.

[12] *Ibid*, p. 145.

[13] *Ibid*, p. 120.

[14] *Ibid*, p. 120.

[15] *Ibid*, p. 123.

self-motivated reading and 60.7% were keen to take up professional certifications.[16]

The Fourth Global Report on Adult Learning and Education (GRALE) issued by UNESCO noted that China has set up an integrated operation mechanism with the features of government-led multidepartment cooperation and social participation and a strategy for advocating seniors' education through pilot trials before a larger rollout supported by pre-existing institutions.[17] Large metropolitan cities like Shanghai, Beijing and the Special Economic Zones (SEZs which kick-started paramount leader Deng's economic reforms) are more well-equipped to manage the socio-economic challenges caused by economic restructuring through skills upgrading and workers' training/education, while China's western and central regions face human resource, funding and technological shortfalls in disseminating much-needed training needs.[18]

In 1998, the State Council approved the Ministry of Education's Action Plans for Revitalizing Education for the 21st Century and established the contemporary distance learning model with the slogan "overall planning, demand driven, promoting deregulation, and improving quality".[19] In 1998, the Ministry of Education approved Tsinghua University, Beijing University of Post and Telecommunications, Zhejiang University, and Hunan University as the initial batch of institutes of higher learning (IHLs) adopting Internet-based distance learning and expanded the list to include Beijing University and the Central Broadcast and TV University in the following year.[20]

---

[16] Xinhua, "Most employed youth in China keep learning after graduation: Survey" dated 5 September 2020 in *Xinhuanet* [downloaded on 5 September 2020], available at http://www.xinhuanet.com/english/2020-09/05/c_139345153.htm.

[17] Xinhua, "UNESCO report welcomes China's efforts in adult learning and education" dated 6 December 2019 in *Xinhuanet* [downloaded on 6 December 2019], available at http://www.xinhuanet.com/english/2019-12/06/c_138608746.htm.

[18] Dahlman, Carl, Douglas Zhihua Zeng and Shuilin Wang, "Enhancing China's competitiveness through lifelong learning", 40525, in the World Bank Institute (WBI) series website (Washington DC: The World Bank), 2019, [downloaded on 1 January 2019], available at https://openknowledge.worldbank.org/bitstream/handle/10986/6702/405250CHA0 Life101OFFICIAL0USE0ONLY1.pdf?sequence=1&isAllowed=y, p. 224.

[19] *Ibid*, p. 123.

[20] *Ibid*, p. 123.

Lifelong Learning and Entrepreneurship

In 2007, the World Bank (WB) report *Enhancing China's Competitiveness Through Lifelong Learning* reminded its readers that age-old Chinese culture has a long tradition of emphasizing learning and continuing education. It cited the ancient Chinese proverb "Never stop learning as long as you live" (*Huodaolao, xuedaolao*) and this mindset had become even more important than in the past when technological changes and epistemological progress proceeded at a much slower pace compared to today's accelerated pace on a daily basis and lifespans are now twice as long as a millennium ago.[21] It appears the age-old saying of non-stop learning applies even today. According to end-2020 survey conducted by *China Youth Daily*, 97% of its respondents identified conceptually with lifelong learning and 97.6% upheld its significance for personal development, citing the reasons it provides more opportunities for personal improvement, attaining competency in the workplace and facilitate students in aligning with the latest developments.[22]

The 1978 Chinese economic reforms released and reinvigorated social labor productivity amongst entrepreneurs and the private enterprises they founded have contributed "56789" to the state economy (meaning 50% of taxes, 60% of GDP, 70% of technological innovations, 80% of urban employment, and 90% of the number of enterprises), indicating the entrepreneurs' significant role in the Chinese economy.[23] Deng Xiaoping's economic reforms unleashed the power of entrepreneurship, innovation, productivity and private enterprise, all of which were based on improving knowledge contents and strengthening skills capabilities.

With the rise of China, Chinese technocrats realized the power and potential of education and an awareness of the need to continually upgrade skills for relevancy to the workforce for the workers and stimulate instincts for entrepreneurship. The planners' instincts moved quickly to

---

[21] *Ibid*, p. xv.

[22] Xinhua, "Most employed youth in China keep learning after graduation: Survey" dated 5 September 2020 in *Xinhuanet* [downloaded on 5 September 2020], available at http://www.xinhuanet.com/english/2020-09/05/c_139345153.htm.

[23] Shi, Dong, "Lifelong Learning, Personality and Entrepreneurial Performance" dated May 2020 in Fordham Research Commons ETD Collection for Fordham University [downloaded on 31 December 2020], available at https://research.library.fordham.edu/dissertations/AAI28148168 and https://www.proquest.com/docview/2460110297, p. 1.

centralize this function. Jiange Li, then Vice-Minister Development Research Center of the State Council, People's Republic of China, articulated this well when he proposed a central mechanism within the State Council to take charge of lifelong learning.

He advocated the need for: "… coordinating the lifelong learning units of the various educational institutions, private enterprises, non-governmental organizations, social organizations, and local communities to improve their interaction and cooperation so that resources can be better utilized; organizing lifelong learning awareness-raising campaigns; setting up learning certification centers to assess learning and training results and issue relevant certificates; and researching and formulating regulations and laws on lifelong learning so that the lifelong learning activities can be carried out in an orderly fashion and be protected by legislation".[24]

On 18 April 2018, Premier Li Keqiang decided in a State Council executive meeting that the country institutes a lifelong professional skills training system to promote entrepreneurship in rural/urban regions of China, adding on to the existing November 2012 national action plan for providing subsidized lessons to 114 million workers for enhancing entrepreneurship.[25] This State Council meeting stated that, for the realization of industrial upgrading, the private sector will play the main role in enhancing workers' skills and carrying out broad professional skills training through initiatives like government-subsidized training, in-house training sessions by companies and commercial courses.[26]

The ministries of education, finance and human resources and social security were mobilized to carry out research on measures to boost enterprises carrying out skills training and accelerate the development of talents through strengthening strong professional qualifications.[27] A new

---

[24]Dahlman, Carl, Douglas Zhihua Zeng and Shuilin Wang, "Enhancing China's competitiveness through lifelong learning", 40525, in the World Bank Institute (WBI) series website (Washington DC: The World Bank), 2019, [downloaded on 1 January 2019], available at https://openknowledge.worldbank.org/bitstream/handle/10986/6702/405250CHA0 Life101OFFICIAL0USE0ONLY1.pdf?sequence=1&isAllowed=y, p. xvii.

[25]Xinhua, "China to promote lifelong professional skills training" dated 19 April 2018 in *Xinhuanet* (edited by Mu Xuequan) [downloaded on 19 April 2018], available at http://www.xinhuanet.com/english/2018-04/19/c_137120726.htm.

[26]*Ibid.*

[27]*Ibid.*

format of apprentice system was put in place to disseminate skills to new workers and those who are re-hired with emphases on cultivating highly skilled talents and facilitating training of senior technicians.[28] Senior workers will become increasingly important in the context of Japan's ageing population and expected manpower shortage. Continuing education for the elderly is also becoming increasingly important in China. In OECD countries, 30% of their citizens between 25 to 64 years old receive continuing education and, as China becomes an elderly society (mainly due to the one-child policy), the acute need for training the aged will increase rapidly.[29]

China's efforts in lifelong learning are internationally recognized. In 2019, the Fourth Global Report on Adult Learning and Education (GRALE) issued in Brussels by the United Nations Educational, Scientific and Cultural Organization (UNESCO) warmly received China's efforts to strengthen the education of seniors and enhance promote their learning, health and well-being.[30] The report cited: "China spends more than 4 percent of its education budget on adult learning and education, and is only one of 13 countries to identify older people as a target group … China has established universities and schools for the elderly at the provincial, municipal and county (district) levels, and rapid progress in the development of community elderly education".[31]

Entrepreneurship training is being emphasized and broadened in China and Shanghai has become a model in this area with eight training facilities, vocational campuses and IHLs offering lessons for the Labour Bureau.[32] The duration of the lessons are 120 hours (1.5 months full-time

---

[28] *Ibid.*

[29] Dahlman, Carl, Douglas Zhihua Zeng and Shuilin Wang, "Enhancing China's competitiveness through lifelong learning", 40525, in the World Bank Institute (WBI) series website (Washington DC: The World Bank), 2019, [downloaded on 1 January 2019], available at https://openknowledge.worldbank.org/bitstream/handle/10986/6702/405250CHA0 Life101OFFICIAL0USE0ONLY1.pdf?sequence=1&isAllowed=y, p. 128.

[30] Xinhua, "UNESCO report welcomes China's efforts in adult learning and education" dated 6 December 2019 in *Xinhuanet* [downloaded on 6 December 2019], available at http://www.xinhuanet.com/english/2019-12/06/c_138608746.htm.

[31] *Ibid.*

[32] Dahlman, Carl, Douglas Zhihua Zeng and Shuilin Wang, "Enhancing China's competitiveness through lifelong learning", 40525, in the World Bank Institute (WBI) series website (Washington DC: The World Bank), 2019, [downloaded on 1 January 2019],

mode) tackling topics like spotting market opportunities, business registration, bank loans applications, writing business plans and rudimentary management skillsets.[33]

The lessons on entrepreneurship are accessible for university graduates, young migrant workers with professional skills integrated into certificate programs while private professional skills lessons offered by training institutions will be encouraged alongside state-subsidized programs available to eligible vocational colleges and training institutions.[34] After the entrepreneurs themselves become successful, they may then work with their workers and executives to identify skills gaps for training, re-training or upskilling workers and then collaborate with trainers to integrate training into their organizational cultures, complementary with state efforts.[35]

Amongst the approximately 2,000 workers trained by the East China Normal University (one of the eight designated training institutes) between 2017 to 2019, many went on to start their enterprises in sectors like retail, food and beverage service, and bike/car mechanical repair, with the most successful individuals recalled as trainers for the courses.[36] East China Normal University continues to assist the entrepreneurs even after they have finished the programmes by dispatching tutors to make frequent calls to the entrepreneurs and connecting those in similar

available at https://openknowledge.worldbank.org/bitstream/handle/10986/6702/405250C
HA0Life101OFFICIAL0USE0ONLY1.pdf?sequence=1&isAllowed=y, p. 223.

[33] *Ibid.*

[34] Xinhua, "China to promote lifelong professional skills training" dated 19 April 2018 in *Xinhuanet* (edited by Mu Xuequan) [downloaded on 19 April 2018], available at http://www.xinhuanet.com/english/2018-04/19/c_137120726.htm.

[35] Woetzel, Jonathan, Jeongmin Seong, Nick Leung, Joe Ngai, Li-Kai Chen, Vera Tang, Shivin Agarwal and Bo Wang, "Reskilling China: Transforming the world's largest workforce into lifelong learners" dated 12 January 2021 in McKinsey Global Institute [downloaded on 12 January 2021], available at https://www.mckinsey.com/featured-insights/china/reskilling-china-transforming-the-worlds-largest-workforce-into-lifelong-learners.

[36] Dahlman, Carl, Douglas Zhihua Zeng and Shuilin Wang, "Enhancing China's competitiveness through lifelong learning", 40525, in the World Bank Institute (WBI) series website (Washington DC: The World Bank), 2019, [downloaded on 1 January 2019], available at https://openknowledge.worldbank.org/bitstream/handle/10986/6702/405250CHA0Life101OFFICIAL0USE0ONLY1.pdf?sequence=1&isAllowed=y, p. 223.

industries or value chains so that they can network to mutually learn from their practices and set up alliances.[37]

The educational institutions including universities are not alone in recycling the knowledge base of successful entrepreneurs who made it big. In eastern Zhejiang, individuals who made it in the big cities are welcomed back to local Communist Party branches as village heads (through elections) to head rural revitalization.[38] Local authorities in the rural areas of China are interested to recruit evangelists of success stories in the urban cities to share their knowledge, skills and experience with the rest of their villagers in the countryside.

Private Sector Opportunities

Until the 1990s in China, the Chinese government was basically the sole supplier of education and training but, in the 21st century, the Chinese education/training system has become more diverse and pluralistic with thousands of private/non-public formal educational institutions and tens of thousands of non-government training providers.[39] One such private trainer is Luo Zhenyu, founder of Dedao, a lifelong learning platform, who has opened up his platform to students who could enroll in the conventional or online app-based lessons on entrepreneurship and other topics. Some of his students are in it for the long haul as Luo explained: "Some members of the audience have already bought the 20-year pass in order to attend the planned series of speeches ... I simply provide them a tool through which they believe that lifelong learning is value for money".[40]

---

[37] *Ibid.*

[38] Quan, Yuan and Sun Qingqing, "China's youth entrepreneurs go back to countryside" dated 9 January 2018 in *Xinhuanet* [downloaded on 9 January 2018], available at http://www.xinhuanet.com/english/2018-01/09/c_136882824.htm.

[39] Dahlman, Carl, Douglas Zhihua Zeng and Shuilin Wang, "Enhancing China's competitiveness through lifelong learning", 40525, in the World Bank Institute (WBI) series website (Washington DC: The World Bank), 2019, [downloaded on 1 January 2019], available at https://openknowledge.worldbank.org/bitstream/handle/10986/6702/405250CHA0 Life101OFFICIAL0USE0ONLY1.pdf?sequence=1&isAllowed=y, p. 22.

[40] He, Wei, "Lecture shows 'lifelong learning is value for money'" dated 5 January 2021 in *China Daily* [downloaded on 5 January 2021], available at https://www.chinadaily.com.cn/a/202101/05/WS5ff3bef6a31024ad0baa0732.html.

The platform carries other courses that are of interest to any would-be entrepreneurs. They include the potential of indigenous R&D of key technologies, resurgence of offline business as growth areas and Luo's methodology of citing entrepreneurs and experts has given credibility and authenticity to his talks.[41] Data from iResearch project indicate the value of the education industry will increase to 4 trillion yuan (US$619.2 billion) in 2023 and the lifelong education section will grow exponentially along with the availability of 5G technologies.[42] Along the way, there are calls to move from simply skills training to developing more competent research universities.[43] This will allow tech entrepreneurs to develop and innovate new technologies as well.

Lifelong learning represents a strong investment opportunity with Chinese tech giants offering lessons/programs to cultivate the next generation of entrepreneurs and teach them market-oriented skills.[44] China's education/training sector has been expanding at 16% annually since 2014, attaining a value of RMB3 trillion in 2019, boosted by China's attention on workforce development and this could provide long-term investment opportunities and economic growth.[45] Many Chinese are accumulating work experience prior to attending in-class education while others are back to the campus to obtain specialized education to enhance their job prospects or increase their productivity.[46] Therefore, China is

---

[41] *Ibid.*

[42] *Ibid.*

[43] Dahlman, Carl, Douglas Zhihua Zeng and Shuilin Wang, "Enhancing China's competitiveness through lifelong learning", 40525, in the World Bank Institute (WBI) series website (Washington DC: The World Bank), 2019, [downloaded on 1 January 2019], available at https://openknowledge.worldbank.org/bitstream/handle/10986/6702/405250CHA0 Life101OFFICIAL0USE0ONLY1.pdf?sequence=1&isAllowed=y, p. 145.

[44] Woetzel, Jonathan, Jeongmin Seong, Nick Leung, Joe Ngai, Li-Kai Chen, Vera Tang, Shivin Agarwal and Bo Wang, "Reskilling China: Transforming the world's largest workforce into lifelong learners" dated 12 January 2021 in McKinsey Global Institute [downloaded on 12 January 2021], available at https://www.mckinsey.com/featured-insights/china/reskilling-china-transforming-the-worlds-largest-workforce-into-lifelong-learners.

[45] *Ibid.*

[46] Dahlman, Carl, Douglas Zhihua Zeng and Shuilin Wang, "Enhancing China's competitiveness through lifelong learning", 40525, in the World Bank Institute (WBI) series website (Washington DC: The World Bank), 2019, [downloaded on 1 January 2019], available at https://openknowledge.worldbank.org/bitstream/handle/10986/6702/405250CHA0 Life101OFFICIAL0USE0ONLY1.pdf?sequence=1&isAllowed=y, p. 4.

experiencing an expansion in higher education demand amongst individuals outside the conventional age groups as more adults head back for specialized degrees necessitated by the dynamic requirements of the global economy/job market.[47]

Maintaining and enhancing China's competitiveness by providing students and workers with the skillsets needed to operate new technologies (especially Industry 4.0) is increasingly important as China gets closer to developing frontier technologies in the global arena in many areas.[48] Focusing more on higher education and specialized skills for developing new technologies (including the tech entrepreneurs) led to the need to upgrade arithmetic, scientific and engineering skills from the elementary to higher educational levels with more attention paid to creativity and entrepreneurship along the way.[49]

Despite the disruptions brought about by the COVID-19 coronavirus pandemic, long-term impacts on employment and innovation can be softened through supporting start-ups and encouraging the emergence of new companies by harnessing recession-era critical economic restructuring to build a stronger and more durable economy.[50] Even though new business registrations declines during economic recessions, innovative start-ups and firms are sometimes created during crises (a testimony to the Chinese character for crisis, consisting of both opportunity and risks), for example, Alibaba's Taobao (established during the severe acute respiratory syndrome (SARS) outbreak in China in 2003).[51] In the current context, start-ups can help with challenging health or economic conditions and adapt businesses to dynamic environmental factors.

---

[47] *Ibid*, p. 4.
[48] *Ibid*, p. 145.
[49] *Ibid*, p. 145.
[50] OECD, "Start-ups in the time of COVID-19: Facing the challenges, seizing the opportunities" dated 13 May 2020 in OECD website [downloaded on 13 May 2020], available at https://read.oecd-ilibrary.org/view/?ref=132_132859-igoa9ao1mc&title=Start-ups-in-the-time-of-COVID-19-Facing-the-challenges-seizing-the-opportunities, p. 3.
[51] *Ibid*.

Chapter 11

Unlikely Entrepreneurs: The North Korean Case Study

Introduction

While the volume looks at China, ASEAN, Japan and other settings in terms of case studies, it may be useful to look at very unconventional case studies for comparative value. One of these unconventional case studies may be North Korea, given its rogue status and international isolation. Kim Young-hui, a defector who studied at South Korea's Korea Development Bank, noted the rise of a new generation of merchants dubbed "donju" (people who have money) investing in factories making food and ammunition, whose funding and technical knowledge accelerated North Korean economic growth.[1] Marketization was increasingly integrated into the North Korean distribution system as profit-oriented investors led competencies into the manufacturing sector to jumpstart its laggard status into a dynamic one that could react to increasing local consumer demand.[2] The *donjus* are leading the way with consumption lifestyles. Some wealthy *donju*s have even adapted capitalistic ways with

---

[1]Lee, Yoolim and Sam Kim, "Entrepreneurs in North Korea? Not as rare as you would think" dated 16 June 2018 in *The Economic Times* [downloaded on 16 June 2018], available at https://economictimes.indiatimes.com/small-biz/startups/newsbuzz/entrepreneurs-in-north-korea-not-as-rare-as-you-would-think/articleshow/64612212.cms?from=mdr.

[2]Salmon, Andrew, "Newly entrepreneurial North Korean economy turns inward" dated 8 July 2019 in *Asia Times* [downloaded on 8 July 2019], available at https://asiatimes.com/2019/07/newly-entrepreneurial-north-korean-economy-turns-inward/.

stipends to housekeepers ranging from KPW 100,000 to KPW 150,000 (approximately US$15–22) monthly to take care of household duties such as preparing food, washing, tidying and caring for their beloved pets.[3]

History

In the 1980s/1990s, the *donju*s had family clan associates operating in the rapidly developing Chinese economy right up to the 2000s as their North Korean ventures retailed and traded in almost all Chinese-made imports, but with increasing domestically produced products, they began to leverage market efficiencies to sell and distribute these goods.[4] Historically, hints of capitalism were found in North Korea in the 1990s when makeshift markets emerged in different region of the reclusive state to manage shortages of food resources arising from famine and North Koreans were compelled by circumstances to barter trade or carry out trading activities for sustenance and other necessities.[5] Another reason behind North Korea's socialist economy decline in the early 1990s was because of a halt in Soviet help and aid after the Soviet Union collapsed in 1992 and eventually North Korea's industrial output went through a 50% reduction within a few years.[6] Against this 1990s backdrop of famines and the breakdown of the state distribution system, the so-called "survival markets" retailed Chinese food items and medicines before gradually opening up to consumer products in the 2000s and operating publicly (500 in

[3] Dong, Hui Mun, "North Korea's wealthy entrepreneurial class facing economic difficulties amid COVID-19 pandemic" in *Daily NK* [downloaded on 6 April 2021], available at https://www.dailynk.com/english/north-korea-wealthy-entrepreneurial-class-facing-economic-difficulties-amid-covid-19-pandemic/.

[4] Salmon, Andrew, "Newly entrepreneurial North Korean economy turns inward" dated 8 July 2019 in *Asia Times* [downloaded on 8 July 2019], available at https://asiatimes.com/2019/07/newly-entrepreneurial-north-korean-economy-turns-inward/.

[5] Wee, Heesun, "North Korea's budding entrepreneurs defy the odds in Kim Jong Un's totalitarian state" dated 14 February 2018 in CNBC website [downloaded on 14 February 2018], available at https://www.cnbc.com/2018/02/14/north-korea-entrepreneurs-defy-odds-in-kim-jong-un-totalitarian-state.html.

[6] Lankov, Andrei, "North Koreans survive on private business — and Kim will fail to stop them" dated 15 February 2021 in NK News edited by James Fretwell [downloaded on 15 February 2021], available at https://www.nknews.org/2021/02/north-koreans-survive-on-private-business-and-kim-will-fail-to-stop-them/.

Pyongyang alone) with the accompanying market practices and efficiencies.[7]

After the government's food distribution system failed in the 1990s, North Koreans relied on market forces for food. In interviews with Sokeel Park (South Korea country director for U.S.-based NGO Liberty in North Korea or LiNK), North Korean defectors/specialists have stated: "Economic liberalization and opening appears to be the only viable survival strategy".[8] The 1990s North Korean famines triggered ambitious Chinese economic/trade activities in mining and textiles incentivized by the latter's desire to avoid a complete breakdown in the North Korean economy.[9] The Chinese did not want large numbers of North Korean refugees fleeing to their border. Chinese goods from the booming Chinese economy unleashed by Chinese paramount leader Deng Xiaoping's market reforms that started in 1978 filled in the gap from this period onward. It also meant that Chinese trade could determine consumer prices in North Korea to a large extent. [For example, when the COVID-19 coronavirus pandemic forced the near shutdown of bilateral trade, denial of access to Chinese goods immediately had the impact of shrinking North Korea consumer markets, which created inflation and lowered household incomes].[10]

Aside from Chinese goods that kept them afloat, North Korea also experimented with semi-entrepreneurship. Despite maximum state mobilization from 2005 to 2010, the North Korean government failed to bring order to the public distribution system and could not prevent informal trade in rice, barley and grain that are the core commodities of the state distribution system because vendor-entrepreneurships found loopholes in

[7]Salmon, Andrew, "Newly entrepreneurial North Korean economy turns inward" dated 8 July 2019 in *Asia Times* [downloaded on 8 July 2019], available at https://asiatimes.com/2019/07/newly-entrepreneurial-north-korean-economy-turns-inward/.

[8]Wee, Heesun, "North Korea's budding entrepreneurs defy the odds in Kim Jong Un's totalitarian state" dated 14 February 2018 in CNBC website [downloaded on 14 February 2018], available at https://www.cnbc.com/2018/02/14/north-korea-entrepreneurs-defy-odds-in-kim-jong-un-totalitarian-state.html.

[9]Salmon, Andrew, "Newly entrepreneurial North Korean economy turns inward" dated 8 July 2019 in *Asia Times* [downloaded on 8 July 2019], available at https://asiatimes.com/2019/07/newly-entrepreneurial-north-korean-economy-turns-inward/.

[10]Dong, Hui Mun, "North Korea's wealthy entrepreneurial class facing economic difficulties amid COVID-19 pandemic" in *Daily NK* [downloaded on 6 April 2021], available at https://www.dailynk.com/english/north-korea-wealthy-entrepreneurial-class-facing-economic-difficulties-amid-covid-19-pandemic/.

state rules and stocked up grains outside the command economy.[11] In the 2000s, North Korean *donju* ("money masters") accumulated funding to invest, and many were former officials with *guanxi* and money to jump-start their ventures and improve manufacturing capabilities, showing bottom-up innovation by reverse-engineering imported Chinese components and then reconstructing them, building up local expertise along the way and forming national hubs that specialize in certain products.[12]

The era of semi-entrepreneurial activities experienced drastic changes when there was a change in top leadership. Kim Jong-il was eventually succeeded by his son Kim Jong-un. Kim Jong-un's early administration was characterized by early successes in economic policy-making that were either modeled after or showed the same features as Chinese economic reforms in the 1980s in the era of paramount leader Deng Xiaoping.[13] Emphasis on local production for local consumption happened approximately in 2012 after Kim Jong-un succeeded his father and he began relaxing regulations, giving managers flexibility and letting enterprises keep a portion of profits, although, by 2019, there appeared to be rising conflict between officials and *donju* nationally over the appropriate ratios of profit or revenue allocation from the ventures.[14]

Sparks of entrepreneurship ignited over time and compelled the regime to pragmatically tolerate the market-oriented practices as they were unable to allocate resources satisfactorily to all denizens, and consequently, the *Daily NK* internet-based daily on North Korean affairs opined that above 5 million North Koreans (20% of the general population) were

---

[11]Lankov, Andrei, "North Koreans survive on private business — and Kim will fail to stop them" dated 15 February 2021 in NK News edited by James Fretwell [downloaded on 15 February 2021], available at https://www.nknews.org/2021/02/north-koreans-survive-on-private-business-and-kim-will-fail-to-stop-them/.

[12]Salmon, Andrew, "Newly entrepreneurial North Korean economy turns inward" dated 8 July 2019 in *Asia Times* [downloaded on 8 July 2019], available at https://asiatimes.com/2019/07/newly-entrepreneurial-north-korean-economy-turns-inward/.

[13]Lankov, Andrei, "North Koreans survive on private business — and Kim will fail to stop them" dated 15 February 2021 in NK News edited by James Fretwell [downloaded on 15 February 2021], available at https://www.nknews.org/2021/02/north-koreans-survive-on-private-business-and-kim-will-fail-to-stop-them/.

[14]Salmon, Andrew, "Newly entrepreneurial North Korean economy turns inward" dated 8 July 2019 in *Asia Times* [downloaded on 8 July 2019], available at https://asiatimes.com/2019/07/newly-entrepreneurial-north-korean-economy-turns-inward/.

directly/indirectly engaged in general market activities.[15] A consumption culture appeared to be emerging in pre-pandemic North Korea. Marketization was increasingly integrated into the North Korean distribution system as profit-oriented investors led competencies into the manufacturing sector to jumpstart its laggard status into a dynamic one that could react to increasing local consumer demand.[16]

Emerging Entrepreneurship

The private sector entrepreneurs had to be very careful in not overplaying their accumulation of cash reserves and foreign currencies. The unpopular November 2009 currency reform abruptly announced the obsolescence of old currency banknotes, compelling North Koreans to mandatorily convert their old banknotes to new banknotes within a tight schedule, in order to destroy North Korea's market fundamentals by de-recognizing the private sector's cash reserves, which resulted in severe disorder, retail collapse and supply shortages even for the elites.[17] In politically calmer eras, however, official tolerance of market-oriented forces has led to more free enterprise outreach to physical, outdoor spaces throughout the cities and the rural areas that were usually made up of open-air stalls and flea markets where small-time entrepreneurs could carry out cash transactions in Korean won, Chinese yuan and even the US dollar.[18]

---

[15] Wee, Heesun, "North Korea's budding entrepreneurs defy the odds in Kim Jong Un's totalitarian state" dated 14 February 2018 in CNBC website [downloaded on 14 Feb 2018], available at https://www.cnbc.com/2018/02/14/north-korea-entrepreneurs-defy-odds-in-kim-jong-un-totalitarian-state.html.

[16] Salmon, Andrew, "Newly entrepreneurial North Korean economy turns inward" dated 8 July 2019 in *Asia Times* [downloaded on 8 July 2019], available at https://asiatimes.com/2019/07/newly-entrepreneurial-north-korean-economy-turns-inward/.

[17] Lankov, Andrei, "North Koreans survive on private business — and Kim will fail to stop them" dated 15 February 2021 in NK News edited by James Fretwell [downloaded on 15 February 2021], available at https://www.nknews.org/2021/02/north-koreans-survive-on-private-business-and-kim-will-fail-to-stop-them/.

[18] Wee, Heesun, "North Korea's budding entrepreneurs defy the odds in Kim Jong Un's totalitarian state" dated 14 February 2018 in CNBC website [downloaded on 14 Feb 2018], available at https://www.cnbc.com/2018/02/14/north-korea-entrepreneurs-defy-odds-in-kim-jong-un-totalitarian-state.html.

The authorities can also shut down foreign sources of trade goods quite easily, especially in extraordinary circumstances. The North Korean state's private sector activities that organically emerged in 2002 were supported by the state's market-led economic reforms, but it was suddenly reversed by the same Kim Jong-il government in 2005 when the great famine subsided and the North's economy recovered with South Korean aid and other external help (in addition to North Korea's entrepreneurial private sector activities).[19] It happened again in 2020. When the North Korean government closed its border with China and stopped virtually the entire bilateral trade with China when the latter was combating the COVID-19 coronavirus pandemic, it directly halted the *donjus*' main revenue and income sources.[20]

All these examples indicated that entrepreneurial activities in North Korea are vulnerable to changes in state policies. It is subject to a cyclical alternation between official encouragement and discouragement of such activities. There were brief moments in which the entrepreneurs' existence could have been threatened. For example, in late 2008, the state issued statements that they were going to shut down or pare down the country's markets starting from January 2009, but this move was transitionally stopped at the last minute because the authorities could not guarantee supply stability of goods and necessities if the markets were closed down.[21] Therefore, the necessity or trade due to domestic shortages lubricated by corruption ensured the sustenance and survivability of capitalist entrepreneurship in North Korea.

According to North Korean defectors (32 informants, including 1/3 reporting from within the country), bribery and corruption can open the gates at the border for goods to ferry through and this fuels what the

---

[19]Lankov, Andrei, "North Koreans survive on private business — and Kim will fail to stop them" dated 15 February 2021 in NK News edited by James Fretwell [downloaded on 15 February 2021], available at https://www.nknews.org/2021/02/north-koreans-survive-on-private-business-and-kim-will-fail-to-stop-them/.

[20]Dong, Hui Mun, "North Korea's wealthy entrepreneurial class facing economic difficulties amid COVID-19 pandemic" in *Daily NK* [downloaded on 6 April 2021], available at https://www.dailynk.com/english/north-korea-wealthy-entrepreneurial-class-facing-economic-difficulties-amid-covid-19-pandemic/.

[21]Lankov, Andrei, "North Koreans survive on private business — and Kim will fail to stop them" dated 15 February 2021 in NK News edited by James Fretwell [downloaded on 15 February 2021], available at https://www.nknews.org/2021/02/north-koreans-survive-on-private-business-and-kim-will-fail-to-stop-them/.

Daily NK detected as 387 officially allowed marketplaces in North Korea retailing from 600,000 stalls in the marketplaces.[22] There is also a growing division of labor in the North Korean production scene with increasing specialization in certain regions, e.g. Sunchon's shoe manufacturing zone, the Rajin Special Economic Zone (SEZ) in the northeastern region with Russian investments in port infrastructure (and Chinese downstream investments), the southeastern tourism resort area of Wonsan and Nampo port (and its three SEZs) specialized in serving Pyongyang.[23]

According to a report on North Korean marketization and intelligence from North Korean defectors, the country's entrepreneurial ventures differ in size and genre, retailing consumer items like food and apparel and services like barber and transportation.[24] In 2019, Joung Eun-lee, a research fellow at the Korea Institute of National Unification, noted that the North Korean economy is diversifying and emphasizing consumer products: "We are seeing a lot of domestic production — such as in food, liquor and tobacco — with many factories making products for domestic consumption."[25] North Korean start-ups include products such as ginseng cosmetic creams and electricity surge protector with boot-camp participants interested in drones and nanotechnology and attending seminars (80-120 per class) on economic policy and entrepreneurship by foreign outfits such as Facebook and *The Economist* in Pyongyang or Pyongsong, north of the capital city.[26] Choson Exchange (a social enterprise looking into economic/

---

[22] Wee, Heesun, "North Korea's budding entrepreneurs defy the odds in Kim Jong Un's totalitarian state" dated 14 February 2018 in CNBC website [downloaded on 14 Feb 2018], available at https://www.cnbc.com/2018/02/14/north-korea-entrepreneurs-defy-odds-in-kim-jong-un-totalitarian-state.html.

[23] Salmon, Andrew, "Newly entrepreneurial North Korean economy turns inward" dated 8 July 2019 in *Asia Times* [downloaded on 8 July 2019], available at https://asiatimes.com/2019/07/newly-entrepreneurial-north-korean-economy-turns-inward/.

[24] Wee, Heesun, "North Korea's budding entrepreneurs defy the odds in Kim Jong Un's totalitarian state" dated 14 February 2018 in CNBC website [downloaded on 14 Feb 2018], available at https://www.cnbc.com/2018/02/14/north-korea-entrepreneurs-defy-odds-in-kim-jong-un-totalitarian-state.html.

[25] Salmon, Andrew, "Newly entrepreneurial North Korean economy turns inward" dated 8 July 2019 in *Asia Times* [downloaded on 8 July 2019], available at https://asiatimes.com/2019/07/newly-entrepreneurial-north-korean-economy-turns-inward/.

[26] Wee, Heesun, "North Korea's budding entrepreneurs defy the odds in Kim Jong Un's totalitarian state" dated 14 February 2018 in CNBC website [downloaded on 14 February 2018], available at https://www.cnbc.com/2018/02/14/north-korea-entrepreneurs-defy-odds-in-kim-jong-un-totalitarian-state.html.

business/legal policies and training for North Koreans youths) had also tried to set up North Korean business incubators by raising capital, installing accounting procedures and providing resources/funding for them after obtaining official approval.[27]

The economy remains vulnerable to supply shocks, especially since North Korea is dependent on external trade (especially with China) for many of its household goods and necessities and also essential commodities such as items where they do not have enough domestic production. The 2020/2021 COVID-19 coronavirus pandemic situation is demonstrative of just how vulnerable supply shocks can be when it comes to North Korea. Prices of food and necessities increased dramatically and became unstable with reduced supply; for example, pork prices in North Korea increased by about 57% from November 2020 to April 2021, and prices of soybean *injogogi* (fake meat), *dububap* (tofu rice) and rice cakes also increased dramatically for smaller portions.[28] In normal times, however, Chinese sources can bring prosperity to those who have access to their goods.

Besides Chinese goods, the infrastructure in North Korean is also not ideal. The local Intranet in North Korea that North Koreans use has restricted information and materials from the outside world, while US tech giants' social media apps are also not available in the Stalinist state, although mobile phones have sped up communication channels between the North Koreans [overseas-based North Koreans use Skype to communicate].[29] Despite UN (United Nations) sanctions, restrictions on cross-boundary trade, US alliance sanctions, missing business infrastructures, absence of logistics, nonexistent online access for most and no bank

---

[27]Drake, Diana, "Entrepreneurship in North Korea? Bringing business concepts to a communist nation" dated 30 July 2012 in Wharton University of Pennsylvania [downloaded on 1 January 2018], available at https://kwhs.wharton.upenn.edu/2012/07/entrepreneurship-in-north-korea-bringing-business-concepts-to-a-communist-nation/.

[28]Dong, Hui Mun, "North Korea's wealthy entrepreneurial class facing economic difficulties amid COVID-19 pandemic" in *Daily NK* [downloaded on 6 April 2021], available at https://www.dailynk.com/english/north-korea-wealthy-entrepreneurial-class-facing-economic-difficulties-amid-covid-19-pandemic/.

[29]Drake, Diana, "Entrepreneurship in North Korea? Bringing business concepts to a communist nation" dated 30 July 2012 in Wharton University of Pennsylvania [downloaded on 1 January 2018], available at https://kwhs.wharton.upenn.edu/2012/07/entrepreneurship-in-north-korea-bringing-business-concepts-to-a-communist-nation/.

loan facilities, small-scale micro entrepreneurs are making do without e-commerce, self-locate their own financing and use personal networks to reach Chinese products seeping through the borders.[30] Some North Korean bankers are picking up more knowledge about the banking system in a capitalist economy from foreign trainers. For example, Choson Exchange's Geoffrey See interacted with a banker in North Korea, who said, "I've read this term in the *Financial Times* and I don't know what it's about, but it sounds very interesting and I've seen it come up quite a few times in the paper... [referring to terms like "private equity" and "exchange trader funds"].[31]

It is important to note that all these activities are only possible with the official nod from the state at the state's pleasure. It could change very quickly if the state determined it imperative to withdraw their support for entrepreneurship. [At the January 2021 Eighth Party Congress, Kim Jong-un promulgated that reformist market orientation measures did not align with state agendas and made the decision (which capitalists in that country disagreed with) that a tight centralized state command of the economy is needed to survive in times of adversities (i.e. COVID-19 coronavirus pandemic)].[32]

Nevertheless, before the January 2021 pronouncement, the Tongil Market in Pyongyang and hundreds of others came into existence after public rationing systems declined in the mid-1990s and most of the products retailed at these markets were China-made food, apparel, education-related items and kitchenware peddled by intermediaries with connections to China and its universe of products.[33] In 2019, China appears to favor

---

[30] Wee, Heesun, "North Korea's budding entrepreneurs defy the odds in Kim Jong Un's totalitarian state" dated 14 February 2018 in CNBC website [downloaded on 14 February 2018], available at https://www.cnbc.com/2018/02/14/north-korea-entrepreneurs-defy-odds-in-kim-jong-un-totalitarian-state.html.

[31] Drake, Diana, "Entrepreneurship in North Korea? Bringing business concepts to a communist nation" dated 30 July 2012 in Wharton University of Pennsylvania [downloaded on 1 January 2018], available at https://kwhs.wharton.upenn.edu/2012/07/entrepreneurship-in-north-korea-bringing-business-concepts-to-a-communist-nation/.

[32] Lankov, Andrei, "North Koreans survive on private business — and Kim will fail to stop them" dated 15 February 2021 in NK News edited by James Fretwell [downloaded on 15 February 2021], available at https://www.nknews.org/2021/02/north-koreans-survive-on-private-business-and-kim-will-fail-to-stop-them/.

[33] Wee, Heesun, "North Korea's budding entrepreneurs defy the odds in Kim Jong Un's totalitarian state" dated 14 February 2018 in CNBC website [downloaded on 14 February

trade over investments in North Korea, affecting further development of Pyongyang's Special Economic Zones (SEZs), and Pyongyang has little choices beyond trading with China,[34] given that the latter is North Korea's most important ally and its backer. According to North Korea observer Stephan Haggard, entrepreneurs are using the North Korean railway system, military detachments and intercity bus system for business logistics and goods transportation, and some observers have noted that government officials are also participating in side businesses, contributing to a hybridized private–state model of market orientation.[35] (Vietnam and China are probably advanced leading examples of such hybrid private sector–state developmental models.)

Sometimes, the state would step into certain market-oriented industries to reassert their control over supply and allocate resources. However, these episodes are cyclical in nature and would return back to market-oriented practices after a period of time. One reason for its reversion back to informal market forces is due to widespread shortages in supplies of a particular product or commodity. For example, North Korea clamped down on the market system in October 2005 (lasted till 2009) when it declared the return of the state distribution system and a ban on privately transacted rice/grains (that was in place since 1957, but broadly disregarded by the populace from the early 1990s onward).[36] Such re-impositions are readjusted when there is an external shock or severe supply challenge. Higher status and wealthier entrepreneurs with bigger-scale businesses and sizable accumulated funding are not the only players in the business world; entrepreneurial housewives cum micro

---

2018], available at https://www.cnbc.com/2018/02/14/north-korea-entrepreneurs-defy-odds-in-kim-jong-un-totalitarian-state.html.

[34] Salmon, Andrew, "Newly entrepreneurial North Korean economy turns inward" dated 8 July 2019 in *Asia Times* [downloaded on 8 July 2019], available at https://asiatimes.com/2019/07/newly-entrepreneurial-north-korean-economy-turns-inward/.

[35] Wee, Heesun, "North Korea's budding entrepreneurs defy the odds in Kim Jong Un's totalitarian state" dated 14 February 2018 in CNBC website [downloaded on 14 February 2018], available at https://www.cnbc.com/2018/02/14/north-korea-entrepreneurs-defy-odds-in-kim-jong-un-totalitarian-state.html.

[36] Lankov, Andrei, "North Koreans survive on private business — and Kim will fail to stop them" dated 15 February 2021 in NK News edited by James Fretwell [downloaded on 15 February 2021], available at https://www.nknews.org/2021/02/north-koreans-survive-on-private-business-and-kim-will-fail-to-stop-them/.

entrepreneurs/merchant middlemen who are tech-savvy with Chinese mobile phones are prominent deal makers too.[37] In the market-oriented trading sector in North Korea, women are indeed the main players. In December 2006, healthy men were prohibited from participation in market-oriented trading activities and returned to work in state-owned factories and agricultural cooperatives (a practice since the era of founding father Kim Il-sung), but this did not impact market-oriented trade since women were the main traders.[38]

Budding tech entrepreneurs in North Korea do not always have access to quality tech infrastructure. Despite such challenges, North Korean individuals persisted with creating the e-commerce website Manmulsang (translated literally as "the everything store"), the m-commerce Okryu, navigation app (Gildongmu 1.0 translated as "road friend") for mobile users in North Korea.[39] Makeshift capitalism and entrepreneurship resulted in adaptations to marketing and retailing as well. For example, entrepreneurial peddlers purchase Chinese clothing through an intermediary, and then use traditional non-digital marketing techniques to invite women acquaintances to model and promote those clothes in an open market, resulting in the term "Jangmadang Generation" (or market generation), first mentioned to the outside world in a defector's new documentary on North Korean millennial entrepreneurs.[40] Ingenuity was also needed in dealing with erratic state regulations. Some foreign outfits have tried to provide training and advisories to North Koreans in an effort to

---

[37] Wee, Heesun, "North Korea's budding entrepreneurs defy the odds in Kim Jong Un's totalitarian state" dated 14 February 2018 in CNBC website [downloaded on 14 February 2018], available at https://www.cnbc.com/2018/02/14/north-korea-entrepreneurs-defy-odds-in-kim-jong-un-totalitarian-state.html.

[38] Lankov, Andrei, "North Koreans survive on private business — and Kim will fail to stop them" dated 15 February 2021 in NK News edited by James Fretwell [downloaded on 15 February 2021], available at https://www.nknews.org/2021/02/north-koreans-survive-on-private-business-and-kim-will-fail-to-stop-them/.

[39] Lee, Yoolim and Sam Kim, "Entrepreneurs in North Korea? Not as rare as you would think" dated 16 June 2018 in *The Economic Times* [downloaded on 16 June 2018], available at https://economictimes.indiatimes.com/small-biz/startups/newsbuzz/entrepreneurs-in-north-korea-not-as-rare-as-you-would-think/articleshow/64612212.cms?from=mdr.

[40] Wee, Heesun, "North Korea's budding entrepreneurs defy the odds in Kim Jong Un's totalitarian state" dated 14 February 2018 in CNBC website [downloaded on 14 February 2018], available at https://www.cnbc.com/2018/02/14/north-korea-entrepreneurs-defy-odds-in-kim-jong-un-totalitarian-state.html.

share perspectives on investor protection in the rule of law. For example, NGO Choson Exchange had imparted training in the concepts and notions of investment laws to North Korean students, and provided suggestions on legal reforms to protect investors.[41]

When the government periodically tightened the screws on capitalism, women entrepreneurs would get around them creatively. The state ban on men from the marketplace was only partially enforceable, while women below 45 or 50 sustained their business activities by informing any legal enforcers that they were simply assisting their in-laws or elderly women who happened to be in the vicinity.[42] The elites of the marketized economy, the *donjus,* have a disproportionate influence on the economy with their sizable private capital, so conversely if their funds run out, it can also have an impact on the economy.[43]

Limitations Imposed by the Regime

An aspect that any would-be entrepreneur in North Korea has to accommodate is constant monitoring and surveillance by the government, even as millennials and the economically empowered professionals are setting up ventures inside North Korea.[44] The developmental strategies in North Korea include: domestic manpower utilization, continuous feedback from vessel owners in the ports, highly-skilled workers' knowledge-sharing,

---

[41]Drake, Diana, "Entrepreneurship in North Korea? Bringing business concepts to a communist nation" dated 30 July 2012 in Wharton University of Pennsylvania [downloaded on 1 January 2018], available at https://kwhs.wharton.upenn.edu/2012/07/entrepreneurship-in-north-korea-bringing-business-concepts-to-a-communist-nation/.

[42]Lankov, Andrei, "North Koreans survive on private business — and Kim will fail to stop them" dated 15 February 2021 in NK News edited by James Fretwell [downloaded on 15 February 2021], available at https://www.nknews.org/2021/02/north-koreans-survive-on-private-business-and-kim-will-fail-to-stop-them/.

[43]Dong, Hui Mun, "North Korea's wealthy entrepreneurial class facing economic difficulties amid COVID-19 pandemic" in *Daily NK* [downloaded on 6 April 2021], available at https://www.dailynk.com/english/north-korea-wealthy-entrepreneurial-class-facing-economic-difficulties-amid-covid-19-pandemic/.

[44]Wee, Heesun, "North Korea's budding entrepreneurs defy the odds in Kim Jong Un's totalitarian state" dated 14 February 2018 in CNBC website [downloaded on 14 February 2018], available at https://www.cnbc.com/2018/02/14/north-korea-entrepreneurs-defy-odds-in-kim-jong-un-totalitarian-state.html.

leveraging business synergies (e.g. managing a sauna proximate to a power station for optimal energy use) and developing a national showcase city with a vibrant service sector, including exquisite shops, coffee places and foreign restaurants (patronized mostly by North Korean elites).[45]

These foreign outlets may be a result of North Koreans travelling overseas and trawling back foreign ideas. According to NGO Choson Exchange, North Koreans who have travelled overseas are wide-eyed about entrepreneurship because they toured and experienced Chinese supermarkets and fast food restaurant, and were attracted by their business model/concept and modernity, and impressed by their cleanliness, affordability of food and speed of service.[46] There are limits to the type of goods that can be sold; for example, retailing foreign media products (e.g. thumb drives with foreign films, data and unfiltered news) is a serious offense and so the entrepreneurs have to toe the line and proceed gradually with officially sanctioned products.[47] In May 2004, Kim Jong-il banned mobile phones formerly permitted in 2002 (with 20,000 users of the official network by December 2003) and this decision was triggered by the April 2004 Ryongchon Station disaster perceived as an assassination attempt by using a mobile phone signal to set off a bomb to destroy Kim Jong-il's armored train.[48]

The *donju* entrepreneurs have taken over or leased the state-owned factories that were operating at below 30% of their capacities, and by introducing market forces and performance pressures that leverages on North Korean affordable labor costs and strong management, these entrepreneurs were able to obtain investment returns in sometimes as fast as

---

[45] Salmon, Andrew, "Newly entrepreneurial North Korean economy turns inward" dated 8 July 2019 in *Asia Times* [downloaded on 8 July 2019], available at https://asiatimes.com/2019/07/newly-entrepreneurial-north-korean-economy-turns-inward/.

[46] Drake, Diana, "Entrepreneurship in North Korea? Bringing business concepts to a communist nation" dated 30 July 2012 in Wharton University of Pennsylvania [downloaded on 1 January 2018], available at https://kwhs.wharton.upenn.edu/2012/07/entrepreneurship-in-north-korea-bringing-business-concepts-to-a-communist-nation/.

[47] Wee, Heesun, "North Korea's budding entrepreneurs defy the odds in Kim Jong Un's totalitarian state" dated 14 February 2018 in CNBC website [downloaded on 14 February 2018], available at https://www.cnbc.com/2018/02/14/north-korea-entrepreneurs-defy-odds-in-kim-jong-un-totalitarian-state.html.

[48] Lankov, Andrei, "North Koreans survive on private business — and Kim will fail to stop them" dated 15 February 2021 in NK News edited by James Fretwell [downloaded on 15 February 2021], available at https://www.nknews.org/2021/02/north-koreans-survive-on-private-business-and-kim-will-fail-to-stop-them/.

two years.[49] Observers, like defector-supporter Sokeel Park, Director of Research and Strategy of NGO Liberty, appear to see the strong capitalistic element in North Korean business dealings: "It's constrained and camouflaged, but it's capitalism nonetheless."[50] There are rare instances of pushbacks against the authorities, but they are few and far between and quickly pacified or the state has unpopular regulations unenforced strictly. In December 2007, Pyongyang prohibited women under 45 (or 50 years old, depending on the local area) from participating in market trade, but ran into difficulties of enforcement and even caused riots to occur throughout the nation.[51] With more domestically driven consumption and encouragement of North Korean currency use, there appears to be greater use of informal market foreign currencies (what some analysts term as "de-dollarization" alongside promoting greater self-reliance away from the desired reliance on Chinese investments).[52]

The state must also be careful not to step on the toes of the citizenry's pragmatic livelihood needs. In early 2010, due to private trade clampdowns/currency reform disruptions, North Koreans agitated against the government with high-ranking officials openly informing foreign sources of their unhappiness; this fear of open revolt (potentially revolution) prompted the Leninist state's leader Kim Jong-il to direct local authorities to accommodate informal markets in May 2010 for the rest of his administration.[53] According to a *Daily NK* report dated 2017, about 20% of North Korea's 25 million-strong population depend on outdoor markets

---

[49] Salmon, Andrew, "Newly entrepreneurial North Korean economy turns inward" dated 8 July 2019 in *Asia Times* [downloaded on 8 July 2019], available at https://asiatimes.com/2019/07/newly-entrepreneurial-north-korean-economy-turns-inward/.

[50] Wee, Heesun, "North Korea's budding entrepreneurs defy the odds in Kim Jong Un's totalitarian state" dated 14 February 2018 in CNBC website [downloaded on 14 February 2018], available at https://www.cnbc.com/2018/02/14/north-korea-entrepreneurs-defy-odds-in-kim-jong-un-totalitarian-state.html.

[51] Lankov, Andrei, "North Koreans survive on private business — and Kim will fail to stop them" dated 15 February 2021 in NK News edited by James Fretwell [downloaded on 15 February 2021], available at https://www.nknews.org/2021/02/north-koreans-survive-on-private-business-and-kim-will-fail-to-stop-them/.

[52] Salmon, Andrew, "Newly entrepreneurial North Korean economy turns inward" dated 8 July 2019 in *Asia Times* [downloaded on 8 July 2019], available at https://asiatimes.com/2019/07/newly-entrepreneurial-north-korean-economy-turns-inward/.

[53] Lankov, Andrei, "North Koreans survive on private business — and Kim will fail to stop them" dated 15 February 2021 in NK News edited by James Fretwell [downloaded on

for livelihoods, while many other North Koreans take part in business training start-up boot-camps operated by Choson Exchange (a non-profit outfit that supports North Korean entrepreneurs) which mentors/incubates 30 start-ups through workshops.[54] Geoffrey See established the Choson Exchange to upgrade the business knowledge of North Korean professionals between 20 and 40 years of age after interacting with North Korean varsity students eager to learn the ways of business and economics and thereafter spent 1.5 years in establishing such programs for young high performers.[55]

The government permits thousands of North Koreans to study entrepreneurship (regardless of ideological conflicts with socialism) with the NPO (Non-Profit Organization) Choson Exchange, which has trained more than 2,000 North Koreans in North Korea between 2008 and 2018 even as they make excursions to overseas locations.[56] Geoffrey See, who set up the NGO to impart business and entrepreneurial skills, worked with North Koreas to set up businesses within the limits of their society and based on the knowledge they have picked up from observing overseas economies despite their restricted access to information.[57] Some analysts opined that there is a utilitarian rationale behind North Korean state toleration of entrepreneurial activities. From the state's point of view, market-oriented expansion may result in losing some

---

15 February 2021], available at https://www.nknews.org/2021/02/north-koreans-survive-on-private-business-and-kim-will-fail-to-stop-them/.

[54]Wee, Heesun, "North Korea's budding entrepreneurs defy the odds in Kim Jong Un's totalitarian state" dated 14 February 2018 in CNBC website [downloaded on 14 February 2018], available at https://www.cnbc.com/2018/02/14/north-korea-entrepreneurs-defy-odds-in-kim-jong-un-totalitarian-state.html.

[55]Drake, Diana, "Entrepreneurship in North Korea? Bringing business concepts to a communist nation" dated 30 July 2012 in Wharton University of Pennsylvania [downloaded on 1 January 2018], available at https://kwhs.wharton.upenn.edu/2012/07/entrepreneurship-in-north-korea-bringing-business-concepts-to-a-communist-nation/.

[56]Lee, Yoolim and Sam Kim, "Entrepreneurs in North Korea? Not as rare as you would think" dated 16 June 2018 in *The Economic Times* [downloaded on 16 June 2018], available at https://economictimes.indiatimes.com/small-biz/startups/newsbuzz/entrepreneurs-in-north-korea-not-as-rare-as-you-would-think/articleshow/64612212.cms?from=mdr.

[57]Drake, Diana, "Entrepreneurship in North Korea? Bringing business concepts to a communist nation" dated 30 July 2012 in Wharton University of Pennsylvania [downloaded on 1 January 2018], available at https://kwhs.wharton.upenn.edu/2012/07/entrepreneurship-in-north-korea-bringing-business-concepts-to-a-communist-nation/.

measure of state control and pose a threat to totalitarian control, but at the same time, it facilitates the government's ability to concentrate on augmenting nuclear weaponization, testing and arsenal, while relying on free market forces to assist the citizens to rely on themselves for necessities.[58]

Choson Exchange's Geoffrey See noted that North Koreans who visited China spotted similarities between the industrial/economic structures of their country and China two decades ago and observed how the Chinese economy grew, improving livelihoods and engaging in interesting ventures; all these observations have a powerful effect on the North Koreans (especially youths who are curious, driven and not risk-averse).[59] With the osmosis of ideas across permeable borders, one can find the transplantation of Chinese-style retail outlets to Pyongyang. Department stores and supermarkets sprouted up in Pyongyang with transactions made using payment cards, while supermarkets and gas stations are popping up in the peripherals of factory regions and provinces turning themselves into tourism locations to benefit from consumption brought about by the new rich.[60] Whatever the reason, the ultimate result of such alleged pragmatic arrangements is an emerging entrepreneurial ecosystem that will grow more significantly beyond traditional housewife-run stalls in the outdoor markets into the next stage of state-supported tech zones and start-up boot camps.[61]

---

[58] Wee, Heesun, "North Korea's budding entrepreneurs defy the odds in Kim Jong Un's totalitarian state" dated 14 February 2018 in CNBC website [downloaded on 14 February 2018], available at https://www.cnbc.com/2018/02/14/north-korea-entrepreneurs-defy-odds-in-kim-jong-un-totalitarian-state.html.

[59] Drake, Diana, "Entrepreneurship in North Korea? Bringing business concepts to a communist nation" dated 30 July 2012 in Wharton University of Pennsylvania [downloaded on 1 January 2018], available at https://kwhs.wharton.upenn.edu/2012/07/entrepreneurship-in-north-korea-bringing-business-concepts-to-a-communist-nation/.

[60] Salmon, Andrew, "Newly entrepreneurial North Korean economy turns inward" dated 8 July 2019 in *Asia Times* [downloaded on 8 July 2019], available at https://asiatimes.com/2019/07/newly-entrepreneurial-north-korean-economy-turns-inward/.

[61] Wee, Heesun, "North Korea's budding entrepreneurs defy the odds in Kim Jong Un's totalitarian state" dated 14 February 2018 in CNBC website [downloaded on 14 February 2018], available at https://www.cnbc.com/2018/02/14/north-korea-entrepreneurs-defy-odds-in-kim-jong-un-totalitarian-state.html.

Pre-Pandemic Period Under Supreme Leader Kim Jong-un

Self-sufficiency and self-reliance or *juche* are the official doctrines of the North Korean state and it appears to be behind the toleration of semi-free enterprise. There are some inevitable tensions in the process of this coexistence. Some detect a challenge in the tensions between Stalinist state agencies and entrepreneurs who manage their assets, who are also careful to toe the official lines/agendas as *donju* entrepreneurs are not permitted to own their productive assets that are on paper under the ownership of state agencies and yet investors have de facto asset control.[62]

Before the COVID-19 coronavirus pandemic outbreak, North Korea appeared to be stepping up on encouraging entrepreneurship. Even when it comes to something as capitalist as entrepreneurship, the state is careful to ensure that the elite leadership is included in publicity campaigns. For example, in 2018, North Korean leader Kim Jong-un gave "field guidance" at Mirae Shop and Health Complex, and in the pre-COVID-19 scenario, despite an authoritarian state and restricted mobility and freedom, it was observable that more North Koreans on the street were understatedly transforming into entrepreneurs.[63] North Korean leader Kim Jong-un often carries out inspection tours to production sites. He visited the Kumsanpho Fish Pickling Factory with his wife Ri Sol Ju in South Hwanghae Province (publicly announced on 8 August 2018).[64]

Profit-making appeared to be a new catch phrase. Ian Bennett, outreach coordinator for Choson Exchange, opined, "There is a hunger in this country for people to start their own business… North Koreans are fairly open in saying they want to open businesses… Profit is not a

---

[62] Salmon, Andrew, "Newly entrepreneurial North Korean economy turns inward" dated 8 July 2019 in *Asia Times* [downloaded on 8 July 2019], available at https://asiatimes.com/2019/07/newly-entrepreneurial-north-korean-economy-turns-inward/.

[63] Wee, Heesun, "North Korea's budding entrepreneurs defy the odds in Kim Jong Un's totalitarian state" dated 14 February 2018 in CNBC website [downloaded on 14 February 2018], available at https://www.cnbc.com/2018/02/14/north-korea-entrepreneurs-defy-odds-in-kim-jong-un-totalitarian-state.html.

[64] Salmon, Andrew, "Newly entrepreneurial North Korean economy turns inward" dated 8 July 2019 in *Asia Times* [downloaded on 8 July 2019], available at https://asiatimes.com/2019/07/newly-entrepreneurial-north-korean-economy-turns-inward/.

dirty word."[65] These ventures are profit-making entities (and not state revenue generators) kept under state surveillance.[66] North Korea does not officially implement taxation, so the *donju* entrepreneurs manage their factories by providing state operators with return ratios of 20–30% and they have accumulated more power and responsibilities in running factories than state managerial appointees, which sees them paying off state agencies that own the factories.[67] Faced with state agendas and monitoring, the *donju*s must also be versatile to adapt to external economic conditions and pare down their spending whenever necessary. For example, the *donju*s may have faced their greatest challenge in the COVID-19 coronavirus pandemic era when even *donju*s with their accumulated wealth were reducing expenditures such as reducing their housekeepers' salaries (by 50%) or even letting them go.[68]

NGO Liberty Director Sokeel Park, who also directed a film "Jangmadang Generation" based on North Korean millennials who are creative entrepreneurs, articulated, "We're seeing initiative from individuals in the pursuit of profit... Trading is human nature... People will find a way," leading to some speculations that entrepreneurship could bring about freedom and reform yearnings.[69] Stephen Haggard opined, however, that ordinary North Koreans who can get rich and purchase items to enjoy like beer and good clothes are dis-incentivized to go against the

---

[65] Wee, Heesun, "North Korea's budding entrepreneurs defy the odds in Kim Jong Un's totalitarian state" dated 14 February 2018 in CNBC website [downloaded on 14 February 2018], available at https://www.cnbc.com/2018/02/14/north-korea-entrepreneurs-defy-odds-in-kim-jong-un-totalitarian-state.html.

[66] *Ibid.*

[67] Salmon, Andrew, "Newly entrepreneurial North Korean economy turns inward" dated 8 July 2019 in *Asia Times* [downloaded on 8 July 2019], available at https://asiatimes.com/2019/07/newly-entrepreneurial-north-korean-economy-turns-inward/.

[68] Dong, Hui Mun, "North Korea's wealthy entrepreneurial class facing economic difficulties amid COVID-19 pandemic" in *Daily NK* [downloaded on 6 April 2021], available at https://www.dailynk.com/english/north-korea-wealthy-entrepreneurial-class-facing-economic-difficulties-amid-covid-19-pandemic/.

[69] Wee, Heesun, "North Korea's budding entrepreneurs defy the odds in Kim Jong Un's totalitarian state" dated 14 February 2018 in CNBC website [downloaded on 14 February 2018], available at https://www.cnbc.com/2018/02/14/north-korea-entrepreneurs-defy-odds-in-kim-jong-un-totalitarian-state.html.

regime: "The increase in marketization is almost certainly contributing to much more pronounced inequality and corruption."[70] Many *donju*s became ardent stakeholders in the regime and the stability of the system. By 2010s, some *donju*s resided in high-rise housing that was valued at tens of thousands of USD, and an unnamed informant in South Pyongan Province noted that "Some *donju* used to boast that 'even if the Taedong River dries up, my pockets never will'."[71] Geoffrey See (founder of Choson Exchange) noted, "Having a channel of communication, even if it's only with entrepreneurs who are not politically influential, gives us a way to communicate what the international community is thinking. It is a way to shape the future of an isolated country."[72]

Prior to information being funneled through NGOs like Choson Exchange, the universities and publications in the libraries were mainly stocked with financial textbooks dating back to the 1970s published in the Soviet Union (USSR), making it difficult to acquire up-to-date information and contributing to North Korean self-consciousness of their isolation and marginalization in the world (according to Choson Exchange).[73] Accumulating sources of information from all outlets available has enabled the North Koreans to build up their academic capabilities over time. State-run Kim Il Sung University/Kim Chaek University of Technology run basic computer science courses using limited internet

---

[70] Wee, Heesun, "North Korea's budding entrepreneurs defy the odds in Kim Jong Un's totalitarian state" dated 14 February 2018 in CNBC website [downloaded on 14 February 2018], available at https://www.cnbc.com/2018/02/14/north-korea-entrepreneurs-defy-odds-in-kim-jong-un-totalitarian-state.html.

[71] Dong, Hui Mun, "North Korea's wealthy entrepreneurial class facing economic difficulties amid COVID-19 pandemic" in *Daily NK* [downloaded on 6 April 2021], available at https://www.dailynk.com/english/north-korea-wealthy-entrepreneurial-class-facing-economic-difficulties-amid-covid-19-pandemic/.

[72] Wee, Heesun, "North Korea's budding entrepreneurs defy the odds in Kim Jong Un's totalitarian state" dated 14 February 2018 in CNBC website [downloaded on 14 February 2018], available at https://www.cnbc.com/2018/02/14/north-korea-entrepreneurs-defy-odds-in-kim-jong-un-totalitarian-state.html.

[73] Drake, Diana, "Entrepreneurship in North Korea? Bringing business concepts to a communist nation" dated 30 July 2012 in Wharton University of Pennsylvania [downloaded on 1 January 2018], available at https://kwhs.wharton.upenn.edu/2012/07/entrepreneurship-in-north-korea-bringing-business-concepts-to-a-communist-nation/.

access, training students who even went on to winning global coding competitions.[74] A North Korean defector from the tech sector noted,

> [North Koreans are just as eager to get ahead as their counterparts in the South]… Expect to see all kinds of geeks trying to make money if their country opens up.[75]

State institutions are not the only ones importing business and entrepreneurial knowledge or offering entrepreneurial advice. Choson Exchange's Geoffrey did a reality check with the North Koreans to let them know what kind of financial services are implementable based on their infrastructure and facilities and took the opportunity to learn about various topical matters and detect North Korean business interests.[76]

The Slowdown

By 2019, however, some observers detected an economic slowdown in the country despite its increasingly adaptable/entrepreneurial economy and manufacturing/importing improved products for local consumption, and this was mainly due to a slowdown in showcasing of national projects, United Nations (UN) sanctions and lower Chinese investment interest.[77] Given the lack of Chinese investment interest, Chinese trade became even more essential to the livelihood lifelines among North Koreans. If Chinese goods stopped coming to North Korea, many entrepreneurs would not be able to trade and eke out their living, especially the masses. Many

---

[74] *Ibid.*

[75] Lee, Yoolim and Sam Kim, "Entrepreneurs in North Korea? Not as rare as you would think" dated 16 June 2018 in *The Economic Times* [downloaded on 16 June 2018], available at https://economictimes.indiatimes.com/small-biz/startups/newsbuzz/entrepreneurs-in-north-korea-not-as-rare-as-you-would-think/articleshow/64612212.cms?from=mdr.

[76] Drake, Diana, "Entrepreneurship in North Korea? Bringing business concepts to a communist nation" dated 30 July 2012 in Wharton University of Pennsylvania [downloaded on 1 January 2018], available at https://kwhs.wharton.upenn.edu/2012/07/entrepreneurship-in-north-korea-bringing-business-concepts-to-a-communist-nation/.

[77] Salmon, Andrew, "Newly entrepreneurial North Korean economy turns inward" dated 8 July 2019 in *Asia Times* [downloaded on 8 July 2019], available at https://asiatimes.com/2019/07/newly-entrepreneurial-north-korean-economy-turns-inward/.

average North Koreans, far more than the *donju*s, are currently experiencing financial difficulties because of COVID-19.[78]

There are few other alternatives to Chinese investments or trade due to other political problems with other countries, including its southern counterpart. The South Korean joint venture Kaesong factory complex which hired North Korean workers to manufacture sport shoes in 2013 (for South Korean companies) as well as Mount Kumgang tourism areas both facilitated skills transfer to the North Koreas; but they were closed after a South Korean tourist was accidentally shot by a DPRK soldier (amid other tensions).[79] In 2020, it appears the pandemic is hurting North Korea's burgeoning *donju* entrepreneurs. The General Administration of Customs of China noted that total trade between China and North Korea came up to US$539,059,000 in 2020 and North Korea imported US$491,059,000 of goods from China in 2020 (both experienced a decline of about 81% compared to 2019).[80] Ultimately, the state, and not the private entrepreneurs, holds the power to the future and destiny of North Korean entrepreneurship. In January 2021, North Korea reversed its reformist economic agenda in place from 2012 to 2017 and turned toward de facto state Leninism focused on central planning and command economy, while stopping private entrepreneurial activity.[81]

---

[78] Dong, Hui Mun, "North Korea's wealthy entrepreneurial class facing economic difficulties amid COVID-19 pandemic" in *Daily NK* [downloaded on 6 April 2021], available at https://www.dailynk.com/english/north-korea-wealthy-entrepreneurial-class-facing-economic-difficulties-amid-covid-19-pandemic/.

[79] Salmon, Andrew, "Newly entrepreneurial North Korean economy turns inward" dated 8 July 2019 in *Asia Times* [downloaded on 8 July 2019], available at https://asiatimes.com/2019/07/newly-entrepreneurial-north-korean-economy-turns-inward/.

[80] Dong, Hui Mun, "North Korea's wealthy entrepreneurial class facing economic difficulties amid COVID-19 pandemic" in *Daily NK* [downloaded on 6 April 2021], available at https://www.dailynk.com/english/north-korea-wealthy-entrepreneurial-class-facing-economic-difficulties-amid-covid-19-pandemic/.

[81] Lankov, Andrei, "North Koreans survive on private business — and Kim will fail to stop them" dated 15 February 2021 in NK News edited by James Fretwell [downloaded on 15 February 2021], available at https://www.nknews.org/2021/02/north-koreans-survive-on-private-business-and-kim-will-fail-to-stop-them/.

Chapter 12

Concluding Remarks

This book started with a succinct and brief literature review of the different definitions of the term "entrepreneurship". Added to conventional ideas, the digital revolution has also created its own version of entrepreneurship, unhindered by physical barriers. With the impending replacement of human jobs by machines, robots and A.I., entrepreneurship has taken on new socially ethical formats like civic techno-preneurship. Civic techno-preneurship is already attracting the attention of venture capitalists in the US and Japan.

The transnational element was also covered in this book with the case study of overseas ethnic Chinese entrepreneurs. In terms of the debate on nature vs nurture, the overseas ethnic Chinese case study shows the powerful factor of circumstances in motivating people to become entrepreneurs simply for survival. Informal networking like *guanxi* has augmented this survival instinct. The overseas ethnic Chinese were an important group of talented foreign entrepreneurs that arrived on the shores of Southeast Asia. Historically, Chinese migration displayed a feature characterized by some observers as "maritime mobility" where generations of Chinese migrants arrived in Southeast Asia in waves and became closely related to the region's economic development.[1]

---

[1] Bräutigam, Deborah, "Local entrepreneurship in Southeast Asia and Subsaharan Africa: Networks and linkages to the global economy" dated 14 July 1998 in United Nations University [downloaded on 1 January 2021], available at https://archive.unu.edu/hq/academic/Pg_area4/Brautigam.html.

Indigenous ruling elites made pragmatic arrangements with Chinese entrepreneurs in facilitating and complementing their business activities. For example, in Malaysia, the rulers "tax farmed" Chinese entrepreneurs for their state revenues while retaining their political power even as the Chinese entrepreneurs zeroed in on an industry or commodity for monopolization (either in output or distribution) by paying a predetermined rent to the sovereign while lucratively pocketing any surplus profits.[2] Many overseas Chinese entrepreneurs became wealthy in this manner. Based on kinship and dialects, overseas Chinese networks provided credit, preferential distribution pacts, business advice, market intelligence and networking among themselves in the 18th and 19th centuries, thereby reducing the costs of doing business, providing trustworthy business partners across generations and buffering the risks needed to go into the manufacturing sector.[3] This historical perspective provides an insight into the chronological development of an ecological system of entrepreneurship.

Guanxi works the other way around as well. Hong Kong's entrepreneurs are also tapping into the informal Bamboo network to access business opportunities in Southeast Asia. Some observers dubbed Hong Kong's investments and entrepreneurial role in Southeast Asia as part of a "Chinese commonwealth" with an "open architecture" providing entry to local resources like information, business connections, raw materials, low labor costs and a diversity of business practices in different business environments, and it is an "interconnected yet potentially open system".[4] Such open architectures are still drawing in Bamboo network–Western company collaborations today.

---

[2] Bräutigam, Deborah, "Local entrepreneurship in Southeast Asia and Subsaharan Africa: Networks and linkages to the global economy" dated 14 July 1998 in United Nations University [downloaded on 1 January 2021], available at https://archive.unu.edu/hq/academic/Pg_area4/Brautigam.html.

[3] Bräutigam, Deborah, "Local entrepreneurship in Southeast Asia and Subsaharan Africa: Networks and linkages to the global economy" dated 14 July 1998 in United Nations University [downloaded on 1 January 2021], available at https://archive.unu.edu/hq/academic/Pg_area4/Brautigam.html.

[4] Kao, John, "The Worldwide Web of Chinese business" dated April 1993 in the Harvard Business Review (HBR) from the Magazine (March–April 1993) [downloaded on 1 January 2020], available at https://hbr.org/1993/03/the-worldwide-web-of-chinese-business.

After examining the different conceptual ideas of entrepreneurship, the ecological system of entrepreneurship was identified with a wide array and universe of stakeholders like the state, venture capitalists, non-profit organizations (NPOs), students, universities, instructors/trainers, educators, local communities, bureaucracy and many other entities. Even Industry 4.0 Tech Giants are pulled into the fray by universities. Some ecological systems are found in hipster locations that breed creativity and community solidarity, like Kamacon in Japan. The involvement of the local community and local officials along with a civic techno-preneur gives the entrepreneurial venture a democratic outlook and encourages contributions back to society. Hackathons are another way to involve a pluralistic spectrum of stakeholders in local techno-preneurial projects.

With its focus on East Asia, this book looked in greater detail at case studies from small economies like Singapore, well known for its cutting-edge approach to entrepreneurship, to economic superpowers like China, which is fast emerging as a global start-up hub, and Japan, fast becoming a global civic techno-preneur hub. China has the heft and economic power to nurture and cultivate promising ideas. It is also tapping into the source of returnee students to capitalize on their creative ideas and skills. Unique features of the Chinese system such as the embeddedness of the Party in the private sector were also studied in this work.

States are not the only entity in the global entrepreneurship game; Southeast Asian economies are banding together to form regional organizations (ROs) to share resources (e.g. educational resources, university courses and credits) to strengthen entrepreneurship within the region. All these initiatives are carried out in good measure to tap into the promise of a common market emerging from the formation of the ASEAN Economic Community (AEC) since December 2015. ASEAN's combined resources are formidable as they hold entrepreneur trade shows together and even work with Northeast Asian partners like the Republic of Korea to hold entrepreneurship contests.

In the East Asian region's desire to tap into entrepreneurship, the economies are also keen to tap formerly marginalized groups to power up the entrepreneurship game like women, energetic youths and reskilled individuals. In the case of women, ASEAN women have formed their own associations for mutual encouragement of entrepreneurship. The formerly marginalized group of overseas ethnic Chinese entrepreneurs is a textbook case study of how entrepreneurs transformed their own destiny through hard work and seizing opportunities, even in foreign and hostile environments. Regardless of the groups discussed, a commonality among them seems to be the need for mind-set change and/or the circumstances of necessity that catalyzed and stimulated individuals with good ideas to pursue their dream of setting up businesses.

Besides external drive and circumstances, there are factors that can be nurtured. They include utilizing mass education and Institutes of Higher Learning (IHLs) to teach practical applied learning courses to students and arm them with the necessary skills to tackle the many challenges of being an entrepreneur. Education can also be in the form of bite-sized units (micro-credentials) that can be consumed easily by working adults, entrepreneurs interested in upgrading a specific skillset and working adults who have little time to spare to study an entire degree. Some cultures like the Confucian influence, it appears, are conducive in stimulating educational pursuits within the community. The same cultural context also appears to encourage Chinese entrepreneurs and the public in general to adopt the idea of lifelong learning.

Both tangible and intangible barriers to entrepreneurship were discussed in this work. One of the intangible barriers discussed was the element of mind-set. In some of the case studies, it appeared that the fear of failure was a major mind-set barrier to would-be entrepreneurs pursuing their business ideas to actualize them. Providing resources through regional and international organizations, mentoring and scenario-planning through entrepreneurship education are just some of the ways to overcome this. Some even suggested making professional services (e.g. legal fees) cheaper to assist financially strapped entrepreneurial projects. Other ways to inspire them is through storytelling by successful entrepreneurs of their previous struggles and learning about the struggles faced by charismatic global entrepreneur stars. All these are done to remove the stigmatization of failure.

Finally, in the case of Japan, entrepreneurship in that country is mainly crisis-driven historically. And, for all countries in the region, the current COVID-19 coronavirus pandemic is a crisis that exerts risks and provides opportunities for entrepreneurship at the same time. Universities like Singapore University of Social Sciences (SUSS) offered free courses during the stay-home circuit breaker, while lockdowns have precipitated home businesses, turning some stay-home enterprises into thriving businesses. In this context, technologies, the necessity of change through crises, and state assistance and policies have become a powerful cocktail for spearheading a whole new generation of entrepreneurs.

In the very last chapter before the conclusion, this book changed gears to look at the last frontier of entrepreneurship-like activities as an interesting case study and contrast with the other case studies discussed in the volume. While this book looks at China, ASEAN, Japan and other settings in terms of case studies, it may be useful to look at very unconventional case studies for comparative value. One of these unconventional case studies may be North Korea, given its rogue status and international isolation. It is interesting to look at how powerful entrepreneurial energies act as a countervailing force to illiberal regimes in adaptive economic development. From the high tech in progressive liberal democratic capitalist economic systems to Stalinist impulses seduced by market forces, this book does not pretend to be comprehensive, but hopes to offer insights into a selected range of case studies for analysis and discussions.

Index

Printed in the United States
by Baker & Taylor Publisher Services